Greece

modern architectures in history

This international series examines the forms and consequences of modern architecture. Modernist visions and revisions are explored in their national context against a backdrop of aesthetic currents, economic developments, political trends and social movements. Written by experts in the architectures of the respective countries, the series provides a fresh, critical reassessment of Modernism's positive and negative effects, as well as the place of architectural design in twentieth-century history and culture.

Series editor: Vivian Constantinopoulos

Already published:

Brazil
Richard J. Williams

Britain
Alan Powers

Finland
Roger Connah

Italy
Diane Ghirardo

Turkey
Sibel Bozdoğan and Esra Akcan

USA
Gwendolyn Wright

Greece

modern architectures in history

Alexander Tzonis & Alcestis P. Rodi

REAKTION BOOKS

Published by Reaktion Books Ltd
33 Great Sutton Street
London EC1V 0DX, UK

www.reaktionbooks.co.uk

First published 2013
Copyright © Alexander Tzonis and Alcestis P. Rodi 2013

The publishers gratefully acknowledge support for the publication of this book by The Hellenic Foundation.

All rights reserved
No part of this publication may be reproduced, stored in a retrieval system, or transmitted, in any form or by any means, electronic, mechanical, photocopying, recording or otherwise, without the prior permission of the publishers.

Printed and bound in Great Britain by Bell & Bain, Glasgow

British Library Cataloguing in Publication Data
Tzonis, Alexander
Greece. – (Modern architectures in history)
1. Architecture – Greece
2. Architecture, Modern
3. Modern movement (Architecture)
I. Title II. Series III. Rodi, Alcestis P.
720.9'495-DC23

ISBN 978 1 86189 379 6

Contents

Introduction

How did modern architecture develop in Greece? The country was dependent on outside centres of economic and institutional power; most modern ideas, modern ways of doing things, and most of the financing needed for modernization were imported from abroad. For modernization to thrive, it depended very much on the way new knowledge, new ways of life and of course foreign investment were absorbed and applied in addition to the preconditions that would permit the process of modernization to begin. In Greece's case – or Hellas, as its citizens chose to call the new state – the War of Independence (1821–32), the struggle to break free from Ottoman rule, succeeded thanks to military intervention by the Great Powers (Britain, France and Russia), notably the sea battle of Navarino (27 October 1827), which followed the Treaty of London earlier that same year. Financial aid was granted with a state loan of 60,000,000 francs, which initiated the long history of Greek debt as well as the history of the influence of the Great Powers in Greece's political affairs.

The planning and building of the new nation state demanded foreign importations as well as improvizations made from scratch. Yet Leo von Klenze, a German architect who travelled to Athens in the early years of Greek independence and submitted plans for the new capital's reconstruction, insisted that 'Greece should not be turned into Bavaria'.[1] He might have added that it is hard to build on the ruins of old empires with the meagre materials they supply. The absence of sufficient institutional and knowledge resources to make Greece a modern state together with a financially weak government that largely relied on private enterprise to carry out basic public services, brought about an impotent state with a pathetic administration unable to conceive or to carry out complex planning operations, a state that resorted to force in order to impose its authority or to mask the absence of any prepared plan. The state's need to apply force created in turn regular public protests and anarchic demonstrations, conditions hardly conducive to carrying out rational modernization of the buildings and cities of any country let alone those in Greece.

View of Athens today.

Modernization in Greece had a further characteristic, that of taking place within a culturally and ethnically heterogeneous population (not dissimilar to nineteenth-century Germany, where a constellation of quasi-independent political units were moulded into a new modern 'imperial' complex). The groups beyond Greeks that had carried out the Greek revolution within the Ottoman empire, like the groups that played a similar role within the Austro-Hungarian empire, were diverse: peasant Albanians, Vlachs, Koutsovlachs, Slavs and Sarakatsani, an urban population scattered in ports and towns across the Ottoman empire, from Constantinople, Salonica, Pontos, the coasts of the Black Sea and Ionian Anatolia, the islands of the Aegean, the commercial centres of the Balkans, the Russian empire, the Austro-Hungarian empire (which included 80,000 Greek families) and Western Europe. They were Christian Orthodox, but they spoke different dialects or even languages, followed different traditions, held communal festivals in different places and at different times, dressed unalike, followed disparate everyday routines and had diverging interests; they had a fuzzy idea about the extent and the borders of the new state,[2] and didn't even share the same name among themselves; the term 'Greek' or Hellene was not yet understood in the sense that it is used today.[3]

Not surprisingly, the War of Independence was not driven by a single cause, a single vision of a new state or a single plan, but was waged by an unlikely assortment of overlapping groups: clannish landlords (*kodjabashides*), notable town representatives (*demogerontes*), peasants (*rayades*), shepherds, seamen, merchants, prelates and priests, bandits (*klephtes*), warlords (*pallikars*) and scholars (*kalamarades*). To these occupational or class divisions one has to add the equally serious splits between micro-regions such as the Peloponnese, Roumeli and Hydra, which later official history books in Greece tried to minimize but to which contemporary accounts and local press testify.[4]

Once Greece had gained its independence and acquired official borders in January 1831, new differences divided Greeks: there were those who lived within the national boundary, the endogenous, and those that remained 'unredeemed' beyond it. New splits also emerged in the population when the Great Powers tried to get the people on their side and establish alliances. Characteristically, the first political parties in Greece adopted party names according to the Power they claimed to represent: the 'English party', the 'French', the 'Russian'. From these divisions new ones developed. Greece remained a divided country right through to modern times.

The goal of constructing an overriding common identity for all the people within the state became a challenge for politicians but also for

The capital of the new nation state in a *View of Athens from the Ilissos River*, watercolour by Johann Michael Wittmer, 1833.

poets, historians and architects, all of whom sought to create a new bonding identity.[5] The various imagined communities ranged from the enlightened analyses that presented the new Greece as a civilizing force tasked with converting a pre-modern, despotic empire into a modern liberal state,[6] to regionalist ethnic and religious bigotry that juxtaposed imagined enemies to imagined friends, and denied the varied ethnic and cultural realities of the new state.[7] These fanciful notions, Ioannis Kolettis's so-called 'Great Idea' of an expanded Greek empire being one of the most dominant ones during the nineteenth century, were translated into blueprints, political and cultural programmes, artefacts of a national collective consciousness through the production of literary works, histories, textbooks, buildings and towns. As this book will show, architecture played a primary role.

Greece is a region endowed with one of the world's richest and most influential architectural heritages and a palimpsest of historical structures. Such a legacy can be an inspiration as well as a hurdle for the making of a modern architecture. The classical buildings that were built in Greece in the first decades following the War of Independence, and which helped to create a 'modern' Greek state, were designs imported from the West. Yet, in the context of the post-Ottoman empire, this new architecture was seen by Greeks as an idiom reborn at home. Similarly, the international white cubic modern architecture introduced in the late 1920s from France and Germany, which we will explore in the following chapters, were seen as having archetypes in Greece's 'humble, small island houses', which displayed a 'perfect match between form and function'.[8] However, numerous economic and political crises, *coups d'état*, civil discord and state bankruptcies resulted in Greece's failure to develop modern technology, organize a civil service, advance an effective welfare state or house the generations of refugees displaced from the time of the War of Independence through to the Second World War and the Civil War that followed. Added to this is the issue of the continuing decline of both the cities and the countryside, containing historic architectural examples and landscapes that for centuries had been left untouched.[9]

The study of Greece and its modern architecture offers insights into many current debates about globalization versus regionalism, community participation versus centralized control, universal values versus Balkanization, one-dimensional, libertarian, short-term economic growth versus normative planning that aims for social and environmental prosperity in the long run.

chapter one

Architecture of Revolution

When Ioannis Kapodistrias,[1] the newly appointed head of state of a fledgling Greece, returned in 1828 from a rallying tour across Europe, he despaired of his new country's widespread poor housing conditions, with people living 'in sheds as nomads or in ruins'.[2] A pioneering scheme called Pronoia was one of many projects commissioned by Kapodistrias as an immediate response to these wretched conditions, and the first example of state social housing in Greece.

Social housing as a building type has been a major preoccupation of modern architects. While *Pronoia* (meaning 'providence' or 'welfare') was not an innovative design solution, it was nonetheless one of the earliest responses to a very modern problem. Commissioned seven years after the Revolution of 1821 that began the overthrow of Ottoman rule, it was intended to provide shelter for refugees who had abandoned their homes on the coast of Asia Minor, as well as on the islands of Chios, Crete, Psara and Rhodes and the towns of Nafpaktos and Souli, which were all devastated by a vindictive Ottoman army.

Realizing that nearly 90 per cent of the peasant population had no land to cultivate, Kapodistrias immediately moved to redistribute land and to set up projects that would raise the basic standard of living and provide education. A year after his appointment he set up an emergency programme of comprehensive urbanization, collecting demographic data and identifying locations where social housing could be undertaken. Although a strong believer in centralized government, he encouraged decentralized regional development, mindful of the particular conditions in Greece. On 3 June 1831 he issued a decree recommending 'the erection of a city or a suburb at a place where only ruins exist or anywhere on Greek soil as soon as a plan is designed'. At the same time he commissioned architects and engineers to draw up plans for new towns.

Kapodistrias was well prepared to carry out this ambitious campaign of building and urbanization. Before coming to Greece he had travelled around western Europe appealing to architects and engineers, both Greeks and non-Greeks, to relocate to Greece to help construct a new independent (one is tempted to say 'utopian') state.[3] Among those who responded were two graduates from Berlin's Technical University: Stamatios Kleanthes and Eduard Schaubert, who became government architects in September 1830, assigned to survey the site of Athens.[4] Kapodistrias also recruited technical experts from the Expédition Scientifique de Morée, a large group of artists, antiquaries, botanists, draughtsmen, geologists, geographers, epigraphers, architects and engineers formed by the French government to survey the Peloponnese.[5] And he hired architects and engineers from the French forces that were fighting the Egyptian troops of the pro-Ottoman Ibrahim Pasha; among them was Stamatis Voulgaris (also documented as Bulgari), who was commissioned to take charge of the Pronoia housing. Voulgaris worked closely with Kapodistrias and received several commissions in addition to Pronoia, such as the projects for Nafplion, Tripolis and Pylos, and in 1828 for the port town of Patras, his most complete and absorbing urban scheme.

In addition to housing and town planning, schools were key to the new state's modernization. In one letter Kapodistrias noted that 'it is not possible to construct public education as fast as needed and as we would

Stamatis Voulgaris, *Plan for Patras*, 1829.

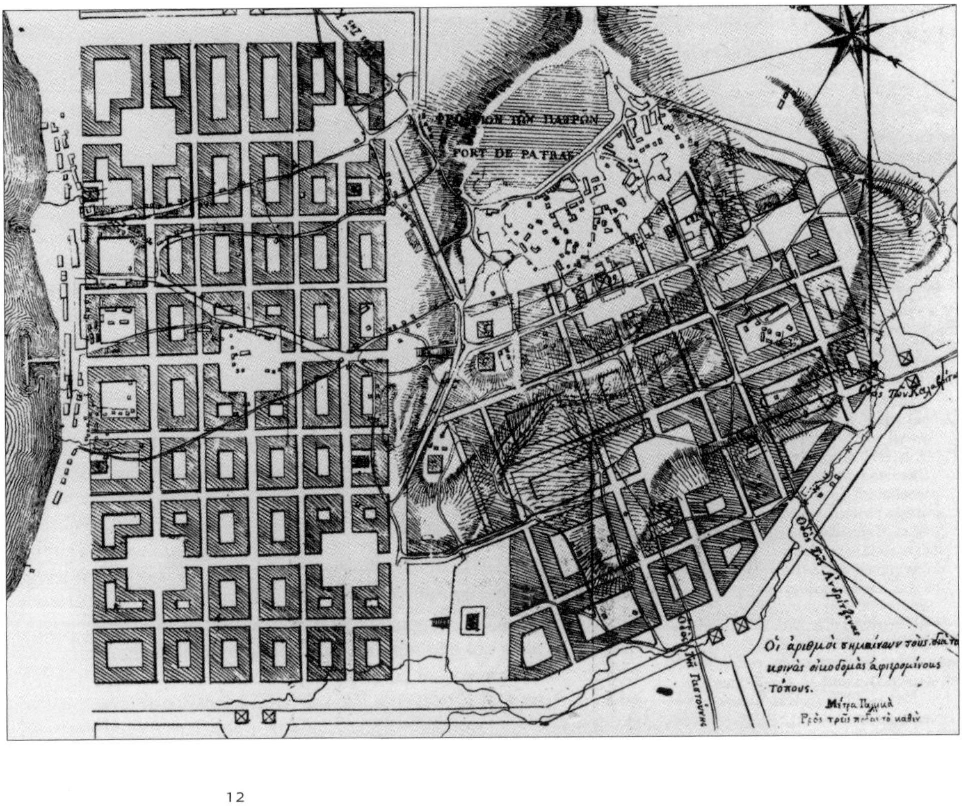

wish it. We must have school buildings . . . when I arrived here what I found were only shacks sheltering crowds of hungry families'.[6] He sent his architects and engineers to the various towns, asking them to select sites, design schools and supervise their construction. These buildings can still be found today scattered throughout Greece; many are still used by schools, prominent early examples of the enduring stamp of modernization.[7]

On 9 October 1831, soon after the Pronoia plan had been assembled, and with other planning and building projects in process, Kapodistrias was assassinated – his death following a plot by landowners who perceived their interests to be threatened by his government. Civil chaos and administrative paralysis followed; Kapodistrias's plans for regional reorganization of the state and land redistribution remained in limbo. Facing enormous financial difficulties, the provisional government offered for sale the properties that had previously belonged to Ottoman landlords. But in spite of their low value, neither the impoverished peasants nor the penniless Greek municipalities had any means for taking up the offer. Thus the lands for sale were snatched instead by wealthy diaspora Greeks, well-to-do local Greeks, rich ship-owners from Hydra, comfortably-off ecclesiastical institutions such as the Petraki Monastery, and a few foreign philhellenes, among them the Anglo-Scot George Finley (a historian of Greece) and Sophie de Marbois-Lebrun, Duchess of Plaisance.[8] The transfer of property to people with better business skills than the former Ottoman landlords but with very little understanding of agriculture or indeed about those who worked on the land did not improve either the fortunes of the labourers or the productivity of the fields. The peasants fought hard for their rights, complaining, according to one local newspaper, against those who 'came to Greece, purchased few estates intending to become seigneurs . . . and treated the Greeks as serfs'.[9]

After six months of inaction and anarchy, in May 1832 Russian and French diplomats were convened by the British Foreign Secretary Lord Palmerston to meet in London. To achieve long-term order, the convention decided that Greece should be a monarchy and the throne was offered to Prince Otto, son of King Ludwig of Bavaria. All these decisions were taken in the absence of a Greek representative. To boost Otto's regime, the Great Powers offered Greece a loan of 60,000,000 francs.[10]

When Otto and his entourage arrived in Nafplion, the question of the future capital of Greece was still undecided. Stamatios Kleanthes and Eduard Schaubert, who had remained in Athens after Kapodistrias's death, continued to work on their new plan for Athens as a capital. Their scheme was structured as a large right-angle triangle, the right-angle opening towards the Acropolis, placing the Palace at the top (the location of Omonoia Square today) and the start of a major axial boulevard directed

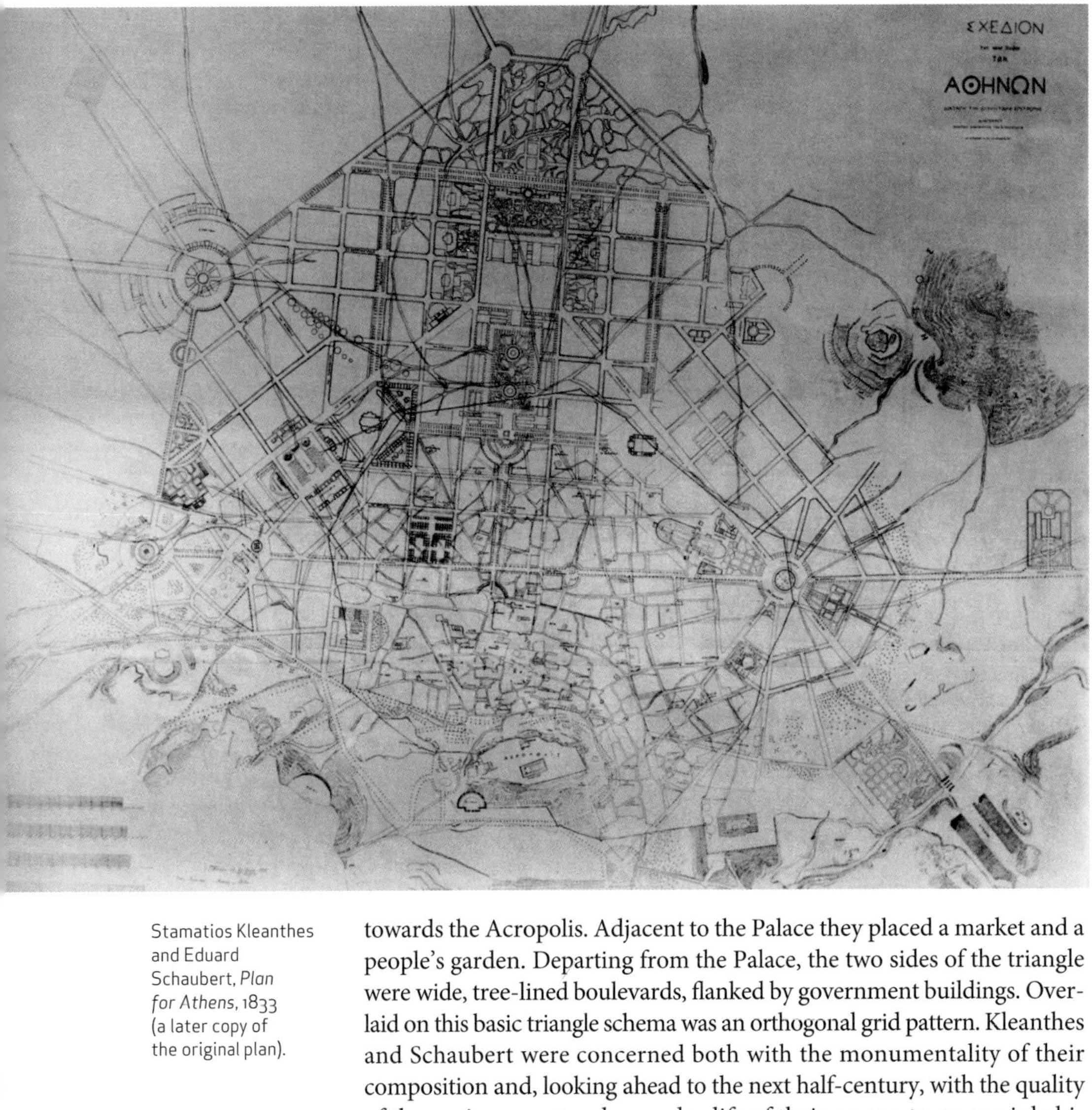

Stamatios Kleanthes and Eduard Schaubert, *Plan for Athens*, 1833 (a later copy of the original plan).

towards the Acropolis. Adjacent to the Palace they placed a market and a people's garden. Departing from the Palace, the two sides of the triangle were wide, tree-lined boulevards, flanked by government buildings. Overlaid on this basic triangle schema was an orthogonal grid pattern. Kleanthes and Schaubert were concerned both with the monumentality of their composition and, looking ahead to the next half-century, with the quality of the environment and everyday life of their 40,000 to 50,000 inhabitants. Thus, they provided a yard or garden for every house, and restricted the height of the houses to two floors. Their plan also respected the archaeological areas and Byzantine churches. It was approved and published as a government decree. Soon after, the landowners who had just purchased most of the land covered in Kleanthes and Schaubert's plan, and who had initially supported the project by offering to contribute land to facilitate its implementation, reacted negatively, removing their backing. By then the plan had been taken to Munich for final approval by King Ludwig.

The revolutionary government of Greece kept changing location according to pressures from interest groups or new opportunities. In 1823 Nafplion had been instituted as the government seat. Three years later the capital was moved to the island of Aegina. In 1829 Kapodistrias brought it back to Nafplion, seeing the town's potential due to its international population of merchants, technicians and scientists. Within the horizon of Ludwig's geopolitical cultural schemes, however, Athens appeared an attractive option.

Ludwig himself had doubts about the Kleanthes and Schaubert scheme and sought the opinion of his architect and confidant, Leo von Klenze, who did not approve it. Indeed, Maximilian I and crown prince Friedrich Wilhelm of Prussia had already asked another leading German architect, Karl Friedrich Schinkel, for a proposal. Schinkel responded with an elaborate palatial complex for the top of the Acropolis.[11] This plan has become renowned as one of the great utopian schemes in the history of architectural design; it is one of the most frequently reproduced images of 'visionary' architecture. Yet it is also a modern manifesto about how to handle architectural heritage and new build together within a given regional context. (Schinkel makes this clear in a letter, in which he recommends that the architect of the future Palace had to study the customs and needs of the place, avoiding the import of 'trivialized . . . Italian and French' prototypes that misunderstood symmetry, 'creating boredom and pretension'.) Schinkel proposed an outdoor scheme of accumulated, interlocking atria, courts and stoas meandering around the Parthenon and the other ancient ruins.[12] Leaving aside the almost blasphemous notion of introducing such a massive complex to the site of such a significant historical monument, the design was in fact functional and well adapted to both the site and local climate. Even so, the more pragmatic and moderate Ludwig rejected the idea, asking his son not to construct anything on the historic hill: 'whatever is built there will be bad both for the Acropolis and for the new buildings'.

In June 1834 the Kleanthes and Schaubert plan was suspended, and Ludwig requested Klenze to travel to Athens, observe the situation, work closely with Otto and his councillors, and report back to him confidentially.[13] Athens then was sparsely populated, little more than an overgrown Mediterranean village; its gentle landscape was undercultivated, dotted with a few ancient ruins and recent wrecks, as many contemporary drawings and engravings reveal. Prior to the 1821 revolution Athens had been home to around 12,000 people: among the Christians living there were a small number of Greeks who claimed ancient descent,

The Choragic Monument of Lysicrates seen walled into the garden end of the Capuchin Monastery, Athens, 1669. Original drawing by James Stuart and Nicholas Revett, 1751–3.

Arvanites (Christian Albanians) who had migrated to southern Greece and settled there between the fourteenth and sixteenth centuries, and a few Western Europeans, among them Franciscans, Dominicans and Jesuits (groups that had lived in Athens for centuries), as well as Ottoman landlords, administrators, peasants, 'slaves' and the soldiers that made up the town's garrison. As was the case in most urban centres of the Ottoman empire, this highly diverse group of peoples existed symbiotically, keeping their respective identities intact. During the Revolution, indigenous Greeks and Arvanites had joined the struggle against the Ottomans and, as a result, in June 1826 Athens was attacked and devastated by the Ottomans, and afterwards abandoned by most of its inhabitants. In 1834, the year Athens was declared the capital of the new state, it had shrunk to a settlement of just 73 houses.

While Klenze tried to carry out his duties despite various diplomatic and political complexities,[14] he also took care of his personal mission – the preservation and reconstruction of the Acropolis monuments. He began work there in August 1834, convincing the government to pass a law (18 August 1838) prohibiting any future military use there. He was also responsible for the first restoration of the Parthenon with the archaeologist Ludwig Ross (curator of the antiquities of Athens), and the restoration of the Temple of Athena Nike and the Erechtheion with his assistants Schaubert and the Danish architect Hans Christian Hansen, who had moved to Athens in 1833. In addition, he organized the protection of the antiquities. Finally, taking as a point of departure the Kleanthes and Schaubert urban scheme, Klenze began developing his own plan

for Athens. He changed the location of the Palace, moving it away from the centre and adjacent to the archaeological area. Klenze developed designs for individual buildings for the new capital, including a monumental design for the Palace. He also designed a building complex to house an art academy together with an archaeological museum. In both projects he tried to combine a rigorous arrangement, following the rules of the classical canon, with a picturesque informal adaptation of the scheme to suit the site.

It has been said that in dealing with the capital's plan Klenze was concerned with reducing the cost of land expropriation required by the Kleanthes and Schaubert scheme. Indeed, his alternative proposal does appear to have reduced the total area their version covered, to have eliminated the boulevards, and to have shrunk many public spaces, seemingly in the interest of the landlords. However, as Alexander Papageorgiou-Venetas has shown in his study of Klenze's involvement at Athens,[15] Klenze's notes and letters reveal that his main disagreement with the Kleanthes and Schaubert plan had to do with its architectural weaknesses. Klenze criticized the geometric rigidity of the others' proposal, one driven by its 'rectilinear regularity' and 'points of view' – as applied in cities like 'Nancy, St Petersburg, Mannheim, and Karlsruhe'[16] – contrasting it to the uniqueness of the character of the Greek landscape, the 'land formation', the 'local direction of the winds', 'the streams', the 'clean forms of the mountains', the 'historicity' and 'poetic character' of Athens, the 'exactitude and plasticity' of the profile of the landscape, 'reminiscent of the sculptures of Phidias and Praxiteles', the 'richness of colours' and the 'harmony, freedom, succession of chiaroscuro tones, play of light'.[17] He maintained that Kleanthes and Schaubert imposed wide streets that reflected modern German engineering ideas about traffic efficiency, ignoring the requirements of the local climate that dictated narrow streets as a means of providing sufficient shade. For him, the plan's wide streets did not accommodate the way of life of people of the South, who enjoy life outdoors and use the streets to come into contact with one another.[18] Thus, while his ideas were seemingly less modern than those

Agios Ioannis stin Kolona (St John at the Column), Athens. Church attached to a column of an old Asklepios temple. Drawing by Theodore du Moncel.

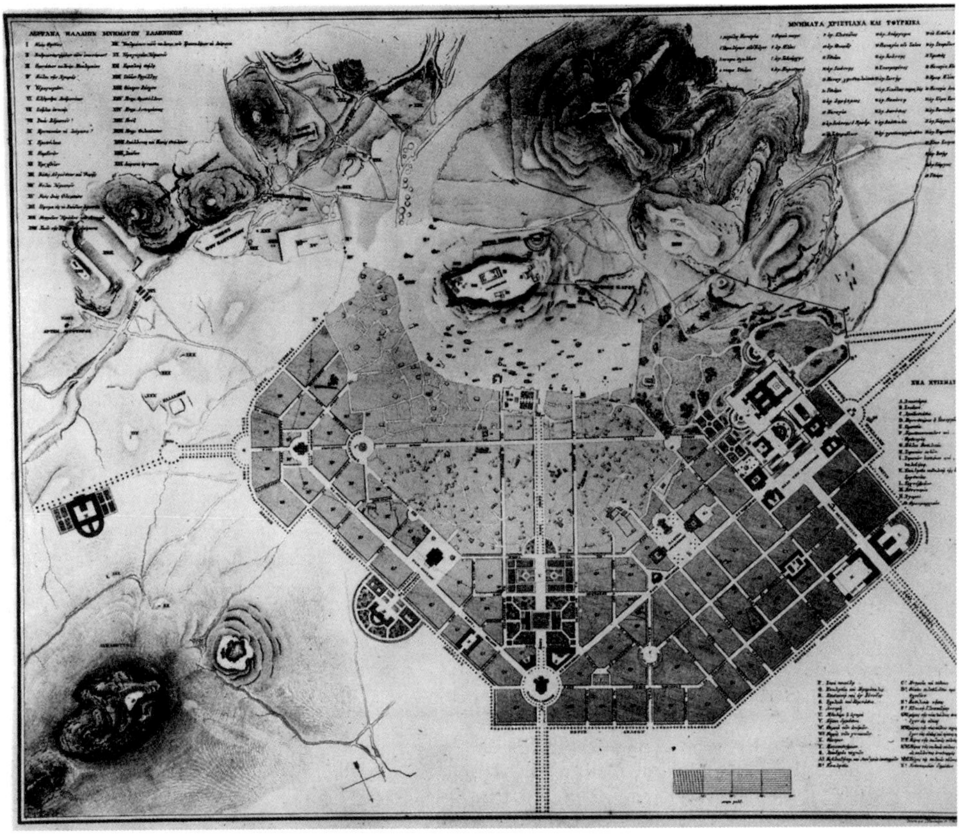

Leo von Klenze, *Plan for the New City of Athens*, counterproposal, 1834.

of Kleanthes and Schaubert, his understanding of the regional requirements were advanced for their time. Yet when a building commission was convened in 1834 to find a solution, Klenze's points were not taken into consideration.[19] The commission was instead mindful to satisfy the interests of the landlords, merely paying lip service to the Kleanthes–Schaubert plan. The pair had no alternative but to resign.

While this controversy was taking place, Otto was making up his mind about moving to Athens. Finally, on 1 December 1834, he officially declared Athens the capital of the kingdom and decided to travel there immediately, despite the fact that nothing was ready to receive either him or his entourage.[20] A year later, Ludwig arrived in Greece accompanied by Friedrich von Gärtner, another of his court architects.[21] During his time there Ludwig took all the necessary decisions about the plan for Athens, the location for his Palace, and the architect who was going to design it: Gärtner, not Klenze. Gärtner notably recommended keeping the Palace site at a distance from the Acropolis and the surrounding archaeological area occupying one of the hills towards the north.

Gärtner designed the scheme in four months during his stay in the capital. On 25 January 1836 Ludwig himself placed the foundation stone, demonstrating the political significance of the project.[22] Construction began two years later and by 1843 the Palace was ready, a disproportionately grandiose project for a state whose coffers were empty and whose population, not more than 800,000, was one of the poorest and least educated in the post-Ottoman empire, and who lived in what had been one of its least productive regions. The Palace design itself was restrained. Inscribed in a prismatic grid, it followed a strict tripartite classical schema, each side containing two large, symmetrically arranged, atria. The spatial composition of the scheme adhered to the classical canon, as did the minimal classical Grecian decorative elements of the flat facades and the Propylaea-like white marble Doric porticos marking the entrances to the building.

Together with Pronoia, Gärtner's Palace is arguably Greece's first major modern architectural project. While it seems, as a neoclassical building, to be in opposition to the modern movement, the critic Henry-Russell Hitchcock found in Gärtner's quadrangular Palace, as in many buildings

Friedrich von Gärtner, King Otto's Palace, Athens, 1836–43 (photograph 1868).

by Schinkel 'and his followers in Germany', in their 'rigorousness', 'regularity', 'unbroken surface', 'austerity' and 'serenity', a 'precursor' of modernist architecture and of the Miesian style.[23] However, an examination of the archives that document the history of the conception of the scheme of Gärtner's Palace reveal that many of the 'proto-modernist' qualities that Hitchcock – who never saw these archives – admired in the scheme were not the result of intentional stylistic decisions. Gärtner had originally worked out facades with elaborate details and rich decorations, but these were deleted by Ludwig, who considered them opulent and costly. Indeed Gärtner was contemptuous of the stripped-down version of his scheme, calling what remained 'just a military encampment'.[24]

The building's unprecedented scale necessitated new methods of management and construction, which Gärtner and his assistants im-ported. They brought in German technicians and carpenters and Italian stonecutters, who worked together with native Athenian builders and Greek builders from the islands, invited to Athens specifically for the project, turning the site into a training ground for new technologies in architectural construction.

The Palace's Neoclassicism also transformed the image of governance of the new Greece from a ricketty Ottoman province to a conservative but none the less 'modern' kingdom. For Schinkel, Klenze and other architects of the time, ancient Greek architecture was, as Klenze wrote, architecture 'par excellence', the highest of its kind, the 'most perfect'.[25] The question of national identity – what the kingdom of Greece (or Hellas, as it was known in Greek) was supposed to be – dominated the early years. The writer and revolutionary Rigas Velestinlis (also known as Rigas Feraios) had called on Bulgarians, Arvanites, Armenians and Greeks to join a multi-ethnic state, 'without discrimination of religion . . . or class'; 'Christianity, Turkism, Judaism and the rest' all having the right to 'free access to work' and education 'for all males and females'. A generation after Rigas, the politician Ioannis Kolettis advocated a different, irredentist, approach, which he termed the 'Great Idea' ('*Megali Idea*'), aimed at the liberation and unification of all 'unredeemed' Greek communities living inside the Ottoman empire (only a quarter of those who called themselves Greek at that time actually lived within Greece's borders). The idea was to bring them together in a Greek state and subsequently to revive the Byzantine empire, with Greece

reconquering Constantinople. Similarly, the historian Constantinos Paparrigopoulos, in his multi-volume *Historia,* tried to explain the polymorphic composition of those who claimed to be or were recognized as being Greeks, linking ancient and modern Greece through Byzantium. But Byzantine architecture and Byzantine culture were generally seen as decadent. Neoclassical architecture encapsulated the new nation's identity. Indeed, even before the Revolution and the official declaration of the 'Great Idea', the classical canon was applied in community and commercial buildings by the 'unredeemed' Greeks living in the various urban centres of the Ottoman empire, such as Salonica, Smyrna, Trebizond and Istanbul.

In 1839, with Prince Otto now King of Hellas, work began on the second major building, the University of Athens, designed by Hans Christian Hansen, who had been appointed court architect by Otto in 1834. Construction lasted almost a quarter of a century due to insufficient, mostly private, funds. As in Gärtner's Palace, the plan and the facades of Hansen's building are stern and minimal, adhering to the classical canon's tripartite scheme. The details are few, simple, the severity of the facades softened through the application of warm colours, mainly those used in antiquity, which blend well with the Athenian sky.[26]

To the right of the University stands the Academy. Its architect was Theophil Hansen, Christian Hansen's brother, who had arrived in Athens in 1838 after studying in Vienna and working with Schinkel. Baron Simon von Sina, the Greek ambassador in Vienna, sponsored the project. The construction of the Academy started in 1859 but, like the University, took a long time to complete, this time because of a five-year interruption due to Sina's disappointment with Otto's dethronement in 1862. It was eventually finished in 1885.

The 'Athens Trilogy': the National Library, 1884–1902, the University, 1839–64, and the Academy of Athens, 1859–85. Watercolour by Theophil Hansen, 1885.

The all-marble Academy is gracefully composed and richly ornamented with Ionic architectural details (mostly originating in the Erechtheion, which Hansen had studied at first hand). It contains sculptures by Leonidas Drossis and Franz Melnitzky and murals by Christian Griepenkerl and Carl Rahl, all elegantly detailed while not especially interesting conceptually, despite the mission of the building. Ernst Ziller, a young architect working in Hansen's office, supervised construction, and would subsequently go on to design numerous Athenian buildings. Given the continuous backwardness of the country, and with most of the promises made directly after the Revolution remaining unfulfilled, not everyone was happy with the project, as with other architectural projects of the period. The journal *Aion* ironically noted on 27 March 1858: 'we have no navy, no army, no roads, yet, we will soon have an Academy: look with fear Turkey. Cheers Byzantium. The Academy is under construction.'

A third building to the left of the University (1839–64) is the National Library (1884–1902), also by Theophil Hansen. The project, the last of the 'Athenian Trilogy', as Hansen called it, is the least successful formally. It has a protruding central entrance component, oversized, and disjointed from the two side parts of the tripartite composition. The Pentelic marble building sits infelicitously on an oversized limestone base. An accumulation of compositional errors followed, not least an equally unrelated oversized curved stair with a bulky ornate balustrade terminated by monumental lamp-posts.[27]

The weakest aspect of the Hansen brothers' designated group is that the three do not make up a 'trilogy'. Theophil Hansen tried to bring their trio of projects together by making them similar, but they remain ununified. Pedantically adhering to the classical canon, each building was mechanically divided into three parts, with each one left standing as an isolated object without reference to a larger compositional whole.

In contrast to the trilogy by the Hansen brothers, the application of a classical tripartite structure to the building complex of the National Metsovion Polytechneion in Athens (or simply Polytechnic, Athens, 1862–76) by Lysandros Kaftanzoglou is a masterpiece of the genre. The 'minimalist' qualities of the Polytechnic admired today were to a great extent the result of budget austerity; like Gärtner, Kaftanzoglou believed that his project was incomplete: 'the buildings erected ought to be seen as skeletons from the aesthetic point of view, the proper ornamentation not yet applied'. On the other hand, what made both buildings among the best works of nineteenth-century architecture was not the absence of ornament but the rigorous spatial organization of the 'skeleton-schema', which stood up even if many detailed elements were never attached to it.

At the Polytechnic, the Ionic and Doric modes are used meaningfully. The centre of the main building is accentuated with an elevated Ionic propylon. Once more, the Erechtheion motif was used as a prototype. The two side buildings (flanking the complex) are differentiated in height and character from the central one. (By contrast, in the case of the trilogy, the Academy is Ionic while the Library is Doric.) Again, the discrepancy with the Hansen trilogy is instructive, the Hansens ignoring the quality of the emergent in-between spaces in their complex, leading to an amorphous total. Finally Kaftanzoglou's design provided interesting open public spaces – loggias, courts and an atrium well-adapted to the Attic climate.

An equally significant building designed by Kaftanzoglou was the Arsakeion (1846–52), a girls' school named after Apostolos Arsakis, the sponsor of the project. Kaftanzoglou also designed two additional buildings next to the Arsakeion – the Tositseion girls' school and the nursery school (both demolished in 1900), once again a complex of admirable simplicity and harmony.

Kaftanzoglou's contribution to the development of Greek architecture was enormous, both through his works and his writings and teaching. A year after his arrival in Athens in 1838 (having studied in Rome and France) he exhibited his work inside the ancient temple of Hephaestus (also called the Hephaisteion and – incorrectly – the Theseion). The show included his personal proposals for the future of Athens: these clearly demarcated the archaeological area for conservation and suggested that east should be the direction for the city's growth. After unsuccessful attempts to establish a practice in Athens, he left for Constantinople, where he stayed for four years. Commissions were not easily come by in Greece, one reason being the competition from those foreign architects who dominated public service positions. The situation changed with the 1844 constitution that Otto was forced to accept, which together with providing a parliament and almost universal suffrage, limited the participation of foreigners in public service, opening major opportunities for Greek professionals. Kaftanzoglou took over the direction of the technical school, Vassiliki Mihanothiki, and transformed it into an applied and fine arts school, the Royal Polytechnic (*Vassilikon Polytechneion*). He stayed on as its director until 1862, when King Otto was forced to leave Greece (his radical ideas and architectural biases didn't prevent him from being both a pro-Otto royalist and a free thinker at the same time). Kaftanzoglou's rigorous classical credo is clear in his designs for ecclesiastical buildings, for which he largely excluded Byzantine elements, completing the Roman Catholic church Agios Dionysios (1852) originally designed by Klenze, and in his own schemes for Agia Irini (1846–92) and his last work, the church of Agios Konstantinos (1879–96). However, his

Lysandros Kaftanzoglou, Athens Polytechnic, 1862–76. Watercolour by Luigi Lanza.

Athens Polytechnic, 1862–76.

opposite: Athens Polytechnic, 1862–76.

Lysandros Kaftanzoglou, Arsakeion Girls' School, Athens, 1846–52 (photograph 1965; shops at ground level are later additions).

Lysandros Kaftanzoglou, Tositseion Girls' School and Nursery School, Athens, 1865 (photograph 1885; building demolished 1900).

opposite: Lysandros Kaftanzoglou, Church of Agios Konstantinos, Athens, 1871–96 / 1905.

work was not dogmatic: the construction of Agios Georgios Karytsis church reused old Byzantine fragments from adjacent ruins. Buildings in Athens at that time using anything remotely linked to Byzantine architecture comprised two rather insignificant examples, the Army Ministry and the Military Pharmacy (1852) by Theophil Hansen, who was not only a master of the classical canon but also of Western medieval and Byzantine idioms. While Kaftanzoglou himself had used Byzantine motifs in his own work, he nonetheless accused Western scholars and architects of being driven by 'completely metaphysical' and 'romantic ideas', 'searching for inspiration in the dark epochs of slavery and decline', admiring 'Byzantines, Normans, Arabs, Goths' irrelevant to the present century of great discoveries and illuminations'. Kaftanzoglou reckoned that the 'Christian temple . . . canon established by our ancestors should be abandoned'.

The 'Castle' in Penteli outside of Athens (1841) and the Villa Ilissia (1848) in Athens, now part of the Byzantine Museum, were both built for Sophie de Marbois Lebrun, Duchess of Plaisance, who had moved to Greece in 1836. For many years the buildings were attributed to Stamatios Kleanthes (a former student of Schinkel in Berlin) without

Christian Hansen, Opthalmology Clinic, Athens, 1847–54.

much proof. Recently, however, Olga Fundulaki, the author of the only monograph on Kleanthes, announced that the designer of the Castle was the Lyon architect André Louis Antoine Couchaud, who spent a considerable period in Greece studying Byzantine buildings (1838–40 and 1842–5), and that Kleanthes supervised its construction.[28] Whoever was the real architect, these are certainly rare cases of works clearly inspired by European medieval or Orientalist motifs (they draw too from J.-N.-L. Durand prototypes in France as well as from Schinkel's Court Gardener's House of 1831 and Roman Baths, 1834, both in Potsdam). Their shady loggias and extended eaves, sometimes bracketed, are also fitting for the environment and climate of Attica.

Equally eclectic in combining elements drawn from precedents of different periods but without the fantasy and the melancholic mood of the Duchess's residences was the luxurious residence for the Dimitriou brothers on Syntagma Square, diagonally across the Palace. Built in 1842, the year of the collapse of the Greek market and the export crisis for wine, olive oil, raisins and silk, this is an elegant example of Rundbogenstil, initiated in Germany by Heinrich Hübsch and Schinkel (who followed Durand and others working in Napoleonic-era France), subsequently pursued by Klenze and Gärtner in Munich, and finally introduced to Athens by Theophil Hansen. Hansen's assistant, Ernst Ziller, also employed it in his Iliou Melathron or House of Troy (1878–80), the residence of the merchant and archaeologist Heinrich Schliemann, the discoverer of Troy, and which housed the finds from his excavations prior to their removal to Berlin. The work is pleasing to the eye though not particularly original.

As a young man Ziller had been involved in serious revolutionary activities. In his architectural practice in Greece, however, he proved to be the most understanding designer of the new elite society. His most successful project was the residence for Othon Stathatos (1895), located like Ilissia and other prestigious residences on the ancient road leading out towards the northern villages of Attica, and within walking distance of the Palace. The Stathatos residence, now part of the Cycladic Museum, was one the most attractive residences built on the Avenue, and even today is one of the most loved buildings in the capital. More than any other work by Ziller it foreshadowed the end of a rigorous, epic era and a turn towards a more hedonistic, Belle Epoque period that would characterize Greek architecture at the end of the nineteenth century. Ziller also designed the more austere and impressively large mansion of Vassilios Melas (1873) next to the city hall.

The most important architect of public buildings of this second generation was Panayiotis Kalkos. The son of a revolutionary, he belonged to

André Louis Antoine Couchaud or Stamatios Kleanthes, The 'Castle', Penteli, Attica, 1841.

André Louis Antoine Couchaud or Stamatios Kleanthes, Villa Ilissia, Athens, 1848 (photograph 1914; remodelled by Aristotelis Zachos, 1928–30, enlarged by Vassilios Douras 1949–52).

Ernst Ziller, Stathatos residence, Athens, 1895.

a new generation of architects in Greece who had experienced the pioneering experiments that introduced the classical canon to the new state and who had assisted in the design and construction of several buildings before they assumed a practice of their own. Among Kalkos's projects are the remarkable Varvakeion High School (1857), the Town Hall (*c.* 1872) and the Municipal Orphanage (*c.* 1872). Kaftanzoglou's qualities of sobriety, coherence and rigour are clearly present in Kalkos's work.

Despite its significance, Piraeus, Athens's port, was perceived by the government and by Athenians as a provincial town, its buildings seemingly lesser to those of Athens. Yet its Town Hall and the Municipal Theatre by Ioannis Lazarimos (1882–95) were austere classical compositions that fitted carefully into the street plan.[29] Whatever the excellence was of these buildings, with the exception of a few coffee-houses they could not make up for the backwardness of public spaces and the absence of any future comprehensive plan for the town.[30]

Ernst Ziller, Hadjikosta Orphanage Church of Agios Georgios, Athens, 1890–1901.

The drive behind the development of Athens was strictly political: the capital was a political 'brand'. Until the First World War, it generated mostly government intrigue and bureaucratic directives, slowly through its educational institutions creating an elite that included only a few individuals with technical knowledge but many more literary scholars, theologians and lawyers, in short, ideologists important for local politics and for the diaspora. Indeed, many Greeks believed that the populace of the capital was not involved in any productive work and merely spent its time in local politics. The productive and commercial centres of Greece were elsewhere – in Patras, Nafplion and Hermoupolis (capital of the island of Syros). Soon after the Revolution, Hermoupolis acquired a plan (1837) by Wilhelm von Weiler, who also designed a number of public buildings with J. Erlacher. Ziller also designed one of his best public buildings for Hermoupolis: the Town Hall (1871–98).[31]

In addition to these relatively substantial projects beyond Athens, a series of modest schools that were part of Kapodistrias's programme continued to be built after his death. Thus we find buildings by D. Stavridis, a military engineer, in Andritsena, Arvanitokerasia, Karytena, Prastos, Tripolis (1829–30) and in Argos (1831); by Wilhelm von Weiler in Hermoupolis, Syros (1836) and Mykonos; by A. Y. Kalandras in Megara

Panayiotis Kalkos, Varvakeion High School, Athens, 1857 (photograph 1936).

Alexandros Georgandas, Customs House, Syros, 1859–61.

(1831–5); and by Kleanthes and Schaubert in Aegina, Hydra, Spetses and Vostitza (now Aigion). To aid the campaign, guidelines were published in 1830 for the design of school buildings. The fundamental design ideas of these schools were grounded in Durand's theory and practice. They were practical, minimal-standard facilities whose elementary organization was based on 'room and corridor' types recombined to fit local sites, whose 'neoclassical' architecture delivered the message of the Enlightenment.[32]

Even less voluminous and monumental were the ordinary residential buildings designed by the builders themselves. These used prefabricated classical architectural details made by the same workshops that produced the classical ornaments for the major public buildings. This helped to create a uniform urban landscape despite the lack of city regulations. They were one- or two-storey structures usually entered via a courtyard that was surrounded by an arrangement of rooms overlooking the yard. Life was mostly lived outdoors, in the covered corridor that gave onto the rooms, in the courtyard, or on the house's front doorstep. But construction could not keep up with the expanding population, even when the pace was not particularly fast.[33]

House in Nafplion, late 1800s.

ΖΑΧΑΡΟΠΛΑΣΤΕΙΟΝ
Κ. ΓΑΛΑΚΤΟΠΩΛΕΙΟΝ
ΓΛΥΚΑ

By 1851 Greece's population was approximately one million, of which around 25,000 individuals lived in Athens. The final years of Otto's reign witnessed the decline of most of the urban centres that flourished before and during the first years of the Revolution in Greece and the burgeoning of Athens, weakening the distributed pattern of urban development and replacing it with a centralized one. As regards Athens, while a royal decree in 1836 had set guidelines for rebuilding the city and an official plan was in place, it continued to be modified. Special exceptions and individual modifications to the rules subscribed by the law for single cases were also constantly introduced. Athens developed unpredictably, even chaotically. The press criticized the situation. Kaftanzoglou fought for the preservation of the old city and its separation from the new by means of a 'green band', pleading for the safeguarding of historical buildings. Going beyond earlier proposals by Ludwig, Ross and Klenze, he recommended that the band be linked to an archaeological promenade that would connect the hills around the Acropolis with part of the banks of the Ilissos river and the Temple of Olympian Zeus. Even by the end of the twentieth century the scheme had only partially been implemented.

The absence of any plan to guide the expanding capital soon began to be felt by most Athenians, but it was most harmful to a particular group – the workers who had arrived in the city to help with the construction of the Palace and the numerous public and private buildings, as well as archaeological digs and restoration projects. They were impoverished fishermen from the Cyclades but they were also very skilled in construction work. Unable to pay their rent, and ignored by the government, they took their destiny in their own hands and occupied an area in a fringe of the city in which they began building basic shelters, thus establishing the so-called 'Proasteion' ('the Suburb'). The Greeks would give a name to these structures developed beyond the law, *authereta*, meaning random, unauthorized and subject to individual caprice.

In 1847 the Proasteion became part of the capital's official plan. Land prices started to rise, leaving very little space for such improvised construction to continue. The homeless were forced to search for other areas in which to settle. One of the very first such *authereta* structures sprang up without permission on the side of the Acropolis hill. According to Dimitrios Kambouroglou, the nineteenth-century historian of medieval Athens, there was a long tradition of illegal occupancy on this side of the Acropolis that went as far back as the age of Pericles. At the beginning of the nineteenth century, prior to the Revolution, the area had been occupied by homeless so-called *arapides*, former Ethiopian slaves who worked for the Ottomans. In an 1832 memo, Kleanthes and Schaubert argued

Ernst Ziller, Town Hall, Syros, Hermoupolis 1871–98.

that these makeshift dwellings were obstacles to the work of the archaeologists. A new illegal occupation started in 1860 with settlers from the Cycladic island of Anafi (one of the poorest islands of Greece, which would later become notorious as a place of exile for political detainees), thus giving the area the name of Anafiotika. Initially, two men violated the building prohibition and, ignoring the protests of the archaeologists, embedded two shacks on the side of the Acropolis and set up their households. Soon after, exploiting an early law that prohibited the demolition of a house that already had a roof over it, more settlers secretly moved into the area. They would dig and build throughout the night in teams in order to roof their dwellings by sunrise. Lack of funds rather than sympathy with the illegal settlers ruled out the expropriation of their shacks.

Because they occupied an area designated for excavations, the settlers received no support from the intelligentsia, with the exception of the Greek novelist Alexandros Papadiamantis, who wrote about the hardships of the Aegean islanders, and the historian Dimitrios Kambouroglou. In 1881 and 1883 archaeologists unsuccessfully petitioned to move the inhabitants of Anafiotika so as to free up the area for digs. However, towards the end of the nineteenth century, when opposition to the bloated bureaucracy of the Greek state was mounting, the attitude towards Anafiotika began to shift, and writers, artists and the public in general began to admire the self-help settlement as an expression of defiance against an incompetent and oppressive authority. But they also respected its authenticity, the absence of embellishments on the buildings, and the talent and skill demonstrated by the builders, who ignored the formulas of classical architecture and drew instead on the vernacular traditions of their own regions. The historian of modern city planning in Athens, Kostas Biris, claimed that the settlers were aided by growing political opposition to King Otto, whose subjects were now demanding a constitution, which at the time created a climate of lawlessness in the city. Biris also admired how the inhabitants of Anafiotika found the opportunity 'to escape the stultifying ambiance of Attica to put up their little houses'; they employed 'their island design instinct of composition and construction, they found a place that nobody else could use and exploited the prohibitive conditions of the site'.[34]

The number of *authereta* homes would continue to grow in Athens as well as on the periphery of towns throughout Greece; they would become one of the defining components of the modern Greek townscape. Gradually, Anafiotika and similar self-help projects began to be perceived by some as a pioneering paradigm that symbolized the ills and consequences of top-down, state-driven construction that disregarded the

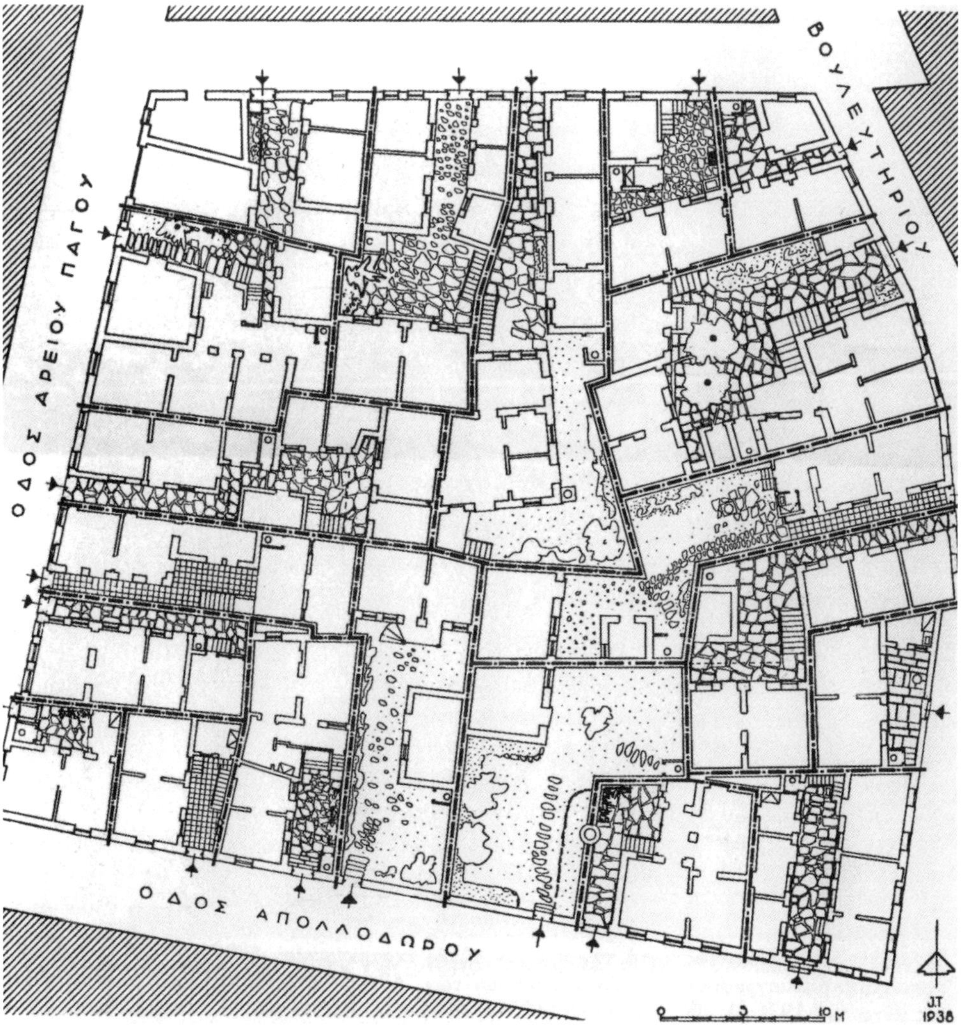

Ground-floor plans of 19th-century vernacular houses north of the Acropolis, Athens. Demolished 1938. Drawing from a survey by I. Travlos.

site and its location; instead, their buildings proved how architecture could be done in an alternative way, ground-up, and local. It also demonstrated how a new settlement could enable a feeling of identity and community, both of which were threatened qualities in the new urban environments of Greece. In an 1894 text, 'Acropolis Selinofotos', the poet Kostis Palamas mused in the moonlight about the plans of the Archaeological Society to demolish Anafiotika in order not simply to excavate the site but 'to plant trees, avenues, gardens, and "paths" around the hill . . . instantly transforming these silent and private places into hubs of

Illegal housing in Anafiotika, Athens. Photograph by Nelly, c. 1927.

noisy visitors and *flâneurs* of any type and taste'. He concluded, 'I do not know why the idea terrified me.' The point would become increasingly relevant not only for modern Greece but for the modern world.

chapter two

'Forward': Infrastructure, City Plans and Buildings

The latter half of the nineteenth century brought with it a series of infrastructure projects to modernize the new nation. The Corinth Canal (begun in 1882) was one of the most significant such schemes in Greece.[1] At the same time, the government commissioned a Belgian company to set up a rail transportation network for Athens. By 1882 trains were transporting Athenians between the city centre and the seaside resort of Faliro; Prime Minister Charilaos Trikoupis lobbied for a rail system that would connect the whole country. At the time around 500 French people were living in Piraeus and Athens, half of them engineers or technical assistants; the high number shows how the country was open to, and heavily dependent on, Western Europe for its technological progress.

Not everyone was happy with modernization's mixed benefits. In 1874 the humourist writer Erineos Asopios invoked the 'sacred mission of Greece', which was the responsibility of 'We, the descendents of Miltiades, Themistocles, Pericles . . . but today, what shameful decadence . . . anthracite, charcoal, coke, lead, copper, blast furnace, extracting, smelting, slag, mining, enrichment, sieve, again slag, and eternal outflows'.[2] Yet, in reality, by the end of the century Greece was far from advanced: Around 70 per cent of its population still lived in villages. The country was dominated by poor peasants who scratched a living from ground that was very hard to cultivate, or was owned by incompetent or absentee landlords who obstructed the exploitation of their land. In contrast to Kapodistrias's earlier vision favouring smallholders, the regime that succeeded him advanced the acquisition of large plots of land by a few local or diaspora Greeks as well as foreigners, a policy that not only led to social tensions but also shrank production, with the new landowners unable to manage effectively their recently acquired property. To overcome these problems, in 1890 Prime Minister Trikoupis passed a law that encouraged banks to support smallholders, which was followed by legislation that permitted peasants to appropriate and cultivate land belonging to absentee landlords and, after a certain period, if such actions were not contested, to possess it legally. Legislation of this sort, based on Roman

Corinth Canal, 1882–93. Designed by Hungarian engineer Béla Gerster, with the assistance of French engineer Vincent Dauzats (photograph 1922).

Steam-driven train named *Therion* ('monster') serving the Athens–Kifissia and N. Herakleion–Laurion lines, 1882–1938.

legal precedents, sought to correct the injustices of the past, bring about wealth redistribution, and more importantly increase the productivity of the land by eliminating uncultivated waste. It turned out to be a populist strategy that resulted in lawlessness and legal disputes that would continue for a century and more. With agriculture so sluggish to develop, villagers were forced to abandon their property, moving en masse to Athens or emigrating to the USA.

Like Kapodistrias before him, Trikoupis considered schools to be more than just places that advanced the population's education, seeing them as the sites at which to construct a common modern national identity. In 1889 his government presented legislation to Parliament asking for a government loan with the 'exclusive aim of constructing school buildings in all municipalities of the state'.

The engineer Dimitrios Kallias wrote a report containing basic design regulations and guidelines in 1894.[3] The material, drawn to a large extent from a recent publication by Jules Ferry, the renowned Minister of Public Instruction in France and father of the institution of *l'école républicaine,* made accessible to architects and teachers a modern typology of school buildings. The report was approved and four types were selected for application, the Ministry of Education distributing drawings of the selected

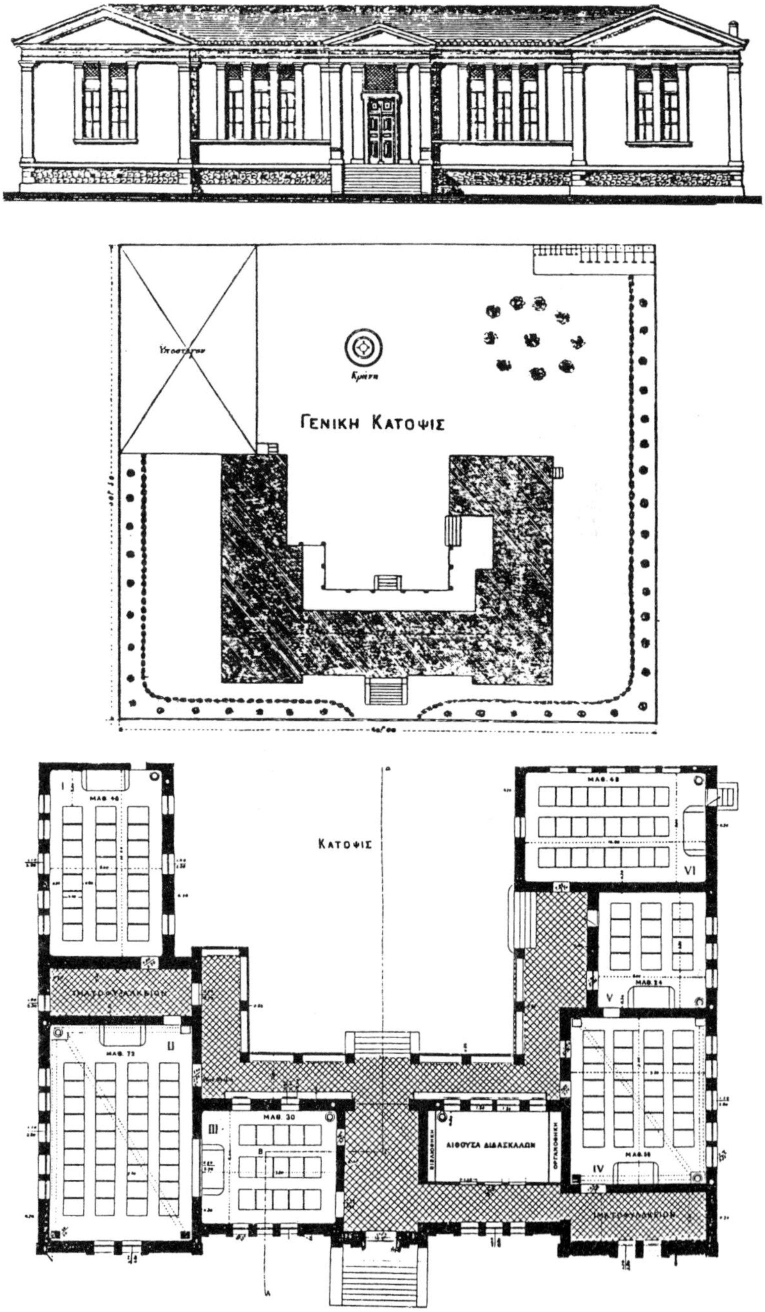

Dimitrios Kallias, *Elementary School Prototype*, 1898. Elevation, site plan and floor plan.

types to all municipal boards. In addition to concerns about health standards, the adopted regulations stressed the architectural appearance of the buildings: their street facades had to emphasize implicitly the significance of the institution and the presence of the new state. Facades and plans had to be plain, stern and symmetrical, and, like the schools built during the short period of Kapodistrias's leadership, Kallias's guidelines were an attempt to present a public face of dignity and orderliness unknown up to that time in most of the countryside. Moreover, the buildings' obvious references to the architecture of classical antiquity provided a 'progressive' national face enhancing a militant and progressive Greek identity in contrast to Ottoman 'backwardness'. After Trikoupis's death in 1896, the Theotokis government continued to support the idea. In order to develop further the programme, in 1899 it introduced an Architectural Service within the Ministry of Education, with Anastasios Metaxas later appointed as the first head of the Service in 1908. Metaxas was a graduate of Dresden's Polytechnic, and his work included the Aegineteion and Syngrou Hospitals, the Ionic and Popular Banks, and the Charokopos House, all plain but graceful buildings adhering to the classical canon. He was thus the ideal architect to activate Kallias's regulations. The 'Kallias'-type schools were constructed for more than a decade (1898–1911) at a slow but regular pace, amounting to 407 schools nationwide, but this was an unsatisfactory figure for a country whose population by then was close to six million. Despite its commitment to modernization, half a century after gaining its independence, Greece remained unable to develop sufficient economic and legal processes to cope with the complex problems of capitalist industrial development.

One of the key reasons for Greece's lag in modernization was the lack of state funds for projects essential for the 'take off' phase and the relative unattractiveness of Greece for foreign investors. The need to raise funds through taxation surprised and distressed the rural population, the easy target for extracting money, who realized that a new, modernizing state demanded more taxes than had the Ottomans. Possessing a severely underdeveloped public administration, lacking any kind of fair programme of taxation or rational framework to plan the economy, Greece had to depend on unpopular loans from the United Kingdom and the Rothschild Bank. Paradoxically, the very weakness of the Greek state, the absence of law enforcement, and the lack of a coherent approach to development, seemed to challenge rather than hinder diaspora Greek and foreign investors who, welcomed by the government, tried piecemeal and perilous industrialization schemes in the midst of rural underdevelopment and the vacuum of state regulation. The notorious Laurion mines founded by an Italian entrepreneur Giovanni Battista Serpieri is one

Facilities of the 'Compagnie Française des Mines du Laurion', Attica, 1876. Photograph c. 1890.

example. The company employed 1,200 labourers, offering them only primitive shacks for shelter, each shack accommodating 30 to 40 men who, given the lack of any relevant legislation, had no right to strike. But strikes erupted: in 1871 the first one in Laurion was also the first strike in Greece, followed in 1874 with a second regarding the right to strike, which was won. Another strike in 1896 caused violent destruction of property and life.[4] Most of the capital for the mine came from enthusiastic investments by the new Greek middle class, encouraged by exaggerated fantasies circulated by the press. Greed, political corruption, precarious management and the constant interference of a non-expert monarch soon led to colossal financial ruin. But there was no response by the state and no administrative attempts to control this new phenomenon at either an economic or planning level.

Private ruin, social malaise and political laxity came to a head with state bankruptcy. In 1893 Trikoupis famously declared in Parliament that Greece was broke – 'Regretfully, we are bankrupt' – while one of his very best friends and supporters, Andreas Syngros, one of those responsible for helping Greece borrow money for its investments in 1881, wondered, as recorded in his autobiography,[5] not why the bankruptcy had happened but why it had taken so long to arrive. Thirteen years earlier, Syngros, in a speech in the Greek Parliament, cynically admitted that under Greek law he paid almost no taxes. Like other libertarian patriotic Greeks, he refused to recognize the connection between unfettered manipulations of the free market, the country's unpaid international debts, and the necessary military support obtained from the Protective Powers.

Greece had found itself unable to pay its debts as far back as 1832, but the first major international crisis linked with military intervention occurred in 1849. It was triggered by the incident of the house in Athens of Don Pacifico, a Jew and close friend and collaborator of the Duchess of Plaisance, which was ransacked and torched by a mob. The motivation was clearly racist. Don Pacifico requested compensation from the Greek government, which was refused. Subsequently, being a British subject, he turned to Britain for protection. When the Greek government turned down an official British request for compensation, the foreign secretary, Lord Palmerston, sent a British fleet to blockade Piraeus, enacting for the first time what came to be called 'gunboat diplomacy'.[6] Intervention was repeated in 1854 when both British and French navies and troops blockaded and occupied Piraeus in order to inhibit Greek support for Russia during the Crimean War, and for payment of outstanding debts. The occupation continued after the Crimean conflict had ended in 1856, the Protecting Powers demanding the establishment of an International Committee of Economic Control that, starting on 18 February 1857, oversaw the economic management of the Greek state.

Despite these humiliating interventions Greece was able to recover and slowly return to development. The Gas Light Company, 'Aeriofos', was founded in 1857 by royal decree. Yet the facility was placed irresponsibly in a key location of the capital, not far from the Theseion, in the vicinity of the ancient cemetery of Keramikos, thus downgrading the quality and value of a central area of Athens for the next century and after. As in most industrial cities at that time, there was no provision in Athens for workers' housing. Workers rented single-storey, low-ceilinged courtyard houses shared by several families, which were arranged in rectilinear streets. But, in contrast to the slums in north European cities, the facades of Athenian houses were pleasantly decorated with ceramic neoclassical details and occasionally by ceramic sculptures. The inhabitants, many of whom had recently arrived from the countryside, crowded the courtyards with domestic animals, flowerpots and jasmine, lemon and orange trees. Social life took place mainly outdoors. Living conditions worsened during the last quarter of the nineteenth century as additional factories were established. A major furniture factory founded by George Georgiadis in 1882 imported technology from Vienna to manufacture bentwood furniture and wooden interior decorations, which supplied most of the significant buildings and households of the time. While the environmental conditions of the 'Gazi' neighbourhood worsened, the press greeted the arrival of industry as evidence of employment, progress and affluence. A hat factory with 250 workers and an impressive smokestack was celebrated by a leading journalist, Vlassis Gavriilides, as an 'unshakeable symbol of industrial progress in Greece'.[7]

Next to the Gazi gasworks in the area of 'Metaxourgeion' (silkworks) emerged workshops and noisy and smelly factories producing carpets, shoes, ironwork and ironware, and carriages.[8] However, it was clear that inadequate services, poor resources, uneducated labour and the risky political climate made Greece unattractive for industrial speculation. Most of the investment by nouveau-riche Greeks and the mainly wealthy diaspora was channelled towards the purchase of real estate and the construction of lavish residences in Athens. This offered major opportunities to contractors, civil engineers and architects, but the pecuniary attitudes of the diaspora Greeks, their refusal to invest their money in Greece, the economic crisis and the apathy of the government became the subjects of critical discussions in the Parliament in 1873 and 1874. In one meeting in February 1874, Petimezas, an MP from the opposition, protested that the government 'built marble palaces in Athens but had turned the whole capital into a home for paupers'. The attack was seconded by the press, with one newspaper accusing the overseas Greeks as having impoverished whole families in order to 'construct grandiose mansions'.[9]

The Poulopoulos hat factory, Athens, 1896.

As economic conditions began to improve towards the end of the century, Ernst Ziller became the leading architect for Athenian elite.[10] In addition to the homes built for Othon Stathatos and Heinrich Schliemann, whose opulent residences were mentioned earlier, Ziller designed more than 500 urban private houses as well as one of the first comfortable modern apartment homes in Greece (1893), on Vasilissis Sofias avenue opposite the Royal Gardens. In the course of a long and prolific professional life, Ziller also designed hotels, among them the Baggeion (*c.* 1890) and the Alexander the Great (*c.* 1889), which gave scale and character to Omonoia Square and, together with a few cafes (some of which were by Ziller), enhanced the capital's social life.[11] He also designed numerous villas in the growing suburb of Kifissia, north of Athens. Here, in contrast to the neoclassical character of the summer residences by the sea, Ziller introduced romantic north European motifs or castellated elements in accordance with the hilly and wooded setting of Kifissia. The result was 'charming', at the very best, creating an operatic mood, but there was neither originality nor experimental innovation in the work.

Ziller was also involved in another project at a difficult moment of Greek history, when, in the words of the newspaper *Helpis* (18 July 1867), 'ancient philhellenism was sunk in the Corinth canal' and the 'Greeks had stopped being in fashion', a fact that did not affect the continuing cultivation of the Great Idea vision, part of the 'imagined community' of new Greece.[12] However, an aspect of Kolettis's Great Idea proved to be seminal: the sometime vision to revive the ancient Greek festivals now assumed a more concrete form, that of restoring the Panathenaic Stadium

Ernst Ziller, project for 'Egyptian Villa', Kifissia, 1899.

Ernst Ziller, Theodorides Villa, Kifissia, 1874. Period photograph of original drawings of elevation and floor plans.

of Athens, which was buried beneath the ground, to house the Olympic Games.[13] Since his early days in Athens in the 1860s, Ziller had planned to excavate the site. His interest was archaeological, but he was also a businessman. A few years earlier, in 1856, Evangelos Zappas, a Greek merchant from Romania, had offered to support the revival of the Games and to restore the Stadium. The government accepted his offer, and King Otto proposed to link the restoration of the Stadium with construction of an exhibition pavilion for agricultural products, envisaging an event that would combine athletics, commerce and politics under the 'brand' of Greek antiquity, strengthening the identity of the new state as the cradle of Western culture but also as a burgeoning hive of production. Zappas agreed with the idea and gave the commission for the pavilion to the French architect Florimond Boulanger, who conceived an interesting functional scheme with a circular atrium within a rectilinear tripartite classical composition.

Initially the plan was to construct the pavilion adjacent to the Stadium, but the idea was soon dropped. Instead the pavilion was placed adjacent to the royal garden, and was to be surrounded by a public garden, which Athens did not have at that time. Construction started in 1874. By then

Panathenaic Stadium, Athens. Restored by Ernst Ziller and Anastasios Metaxas, 1894. Spiridon Louis entering the Stadium at the end of the marathon during the 1896 Athens Olympics.

Otto had abdicated and Prince George of Denmark was king. Zappas had died in 1865 and Boulanger followed him in 1875. There was an attempt by the military engineer Yerasimos Metaxas, who supervised construction, to take over the project. But Konstantinos Zappas, the heir of Evangelos, commissioned Theophil Hansen in 1876 with Ziller as advisor.[14]

Hansen based his design on the executed part of Boulanger's scheme and left Ziller to continue the work. The building was completed in 1888 but Ziller had walked out on the project after a dispute with the government. Ziller, however, having bought the whole site for the Panathenaic Stadium from a local landlord in 1868, was busy with his old idea of excavating the monument. Technically the excavation was not a difficult task, yet Ziller could not afford to finish it on his own. Unable to continue financing the project, which was yielding very satisfactory finds, he sold the site without profit to King George. The Stadium was uncovered completely in February 1870. The businessman George Averoff volunteered to undertake financing the project, which permitted the government to ask the Olympic Games Committee to bring the first international Olympic Games to Athens. Pierre de Coubertin, who had intended to hold an 1894 Games in Paris, agreed with the Greeks. The legendary German guidebook publisher Baedeker issued a special volume for Athens, ancient and modern. Palamas, the national poet of Greece, was invited to write the Olympic Anthem. Ziller was again left out of the final design and

Anastasios Metaxas was brought in to design the gate to the Stadium, whereupon he produced an uninspired scheme. The Games took place in 1896 with great success, and returned to the Stadium in 1906, the structure having become an international icon of the modern Western idea of sports culture, with Ziller having contributed significantly to this important diplomatic success.[15]

The new generation experienced the 1897–1911 economic recovery and a more lasting industrialization with the founding of new companies such as Achaia Clauss in Patras and Fix for wine and beer production respectively.[16] But it also went through humiliating bankruptcies, the 'disappointing victory' of the Thessaly War (1881), a conflict that ended with Greece's acquisition of the regional breadbasket but which at the same time increased the price of bread,[17] and traumatic military defeat in the Greco-Turkish War (1897), initiated by Greece's attempt to wrest Crete from Ottoman control. This martial failure overshadowed the triumph of holding Athens's first Olympic Games the previous year.

As a result of the debacle in Crete, nationalist students organized a violent uprising and occupation of the University building, provoking a bloody reaction by the government. The students and their sympathizers challenged the passivity of the government and the anti-patriotic establishment in 1901. However, the controversy centred on the problem of establishing an official language for the new state, given that there were numerous dialects in use by the heterogeneous population of new Greece. The problem was practical: an efficient linguistic medium was crucial for communicating knowledge in a manner suitable for an under-educated population rushing to become modern. But it was also sociopolitical: an effective language was necessary to help shape a common identity and facilitate a shared motivation for this population.

By the second part of the nineteenth century the debate had become polarized: there was *Katharevousa* (purist), an artificial, scholarly idiom heavily dependent on ancient and medieval Greek texts, 'cleansed' from foreign elements, representing symbolically the continuity of the nation and 'purity' of its people; and there was *Demotiki* (demotic), an amalgam, also artificial, created from commonly spoken dialects, and in this sense close to the people, enabling their enlightenment and emancipation, manifesting the democratic nature of the new nation.

In 1901 a group of fanatical, conservative and nationalistic university students violently opposed to any kind of reform organized massive protests against the translation of the New Testament into *Demotiki* (the translation had been requested by Queen Olga, who was more open minded and more concerned about the low level of literacy in Greece than were those students). Two years later a similar event took place, this time in reaction to a translation of Aeschylus' trilogy, the *Oresteia*. Similar efforts to modernize the language incited similar responses by conservative university students. The impression these chauvinist events had on Western Europeans was negative. Writing in the *Süddeutsche Monatshefte* in March 1912, the eminent Strasbourg Professor of Linguistics, Albert Thumb, called the confrontational means of the Greek reactionaries 'garbage', remarking that 'questions of culture cannot be resolved through violence'. The controversy did not directly touch the smaller world of architecture, but it did dominate every political, social and cultural expression at that time. In addition, the two sides of the linguistic debate did not match the divisions that existed between right and left politics in Greece – the conservative traditionalists and the radical modernizers. While no left-leaning modernizers adhered to *Katharevousa*, quite a few conservative chauvinists became fanatic supporters of the demotic.

One demotic adherent was Pericles Giannopoulos (1870–1910), whose writings comprise a series of articles published in *Akropolis*, a leading newspaper. They were gathered together after his premature death in the literary review *Ta Nea Grammata* in 1938, entitled 'The Greek Line', with the poet George Seferis one of the initiators of the revival. Despite its extreme nationalist spirit, the 1938 text was censored by Metaxas's government.[18] Like Melas and Dragoumes, Giannopoulos believed in force and called for action: 'never cry . . . fight', he said. 'Your place is *Forward*!' he declared (a sentiment not dissimilar to the German socialist paper *Vorwärts* and the Italian socialist *Avanti*). But Giannopoulos was neither a socialist nor a politician: 'Keep away from politics', he countered. Be 'like men of their own will, free, and alive'. Like many writers and artists of his time, say Walter Pater or Oscar Wilde, he regarded his very existence as a work of art. He used to wear a wreath on his head and pray on the Acropolis. He also met a violent end: in keeping with his 'aestheticism', he staged his own death by drowing himself on horseback in the sea of Eleusis.

Giannopoulos's influence on artists and architects was hugely significant despite the fact that he wrote very little on the subject of architecture.[19] He was able to pin down concretely a number of observations about fundamental characteristics of the Greek landscape, linking them with a vision of a way of life and values that he characterized as uniquely Greek. Convinced that 'the ignorance of contemporary life in all its expressions is beyond words . . . the ignorance of contemporary Greece is unbelievable', he came to the conclusion that the primary 'duty is to study ourselves, our past, and our present'. For him, the discipline of history, which he claimed did not exist at that time in his country, was crucial. It is 'prerequisite for reflection ... [and] communication'. Before action, he stressed, one has to ask *what* one plans to do: 'from where does [this action] originate, what did it do before, what is it to be done, how does [this action achieve] it?'

A large number of his observations were regionalist without being associated with chauvinistic ideas. He wasn't calling for a return to nationalist roots but for effective engagement in order to grasp the intangible quality of natural and cultural objects, 'the invisible, incomprehensible nature [of] anything Greek from the Parthenon to the brigand's cabin, the peasant from Megara', being 'one' with the 'GREEK EARTH', 'without any thought, any goal, your spirit free' with 'the Greek Land ... the most Beautiful Land in the World'.[20]

The concept of 'the Greek Line' stands for his method of analyzing the formal and spatial qualities of the Greek environment: 'everywhere a most simple line a soft curve, liquid, and fleeting like the large and calm breathing of the sea, the large and calm waves of the sea'; 'one line appears to ascend softly, descend sweetly, waving . . . climbing harmoniously, sliding symmetrically . . . a single line like our ancient art whereby the

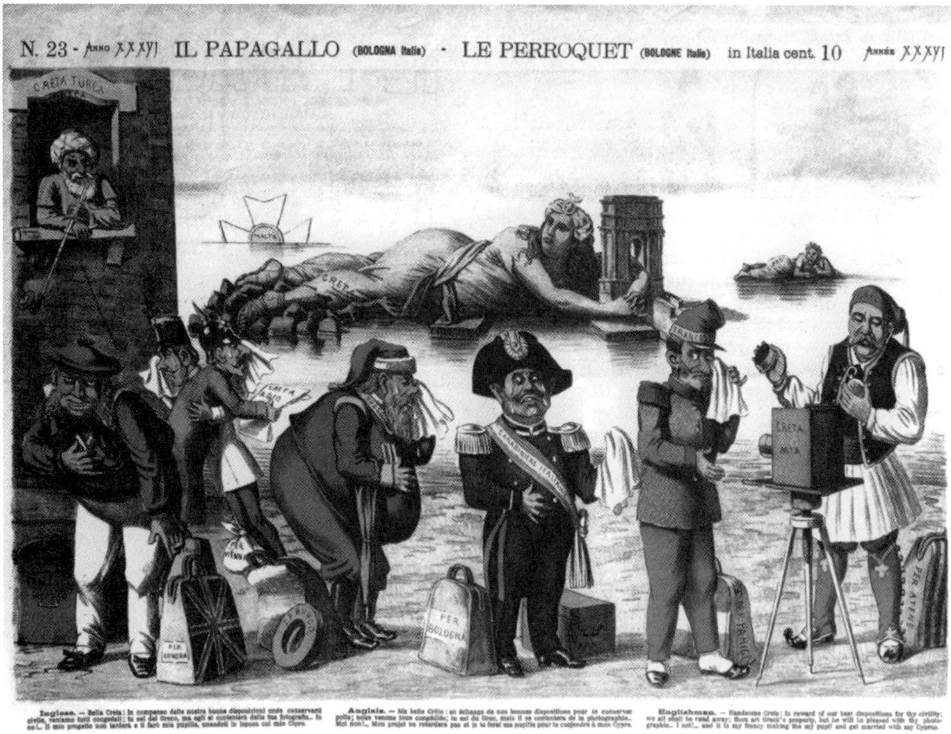

Satirical cartoon. Crete was partitioned into four quarters by the four main powers (Italy, Russia, Britain and France) before it was joined in union with Greece on 1 December 1913.

buildings appear brotherly with each other yet none like the other'. The second element characteristic of the Greek environment is light, he thought, 'the burning ocean of light', the 'joyful light', 'omnipresent light', 'enveloping light', 'hedonic light'. Moving from theory to criticism Giannopoulos became explicitly opposed to the environmental cacophony of Athens. He contrasted the 'cheerful little houses' of the island of Syros 'climbing one on the top of the shoulders of the other' with the architecture of the major commercial avenues in Athens, Stadiou and Hermou, which he called 'barbarography'. The term is one of the many words he coined, stretching the possibilities of the Greek language to the extreme; this and his stream of consciousness syntax often makes his texts difficult to translate, for example his description of the ugliness of the capital's urban environment: 'the lines of one, two, five, ten houses . . . protruding volumes, heavy, rough, scrawny lines, angular, crisscrossing, broken, collision, confusion of lines, collision, confusion of volumes, swarm of lines . . . cacophony of lines . . . all the drunk houses with the crowds, with all their lines, colliding under the sun', they all suggest the idea to 'a philanthropist to start a madhouse for the mad houses'.

'The Greek Line' captured fundamental environmental characteristics in an original and precise way. More the text of a patriot and a moralist than of a nationalist, it dealt with the conflict between globalism and regionalism and the question of an emerging identity of a modernization that can be applied to modern Greeks but also to many other peoples around the world during both his time and our own. Besides his acute formal analysis of artefacts and landscape, his aestheticism was tied to moral values, the authentic, sensory participation with the outdoor environment as a way of life, a truly Greek value. For this reason in times of deep crisis, for example during the dictatorship prior to the Second World War and subsequent post-war reconstruction, his writings became an inspiration for the great poets Odysseus Elytis and George Seferis, and for the architects Dimitris Pikionis and Aris Konstantinidis.

The new generation of Greek architects appearing on the scene around the time of Giannopoulos's suicide were driven by the same desire for action, but action in the pragmatic, professional sense. Of course they were nationalists, but their nationalism in relation to architecture consisted in support for the coming about of a prosperous greater Greece adorned and served by architecture. Their buildings appeared ornate and verbose, but what they uttered was functional prose rather than drama or poetry.

Most of these architects came from elsewhere. Before the reorganization in 1913 of the Polytechnic, Greece did not offer a degree in architecture, for architecture was taught within the school of civil engineering. The School of Architecture was established in 1917, and in the following year the first chairs were occupied by Alexandros Nikoloudes (1875–1944), who was responsible for the School's organization and educational programme, Emmanuel Kriezis (building technology), Anastasios Orlandos (a former student of engineering at the Polytechnic and subsequently of archaeology under Dörpfeld, who taught the 'orders'), and Ernest Hébrard (who by special permission lectured at the Polytechnic in French). A few of these architects had been educated in Constantinople at the Imperial Academy of Fine Arts (*Mekteb-i Sanayi-i Nefise-i Şahane*).[21] Founded in 1882, this Academy offered an architectural programme of studies and a degree. In contrast to the engineers who practised architecture and had been trained exclusively in Athens, the Constantinopolitan architects had first-hand experience of a metropolis. Others had been educated in Western Europe, among them Nikoloudes, who had trained in architecture in the Ecole des Beaux-Arts in Paris. After graduating in 1905, Nikoloudes arrived on the Greek architectural scene, submitting entries to two competitions – a courthouse (1910) and a jail (1913) – both initiated by the newly appointed prime minister, Eleftherios Venizelos.

Venizelos, a lawyer by education, was seen as a successor to Charilaos Trikoupis in the struggle to modernize Greece.[22] Having gained a reputation as a dynamic leader, a charismatic politician and a talented diplomat during the struggles over Crete, he was invited to oversee the implementation of a major reform programme put forward by a group of young officers known as the Military League. Inspired by a military association in the Ottoman empire, the Young Turks, who had rebelled the previous year, 1908, the Military League rose against the Greek government on 28 August 1909. The League had interests that went beyond political and military issues. Among its very first moves was to request advice from the Sociology Company about the problem of language.[23]

Venizelos accepted the League's invitation, arriving in Athens on 28 December of that year. However, neither the League nor he were interested in a dictatorship; he immediately called for elections, became prime minister in October 1910, and proceeded with basic reforms. The man who had impressed the leaders of the world at the Peace Conference in Paris in 1919 by 'showering his audience' with 'notes, statistics, even photograph albums', 'facts, figures, all woven artfully together',[24] had concrete projects already in mind, such as reform of both the army and the education system, starting with the resolution of the language conflict between *Katharevousa* and *Demotiki* and modernization of the teaching system – the Sociology Company being one of his close consultants for both language and instruction. Around the summer of 1912 one of the young members of the School Company, Dimitris Glinos, drafted 'A Concept for a Short Memorandum' that interestingly stresses next to

Alexandros Nicoloudes, multi-use building with arcade, 41 Panepistimiou Street, 1916–18.

the importance of books for instruction, the significance of 'school buildings' and 'gardens'.[25]

Venizelos also promoted the establishment of a modern judicial system, hence his immediate interest in building a courthouse (in fact a Palace of Justice) and a jail, both in Athens. Again, constructing adequate modern buildings was one of his main concerns. In both competitions Nikoloudes was awarded first prize. While neither of his projects were constructed, the prizes helped Nikoloudes to become known as a talented designer able to conceive major public buildings, even if he was not very innovative when measured against the latest Paris fashion. Soon after his arrival Nikoloudes was commissioned to design the Livieratos Mansion (1906) on fashionable Patission Street across from the National Museum and the Polytechnic. There is an interesting contrast between this residence and these two neoclassical structures. While the National Museum and the Polytechnic are conceived as public buildings in the manner of 'temples in a grove', the Livieratos residence is an urban building and part of the fabric of a city street, acknowledging the corner of the building block in a way earlier classical buildings did not.

Certainly, accentuating the angle of a building on a street corner in this way was not Nikoloudes's invention, for it was a fashionable trope in architecture from Paris to Madrid to Buenos Aires. But Nikoloudes made it popular in Athens, giving the city an up-to-date, cosmopolitan look. He also made a more tangible contribution to the modernization of architecture in Greece by designing and executing competently large-scale, multipart, multi-functional works of an unprecedented complexity for his country. Such was the apartment building on Panepistimiou Street in Athens (1916–18), where he had his own apartment on the top floor and offices and an elegant commercial arcade at ground level, and the University Student Club (1926) also in Athens, which contained shops, offices, meeting rooms and an auditorium. His somewhat voguish and pompous facades followed the commercial trends of French architecture. But, despite the fact that in many respects it remained an unfinished solution, the apartment on Panepistimiou Street was not only Nikoloudes's best work, it enriched the city, contributing a novel architectural presence.

By contrast, the Sarogleion Megaron, Military Officers' Club (1929–33), Nikoloudes's most ambitious project, also revealed his weaknesses: a superficial use of architectural 'quotations' without deep historical knowledge or much sense of appropriateness and scale; an absence of inventive exploration or originality; and an indifference to the broader problems of developing architectural culture in modern Greece. Nikoloudes became professor at the School of Architecture in 1918, just a year after the school's foundation, and he continued teaching until 1923. In 1936

ΓΚΥΓΙΩΜ
Μαστίχ
ΣΤΑΜ. Σ
ΛΟΓΩ ΚΑΤΑ

Nasos Giannaros, Apartment building, Athens, designed in 1917, completed by Anastasios Metaxas, 1927, introducing reinforced concrete for the first time in a residential building in Athens.

he returned to teach until his death in 1944. He maintained a successful professional practice, designing more than 200 buildings, a large number of residences, including his own seaside home (at Glyfada, 1924), and the plan for a new upper-middle-class suburb, Psychico (1923–5). Within this suburb, in collaboration with his brother-in-law, Soterios Mayiassis, Nikoloudes also designed a market, an unadorned neo-Roman building, reminiscent of those seen in paintings by the Italian artist Giorgio De Chirico, who had studied art in Athens in 1903–5 while in his teens. Mayiassis was younger and, like Nikoloudes, had graduated from the Ecole des Beaux-Arts. He shared with Nikoloudes the same weaknesses and strengths. His multi-storey Hotel Acropole Palace (1926–8) on Patission Street (not far from the Livieratos residence) was a conventional building, but it pleasantly fits the corner it occupies and has a better sense of scale and proportion than works by Nikoloudes. Those architects like Nikoloudes and Mayiassis, and others of their generation who tried to break away from the rigorous rules of neoclassicism to design buildings more adaptable to modern urban living, paid very little attention to the development of the city within which they practised. Concurrently, a small number of architects, notably Anastasios Metaxas, proceeded with a safe but reductive and tired version of classicism, trying to create a compromise between a 'hellenic identity' and new functional and technological demands (for example the Charokopos residence, subsequently known as the Benaki Museum and the Merlin residence, which later became the French Embassy).

An important innovation occurred when the first seven-floor apartment building in Athens was constructed on Filellinon and Othonos streets in 1917. This design by the civil engineer Nasos Giannaros introduced the use of reinforced concrete in the city; it also raised protests since it blocked the view of the Acropolis. (The building was finished ten years later by Anastasios Metaxas, who concealed the structure behind a conventional neoclassical facade.) The complaints triggered the enforcement of a regulation in November 1919 controlling the maximum height of buildings in relation to the street and the open area of a site in relation to the building.

However, in the absence of a more general and more detailed plan for the capital, the mass of buildings kept on accumulating and sprawling, following the whims of those land speculators who controlled the direction and pattern of growth of the city by buying land and then applying political pressure to expand the city's boundary so as to include their property within it.[26] Most of the few fragmented proposals put forth were naive in urbanistic terms and oblivious to the new technological, environmental and social problems the capital and the state posed at that moment.[27] A serious plan for the reorganization and future expansion of Athens became more urgent as Greece emerged victorious from a war against the Ottoman empire in 1914.

At the suggestion of Queen Sofia, the Mayor of Athens, Spyros Mercouris, commissioned Ludwig Hoffmann in 1908 to work on a plan for the capital. In 1910 Hoffmann presented a scheme displaying grandiose avenues, squares embellished by obelisks, radial roads and broad peripheral streets. The proposal contained a few important suggestions, among them the centralization of train stations and the expansion of the city towards the sea and Patissia, as well as a controversial one, the demolition of the old remnants of the medieval and Ottoman city.[28] A more sophisticated plan was presented by Aristides Balanos in 1917, which focused on the expansion of Athens as a garden city. An interesting view was introduced by Stylianos Leloudas (in his studies of 1918 and 1921), who tried to define the city proper for the first time as part of a larger system of the region of Attica, including a harbour and areas set aside for sports, agriculture and a military centre. He also suggested developing a 'chain of gardens along the banks of the Ilissos'.[29]

An exception in the list of names of those at that time who submitted proposals for the future of Athens was the acclaimed British landscape architect Thomas H. Mawson, who was invited by Mercouris in 1914, again following a royal suggestion. Mawson's proposal, presented in 1918, had the qualities the previous suggestions lacked. It was creative, state of the art and socially conscious. Mawson was an established designer who had laid out numerous gardens in Britain and elsewhere; he was also a writer and a prominent figure in the emerging town-planning movement.[30] Moreover he was candid about the way Athens was spreading in a destructive 'build-as-you-please policy', which was leading to chaos. He saw Athens, 'populated by Greeks and Albanians', as 'one of the most attractive towns in the Levant', which in the near future, as soon as a 'direct communication' (a railway) was established with Thessaloniki, would be 'only sixty hours from Paris'; as a consequence a 'stream of wealthy tourists' would be arriving not only to visit Greece but also to use the city as 'the overland route to India'.[31]

Mawson argued that Athens should not be seen as a small city to be improved and developed piecemeal: it had to be planned as a 'metropolis'. Mawson's scheme combined a well-articulated spatial urban organization with a social and political programme embedded in the environmental conditions of the region. It was a system – without whose unity, he believed, the 'noblest' architecture looks commonplace – that consisted of boulevards, parks and playgrounds. These leisure areas were not leftover spaces depending for their survival on chance and charity; they were an integral

Thomas H. Mawson, *Proposal for New Athens*, 1914–18.

and coherent part of the city plan and they foreshadowed planning ideas that appeared after the end of the Second World War. The scheme also included 'workers areas' for nearly 200,000 people, a strategic control over the allocation of factories, workshops and the civic, commercial and academic sub-centres, all coordinated in relation to the railway station(s) and to the Acropolis. His proposals were received with great enthusiasm. They were called a 'miracle plan', but they were also criticized as hard to apply within the limited means Greece had to hand.

In addition to the plan for Athens, Mawson's scheme contained suggestions concerning Thessaloniki's future. Salonica (its other name) had ceased to be part of the Ottoman empire when it was seized on 26 November 1912, becoming de facto Greek. Mawson was appointed to his new task by the new-founded Ministry of Transportation, which assumed responsibility for urban and regional planning. Salonica became the new focus of planning for Greece for several reasons: by location and history its potential for modernization was much higher than that of Athens. But there was also a geopolitical problem. Because of its economic advantages it was also a highly desirable prize for other emerging Balkan states.

When the Greek army captured Salonica, its population was mixed, and the Greeks were in a minority: according to the statistics collected by the Greek Consulate there were 25,793 Greek Ottoman citizens, 3,593 Greek citizens, 54,718 Ottoman Mohammedans and 93,338 Jews. In addition, there were Dönmeh (crypto-Jews who openly affiliated with Islam),

Armenians, Albanians, Vlachs, Serbs and Bulgarians, whose number and importance had grown during the nineteenth century. Such statistics began to play an important role in a world that had begun to recognize the rights to self-determination.[32]

In contrast to Athens, by the end of the nineteenth century the port of Salonica was the hub of a network of trade conduits spreading out to Vienna, Varna, Alexandria, Constantinople, Smyrna, Aleppo, Marseille and Gibraltar, to name a few of the cities with which Salonica had close contact. Keeping its tradition of hospitality, between 1884 and 1902 the population of Salonica increased from 85,000 to 126,000, 14,000 of which were Jews. In one year, 1891, Salonica received 2,000 Russian Jews escaping pogroms, adding to the demand for more housing.[33] But parallel to its booming construction the city also suffered destruction by the Great Fire of August 1917, the largest conflagration in its history.

Fire was endemic to Salonica. More than 5,000 houses in the Jewish neighbourhood of the city had been destroyed by fire in 1510, while in 1856 a large part of the centre was destroyed. Another disaster in 1890 burned Byzantine churches and more than 2,000 houses in the poorest areas, mostly inhabited by Jews. (The so-called Hirsch Settlement, which rehoused a great number of the victims of the fire, had the highest standards of housing for the poor in the Ottoman empire.[34]) The Great Fire of August 1917 began in the afternoon, lasted 32 hours, and destroyed 120 hectares in the heart of the city: 9,500 buildings, 7,000 of which

Hirsch social housing for fire victims of the Jewish community, Salonica, 1898.

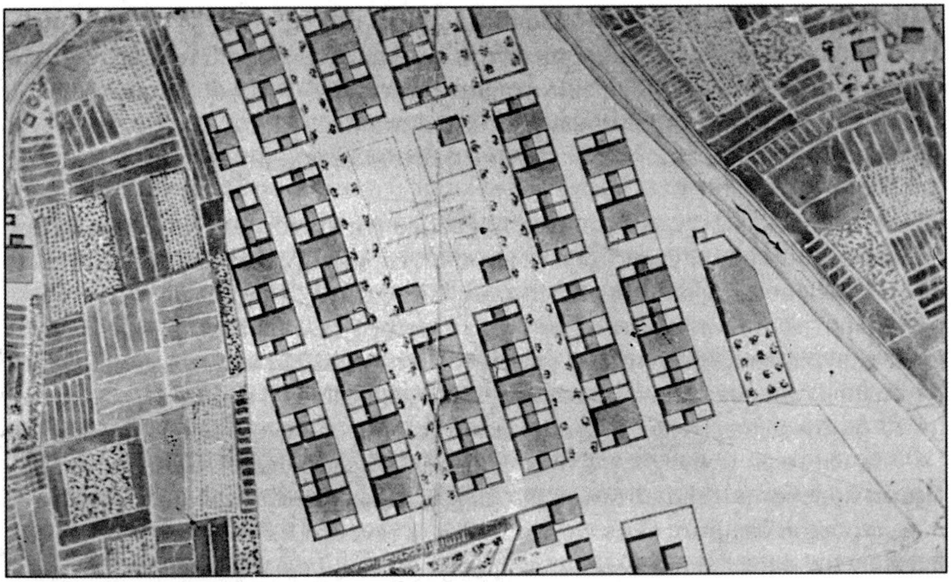

The Great Fire of Salonica, 1917.

belonged to Jews, and 30 synagogues, leaving 70,000 people homeless in a city of 278,749.[35]

Six days after the fire, on 11 August, Alexandros Papanastasiou, Minister of Transportation, called a meeting of experts to discuss the problem and propose solutions. It appears that during this initial meeting, at which local residents were not represented, the fate of the new city was decided and the idea of reconstructing it on the basis of a radically new plan was taken.[36] But producing and implementing such a plan presented problems that planning and construction in Athens had not occasioned. In contrast to modern Athens, Salonica did not emerge from a sparsely populated tabula rasa. It was a vital urban centre with a long and complex history.

A modern link between the Ottoman empire and Western Europe had been established in 1888 when the Orient Express train from Paris arrived for the first time at Salonica. Athens had no such link. The construction of new hotels followed, including the Splendid Palace on the sea promenade, which was instantly adopted by the cosmopolitan crowd passing through the city for business and by the local elite. It was there that the Young Turks, the group of reformists opposed to the conservative Ottoman establishment, set up their strategic base in preparation for their revolution; a native of Salonica, Mustafa Kemal, later to be known as Atatürk, was one of them.

In addition to hotels, restaurants, brasseries and shops were constructed along with hospitals and Ottoman administration offices. Many of these were designed by architects and engineers who had studied in Constantinople (the exchange of experts between Salonica and Constantinople was very close at that time). Some of these architects had also received training in Europe, among them Eli Modiano, among whose buildings were the commercial Arcades Carasso, Davidetto, Kyrtsi, Lombardo and the Cité Saul. Xenophon Paeonides had studied at the Polytechnic in Athens and in Munich, and practised occasionally an over-ornamented classical architecture, adapted to the 'oriental' taste of his clients. His most important projects in Salonica were the Greek Papafeion Orphanage (1893–1903), the mansion now housing the Italian Consulate and the more austere neoclassical Ioannides School (1900). The Italian architect Piero Arrigoni (1856–1940) designed the Jewish Hospital (1902), financed by Baron Hirsch, and the Italian Hospital Regina Marguerita (1894). The Sicilian Vitaliano Poselli (1839–1918) was brought to Salonica from Constantinople by the Ottoman Governor, where he designed the church of Santo Stefano (1886).[37] Among his other works were the Idadie School (1887), which was his first Salonikean commission, the Lycée Impérial, an impressively sombre, monumental building (also 1887), the Government Headquarters (1891), a massive multi-functional building that included several administrative facilities, among them a prison, and the over-ornamented, but technically up-to-date Ottoman Bank (1906–8). All these works have a monumental air, and all deployed the classical canon rather liberally. The most interesting were the Yeni Djami (1902) for Dönmehs, the Synagogue Bet-Saul of 1898, and the Orientalist Moorish-style Hotel Méditerranée. After the fire of 1898 the Allatini brothers commissioned Poselli to design a new structure, which was one

The seafront promenade, Salonica, 1916.

Vitaliano Poselli, Allatini flour mills, Salonica, 1898–1900.

of the largest, if not the largest, industrial building in the Orient, and Poselli's most impressive work. Ziller also contributed to the city, designing the Greek School and Consulate (1890–93) and possibly the Greek Orthodox Cathedral (1891–1914).

Heading the list of designers of private residences to line the new avenues of the city were Soterios Siagas and Ioannis Siagas, as well as the architects of the villas built towards the western side of the city, such as the Villa Allatini designed by Vitaliano Poselli, built in 1888 (donated by the Allatini family to the Ottoman state to serve as the residence of the Sultan Abdülhamid II during his exile in Salonica in 1908); the Villa Mordoch (1905), designed by Paeonides; the Villa Jacob Modiano (1906) by the engineer Eli Modiano; and the most beloved by the public even today, the Casa Bianca or Villa Fernandez of 1911–12 by Piero Arrigoni, a typical Salonikean version of Art Nouveau.

Despite the vitality of Salonica, the fortunes of the Ottoman empire did not appear to improve. Investments in public works failed to yield the expected results. Corruption went unchecked. And the hinterland was afflicted with bandits – Greeks, Bulgarians, Serbs, Albanians. Inside the city the minorities, who were the beneficiaries of economic development, began to turn against one other. Given the centrality of its location, the variety of services it offered, and the mobility of its population, Salonica tended to attract dissidents, visionaries, schemers and revolutionaries,

Piero Arrigoni, Casa Bianca or Fernandez residence, Salonica, 1911–12.

each with their own agendas. On 28 April 1903, a small group of anarchist / nationalist Bulgarian 'conspirators', known as the Boatmen, succeed in creating panic and chaos throughout the city with a series of explosions that set fire to various buildings, including the Imperial Ottoman Bank. Disappointed with the ineffectiveness of the reforms of *tanzimat,* in 1909, the young officers of the hotel Splendid Palace mentioned earlier, part of a much wider network of military revolutionaries, the Young Turks as they were known later, declared the end of the Ottoman *ancien régime.* On 24 July, Abdülhamid II announced the restoration of the constitution. In the overcrowded Selimie Square (which later became Freedom Square), the speeches were in Turkish, Greek, Bulgarian and Ladino, celebrating the uprising with the cry *yasasin milliet!,* long live the autonomy of nationalities, Equality, Freedom, Brotherhood. The same year, however, in early June, another mass demonstration took place in Salonica, organized via fliers written in five languages, Ladino, Greek, Turkish, Bulgarian and French – the first in the history of the Ottoman Empire – which was planned by Fédération, a new labour organization founded in Salonica, with tobacco workers, bakers, waiters and typographers among its members. In 1912 Salonica became the exporter of the union movement to Athens.[38]

This history shows just how complex the task of the Greek government was in taking decisions about the future of Salonica without getting entangled in complicated conflicts despite the urgent needs of the population. However, as mentioned above, Minister of Transportation Papanastasiou acted quickly and put in place an International Commission to carry out the New Plan of Thessaloniki by 11 October 1917. The foundation of an urban planning organization of this kind was a major innovation for Greece. The Commission was chaired by the mayor of the city, Constantinos Aggelakis, and included Jean Pleyber, a French military engineer, Angelos Ghinis, another engineer, and Kostas Kitsikis (1892–1969), a graduate of Berlin's Technische Universität, who had worked in the Technical Services of Berlin's central City Hall under Ludwig Hoffmann, the designer of the unexecuted urban renewal plan for the city of Athens in 1910. Finally, there were the architects Aristotelis Zachos and Ernest Hébrard, the latter the most experienced regarding the problems and potentialities of both the city and the region. Thomas H. Mawson joined the Commission later.

Following Town Planning Movement principles, Mawson proposed an informal spatial plan that required ample public green spaces. He considered the New Plan for Thessaloniki to a great extent to be his project, and he was to use it in his reception speech in 1923 as president of the Town Planning Institute to demonstrate the latest progress in the 'science' of city planning. But the competitive coexistence with Hébrard did not last long and an irritated Mawson returned to Britain, leaving behind his two sons to work on the project and Hébrard free to promote his ideas. The New Plan in its final version is considered to be Hébrard's. Essentially it was characterized by a central grid following Hellenistic and Roman street arrangements, intercepted by diagonal avenues generating small squares and featuring corner apartment buildings at the intersections. The small public areas not only created spatial variety but offered the opportunity for local commercial activities and communal encounters too. A special feature of the scheme was a central broad boulevard, Leoforos Agiou Dimitriou (now Aristotelous Street), perpendicular to the waterfront, surrounded by monumental arcaded apartment buildings serving as the cultural and social hub of the city. The street pattern linked the major Roman and Byzantine monuments. The port activities were concentrated to the west end of the seafront, with cultural and entertainment activities in the east towards the White Tower and beyond. What is striking about the plan is the overall spatial unity within which a variety of building types could be placed.

Venizelos was keen to use the New Plan as a means of attracting investment. He was quick to understand that the real significance and landmarks of the remade city was the plan itself, the new public spaces it provided, and the new activities it would enable. The New Plan radically modernized the city, increasing its density and enhancing its circulation. However, all these improvements benefited the middle class, whose number and wealth Venizelos wanted to raise. By contrast very little was done about social housing, with the exception of peripheral developments such as the Workers Housing Vardari, for victims of the fire, by Hébrard and Kitsikis (1919), and later the suburban quarter Chortiatis by Jean Pleyber (1934). Both projects were influenced by Garden City ideas, emphasising the balance of buildings and green areas and providing an informal layout of the streets.

The Hellenization of Salonica involved undoing the structures and customs of the Ottoman multi-ethnic city. In 1913 Greek administration of the city changed and Hellenized all names of the streets and squares. The following year it required the introduction of new laws concerning working days, imposing Sunday as a compulsory holiday, while Friday was that for the Muslims and Saturday for the Jews. This obliged Jews to keep their businesses shut for two days of the week. In April 1914, 800 Jews left for Jaffa, with 400 leaving later that year, followed by another 500. To discuss the problem of appropriation of Jewish properties in the burned zone of Salonica as well as to obtain funds for its reconstruction, in December 1917 Venizelos met Baron Rothschild in London, but the

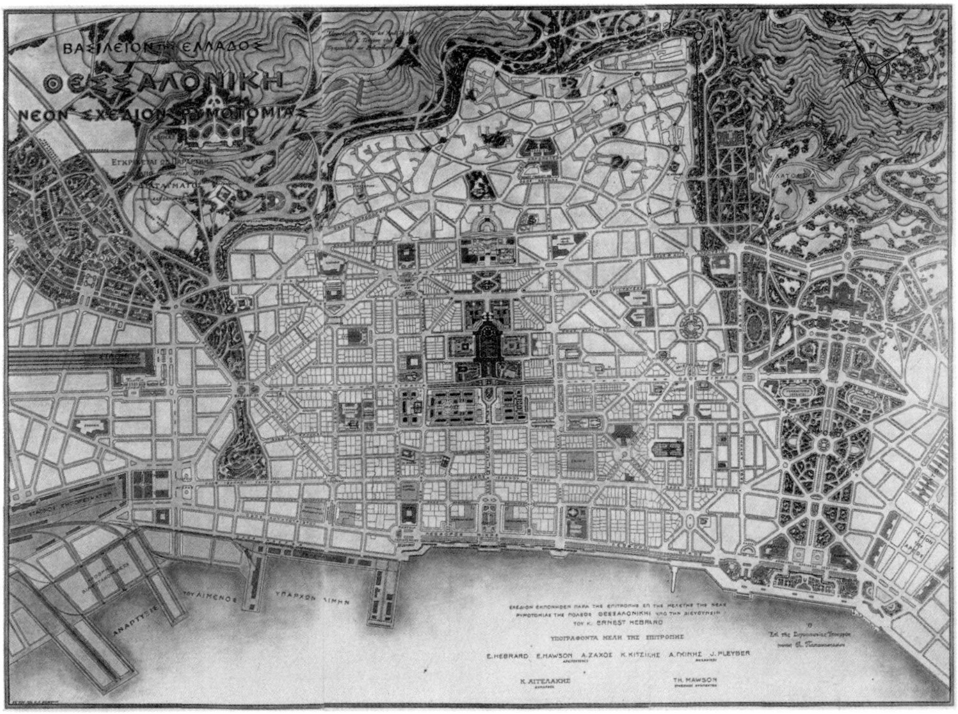

Ernest Hébrard, new Plan for the historic centre of Salonica, 1918.

meeting did not put an end to the tensions and insecurity as Papanastasiou, after reviewing the latest legislation on appropriation from Britain, France, Germany and the United States, continued to apply pressure to implement the New Plan, asking Parliament to pass a new law on 3 April 1918. Thus the new lots were not given back to their initial owners but were auctioned. However, the New Plan was not immediately implemented.

In the 1 November 1920 elections, Venizelos was massively voted down and the Popular Party won. To some degree the disagreements with the plan played a role in this outcome. After this the new prime minister Dimitrios Gounaris, who had included in his electoral campaign the revision of the New Plan, announced that the area allocated to public space was to be reduced. Encouraged by their victory many of the owners of buildings that had been destroyed by the fire started to restore them. Much to their surprise, Gounaris, at the end of December, after visiting Thessaloniki, declared his admiration for the New Plan. In the end a compromise was reached. The public spaces, streets and squares would be reduced from 52 per cent of the total area to 40 per cent. But Hébrard, who was obliged to redraw the Plan, managed to increase the public spaces to 42 per cent.

The New Plan helped Salonica become less segregated ethnically and religiously, the old segregation slowly replaced by spatial separation according to economic stratification; for example the poorer Jews were allocated together with impoverished Greek war refugees to marginal urban areas. The New Plan also enabled the modernization of everyday life. A contemporary Sephardic song commented nostalgically on the change: 'Salonica has changed. There is no more Karavan Serai, no more houses with *sahnisia* [elaborate interior wood details], women of the neighbourhood sitting in a row . . . the north wind blows now, lifting our skirts'.

One of the means for the hellenization of Salonica was to give to buildings a Greek identity. During the last years of the Ottoman empire most buildings financed by Greeks in the city, like the Ioannides School by Paeonides or the Greek School and Consulate (1893) by Ziller, were 'neo-Grec classical'; so were the buildings in Smyrna, Trebizond or Constantinople. The idea of a new Greece was represented in general through neo-Grec architecture up to 1900, when the Greek Pavilion in the Exposition Universelle in Paris was Byzantine in style. On the other hand, Hébrard's arcaded apartment buildings on Leoforos Agiou Dimitriou dominating new Salonica were regionalist Mediterranean – more Iberian than Byzantine-Greek. Another course to hellenize the city through architecture was to restore the city's Byzantine monuments, giving them prominence and, what was thought, their original 'Greekness'. One of these buildings was the seventh-century Basilica of St Dimitrios, which had been converted into a mosque in 1493 and then destroyed by the 1917 fire. After a long delay, restoration was started in 1926 by the architect Aristotelis Zachos, one of the seven members of the International Commission for the New Plan.

In 1911 Zachos had published a polemic article 'Vernacular Architecture' that publicized his beliefs on folk design. Though his ideas lagged behind the brilliance of Pericles Giannopoulos, Zachos was nonetheless the first practising designer to publicly advance the cause of a regionalist architecture and link it to vernacular precedents. In 1913–14 he was the single architectural voice that prevented the demolition of the White Tower in Thessaloniki. But his understanding of folk and medieval architecture was superficial and patronizing, for example in the restoration of the church of St Dimitrios he sought to make the building more relevant to contemporary Greeks by adding a bell tower, an alien element to the architecture of the period.

Zachos had dedicated clients. He built a country house for the banker Dionysios Loverdos in Varymbombi (across from the Tatoi royal estate) in 1928–9 that was published in the magazine *Washmuths Monatshefte*

Leoforos Agiou Dimitriou, now Aristotelous Street, Salonica, based on the scheme by Ernest Hébrard.

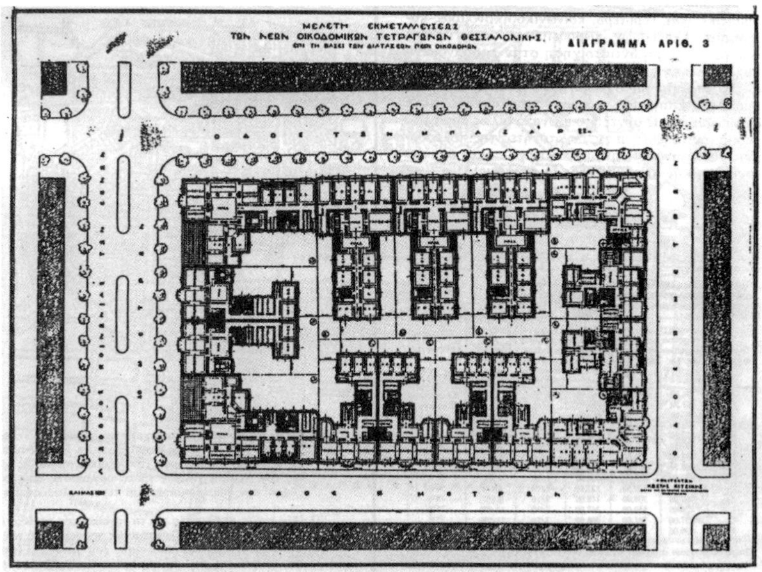

Kostas Kitsikis, Prototype for a residential block, Salonica, 1919. with typical floor plans.

Aristotelis Zachos, Angeliki Hadjimichali residence, Plaka, Athens, 1924–7.

für Architektur und Städtebau (2 February 1930), with the magazine's comment stressing the regionalist character of the project: 'A Greek summer house, not by Le Corbusier, but by a local architect'. For his client Angeliki Hadjimichali he built a house in Plaka, the centre of old Athens; she gave him free rein and the means to apply costly construction details and hand-crafted decor. Zachos tried to design a 'regionalist' interior, neo-Byzantine living rooms furnished with Skyrian chairs, Thracian hearths, island tables and antique chests, all put together in a highly staged but superficial manner.

The elegant neo-Byzantine/neo-Catalonian buildings across Aristotelous Street in Salonica were also 'regionalist' and not influenced by Zachos's ideas. They followed instead Hébrard's design guidelines: the apartment house by Jacques Moshé, the Hadjidimoulas apartment house (1924) by D. Fillitzis, the Longos apartment house (1925) designed by L. Zenari. The same was so with the Thessaloniki Club by Angelos Siagas (1925). Less regionalist and more concerned with the modernisation of Greek architecture were the plans for a new type of residential block also in Salonica designed by Kostas Kitsikis based on current Berlin prototypes.

The victory of the Popular Party in the elections and the return of King Constantine on 11 December 1920 brought delays in the reconstruction of Thessaloniki. There were internal political problems but also a major diplomatic development, the resumption of hostilities against the Ottoman empire. In defiance of the 1918 agreements with their allies, the Greek army attacked in 1921, aiming to capture the interior of Anatolia and Pontus. For a moment, many enthusiastic Greeks believed the time had come to resuscitate the forlorn Byzantine empire. The outcome of the campaign turned out to be very different: a disastrous defeat of the Greek army by the Turks. On 27 August 1922 the Turkish army entered Smyrna. What followed was one of the greatest destructions of human life and property of the twentieth century. Smyrna burned for days. Numerous villages and towns in Ionia followed.[39] By September 1922 the Greek army was destroyed and hundreds of thousands of refugees – indigenous Greeks of Ionia, who had lived for centuries under the Ottoman empire – were flooding Greece. On 11 September the army mutinied. The king resigned and the five royalist politicians, who included former prime minister Dimitrios Gounaris, were tried and executed on 28 November. The 1923 Treaty of Lausanne that followed imposed a compulsory exchange of populations between Greece and Turkey. More

Aristotelis Zachos, Dionysios Loverdos country house, Varymbombi, Attica, 1928–9.

displaced persons arrived in Greece, the refugee population reaching 1,069,957. Of these 350,000 refugees settled in Athens, whose entire population, according to the 1920 census, was only 453,042.

To ease the situation the 15 February 1923 law was passed asking for the redistribution of 1,724 large farms and monastery estates out of a total of 2,259 (as recorded by the 1917 census). In the meantime, schools and other public buildings, even the opera house and the national theatre, were occupied by refugees. People also sheltered in tents under the Acropolis and next to other ancient monuments in caves and on the slopes of the surrounding hills of Athens, many in the company of farm animals. Their identity was Greek, but they spoke many languages, Pontic, Circasian, Armenian, Turkish dialects, but also French, and had strange ways of thinking, and alien ways both of cultivation and of doing business. In his memoirs Morgenthau called the event the 'Great Exodus' of the Greeks, making the analogy with the Exodus from Egypt. Morgenthau was the U.S. Ambassador during the First World War in the Ottoman empire. An intriguing personality, a businessman, philanthropist and writer, close to Woodrow Wilson, and financial Chairman of the Democratic Party, he served in the American Red Cross and the 'Relief Fund for the Refugees' after the war,[40] which provided hospitalization and construction of temporary accommodation for refugees, and the League of Nations 'Committee of Refugees Rehabilitation' founded in 1924.[41] In this later capacity, he was able to organize the building of settlements for the refugees. His writings clearly describe the conditions of the refugees but are also full of candid sketches of Greek administrators, politicians and King George, whom he blames for his narrow-mindedness, foreshadowing the crises to come in Greece in the following years. In his documentation of the efforts made to provide shelter for the refugees, Morgenthau refers with great admiration to the Greek architect Constantine Sgoutas, who succeeded in building with a small team five settlements on the periphery of Athens using simple inexpensive materials, bricks made of mortar and straw, and employing mostly refugees. Sgoutas became later a very successful professional, among whose many buildings were Athens College (1929), designed in collaboration with Kyriakides and Soulis.

In most cases, the settlements were rudimentary, put together without much professional help. They emerged on the city's margins, wherever there was a void between physical obstacles and utility buildings; but there were also rumours that they were allocated to special sites serving political interests or to be close to manufacturing facilities (as in the case of Nea Ionia, Podarades and Perissos), offering cheap labour, forming a city within the city. Because of the nature of their materials they were given the name *tenekedoupoli*, 'tinplate cities', characterized as the 'lowest level of civilized living'. But Morgenthau also remarked how impressive was the quality of social life that came about there, the way the refugees cared about the meagre public space available to them, and the immediate appearance of flowerpots and curtains at the openings of their temporary shacks. The shacks, however, became less temporary than the authorities claimed they would be. Most of them remained in use until the 1960s. The Attica areas of Dourgouti, Drapetsona, Koundouriotika, Kaisariani, Aegaleo, Asyrmatos, Tavros, Korydallos and Peristeri became legendary names associated with both the unfinished shabby structures and a culture of political dissent.[42]

By 1922 the political and social situation in Greece had worsened. The combative ideas of the poet Kostis Palamas had very little to say about the unprecedented crisis of the new nation. Instead it was a 'decadent' poet, Constantine Cavafy, who was able to express the vacuum of leadership with clarity and irony, pointing to its unpreparedness to assume responsibility to change the structure of its institutions and economy, its overdependence on politician-reformers. In his ambivalent 'In a Large Greek Colony, 200 BC', written in 1928, Cavafy commented on the situation: 'That things . . . are not what they should be / nobody can doubt any more . . . maybe . . . the time has come / to bring in a Political Reformer'. And this despite the fact that it is known that 'They make a tremendous fuss / about everything . . .', and after finding an 'endless number of useless things to eliminate' applying their 'surgical efficiency', they part the moment people realize that they should not have been invited after all. 'You see', Cavafy concludes cynically, 'we do move forward'.

Greece indeed was pressing forward. On 24 August 1922 a decree was passed imposing a minimum of unbuilt space in building blocks and increasing the maximum height of buildings in relation to the width of the streets. A law imported from Berlin in 1923 controlled the projection of built volumes from the facade.[43] The same year a new directive divided Greece into three zones, associating each zone with a type of control.[44] As a result of these legal measures the efficiency of the urban tissue increased, while at the same time some guarantees of environmental quality were introduced. Legislation was also passed to protect the view of monuments from being obstructed by high structures. But was that enough to modernize the country? Of course Cavafy's poetry has universal value. It refers to universal human, personal and institutional conditions; still, one is tempted to see in his poem a depiction of the situation in Greece during the years following the collapse of 1922. The poem is dated 1928, but is in the spirit of the political chaos and social anomy of the first part of the 1920s, alluding to the failed dictatorial regime in 1926 of 'reformer'

Smyrna ablaze, 1922.

Theodoros Pangalos, who endangered even the meagre achievements of the first century of New Greece in actions such as the decision to divide into lots the Royal Garden in Athens and sell them to supporters of his regime. Fortunately, vigorous protests by the architect Zachos succeeded in stopping it happen. Yet, neither such conservationist regionalist protests by Zachos nor the cosmopolitanism of Nikoloudes could offer any solutions to the problems of Athens or Thessaloniki. Together with the old solutions becoming obsolete the old problems were gone too, their place taken by new difficulties. The constructs of Kolettis's Great Idea, and Venizelos's Great Greece of Two Continents and Five Seas, were irrelevant. The 'irredentist' regions and the unredeemed Greeks were within Greek land proper now. And they were unemployed, alienated, without shelter, deprived of schools and public space, and their condition was worsening, with demobilization having a negative impact on the labour market and housing. In addition, the 1921 economic crisis in the West prohibited both local Greeks and those of the Ottoman empire to emigrate to the United States. Thus the traditional economic safety valve of modern Greece was making unemployment and homelessness worse. There was no surprise when, in 1923, 150,000 workers went on strike in Athens. Salonica was also restless. But while the crisis was evolving, Venizelos was back in 1924 as Prime Minister, promptly resigning in less than a month and returning to Paris. While there he translated Thucydides into demotic Greek: 'Pericles' Funeral Oration' was an appropriate text to reflect not only on questions of democracy and good governance but, through the implicit parallels between the ancient Athenian devastation of the Peloponnesian War and the Asia Minor Catastrophe of 1922, on the tragedy of war too. These were appropriate topics to occupy the mind of Venizelos while

The National Theatre sheltering refugees, Athens, 1925.

waiting to return to Greece; he was now more than ever committed to force a reformist modernization on Greece. While Venizelos bided his time in Paris, a new generation of artists, intellectuals and architects had come of age and was poised to make its mark.

Refugee settlement by the Temple of Hephaestus, Athens, 1925.

chapter three

Open Wide the Windows – Let the Sun Come In!

The generation of the 1930s had shared the experience of the national 'catastrophe' and the deprivation and political disasters that followed. For them the school became the building type that would embody the nation's aspirations. The military defeat that put an end to the Great Idea and caused the 'great exodus' that wiped out the centuries' old communities of Asia Minor, the drop in living standards, the succession of botched regimes manifested in the penury and ignorance of the Greeks all resulted in the Greek people placing all their hopes for survival in education. As Kapodistrias had declared almost a century earlier in his letter to Korais,[1] good buildings were indispensable to good education. The national poet, Kostis Palamas, encouraged the new generation 'to build schools not war castles . . . build them plain, roomy, big . . . open wide the windows and doors to let the . . . sun come in and govern'.[2]

There had been nothing to suggest such a need at the Peace Conference in Paris in 1919. At that time, before the Asia Minor Catastrophe of 1922, in an attempt to whip up allied support for Greece's takeover of Anatolia, Venizelos gave a speech boasting about the capability of the Greeks to 'civilize the Turks, just as the British and French were civilizing Africans and Asians'.[3] But even then Venizelos knew that the reality was different. He was aware of the dismal figures from his minister of education, Constantinos Gondikas, which showed that 36 per cent of the male Greek population and 52 per cent (perhaps as many as 70 per cent) of the female, were illiterate.[4] Venizelos understood that a programme of education was urgently needed; he knew that the buildings in which young Greeks were being educated dated from the time of Kapodistrias and Trikoupis. During the preceding decade, Venizelos's government had built 54 schools and repaired 174 throughout Greece, so the building programme was still in the hands of competent engineers.[5]

Nikolaos Balanos, an engineer who previously had worked for the railways, together with G. Soulis, developed guidelines for schoolroom architecture that modified Kallias's basic types. They discouraged the use of neoclassical ornament (such as capitals and pediments) for the facades

Nikolaos Mitsakis, Primary School, Koletti Street, Athens, 1932.

of the schools, but insisted on the formality and classical character of the overall composition of each scheme, with the conscious intention to project through this image of order and stability the idea of new state.[6] In addition they criticized the very principle of applying a standard type of school building for all locations in Greece and suggested adopting a new design policy. Rather than a top-down method of universal spatial patterns, deployed since the time of Kapodistrias, they suggested a bottom-up approach that took into account the specifics of the environment of each region and even each site. In 1904, and again in 1913, Dimitris Saratsis proposed a new kind of school building that took its environmental setting into consideration.[7] In a review of Saratsis's book, a young teacher, Dimitris Glinos, critical of the 'humid', 'dark' and 'poisonous' spaces in 'most European houses and cities', and in most of the existing school buildings in Greece, defended the idea of a regional kind of architecture, asking for outdoor spaces, courts and porches, in a country where for 150 days each year courses could be taught outdoors.[8] He also advocated both day and night use of the buildings.

Rather than debating the school buildings, people were mostly preoccupied with the school curriculum reform promoted by Venizelos, especially his efforts to replace *katharevousa* by *demotiki*. While nobody doubted the important role buildings for instruction were going to play in modernizing Greece, language reform was seen as the most important prerequisite to the development of a technological and commercial culture, and, for a large part of Venizelos's party, a necessary condition for the creation of a more open and egalitarian society.[9]

Towards this end, Venizelos's small group of intellectual advisors (among them Nikos Kazantzakis, Alexandros Delmouzos, Manolis Triantafyllides and Dimitris Glinos), began to compose their own books in demotic Greek, as well as limiting the amount of instruction dedicated to traditional 'classical education'. They wanted classic authors introduced via translations, and they assigned more time to the teaching of sciences and foreign languages. In the same spirit, higher education departments dedicated to philology and theology were reduced, while night schools and new vocational schools offering practical crafts were founded. A major innovation was the creation of a school to 'educate the educators', a new experimental facility, the Marasleion Academy, independent of the University of Athens. Finally, an additional novelty was the establishment by Royal Decree of the School of Architecture on 26 March 1916.

Unsurprisingly, in the process of implementing his education agenda, Venizelos had made enemies, and this, together with the other controversial changes he pursued, resulted in his defeat in the November 1920 elections. A national plebiscite brought back King Constantine. Venizelos left Greece, and many of his young collaborators in education were fired, some like Venizelos choosing to leave the country. Consequently, most of the educational reforms were suspended. Even worse, a movement began to undo educational achievements. Without wasting time, Spyros M. Kalliafas, a school-teacher (whose chief credential was having had the privilege of educating King Constantine), led a campaign to roll back whatever improvement Venizelos had tried to implement, which he claimed were 'charlatanisms' incited by *xenocrates* (promoters of foreign ideas). Kalliafas went so far as to burn the textbooks written in *demotiki* that had been prepared by the Venizelos team.

Concurrent with this reaction was a more disastrous event, the ill-fated turn of the war against the Ottoman empire. This conflict continued after the First World War was over, and led to Greece's defeat in the Asia Minor Catastrophe of 1922. A year later, Venizelos was back in Greece once more as Prime Minister. In spite of the reaction against his education reforms he had no difficulties in reactivating his original campaign. With his previous collaborators reinstated, one of his first actions was to try to evacuate the schools still occupied by war refugees. In 1923 the Technical Chamber of Greece, the professional body of Greek engineers, was established and included architecture, giving a boost to the improvement of construction and design of buildings.

Venizelos now had to wrestle with both his conservative opponents and the radicals – the Socialist Party and the Workers' Union. These were newly emerging powers causing serious trouble in many areas of his reform programme, including education. In 1920 a Socialist/Labour candidate was elected for the first time to Parliament. In 1923 the Socialist Party was strong enough to call a strike, and although not strong enough to make it succeed, its voice was heard: it criticized Venizelos for being too narrow in his reforms, not considering them as part of a broader and more fundamental social change, and it attacked his failure to construct 'healthy school buildings in cities and villages'. The dispute split Venizelos's collaborators. Delmouzos, taking a more centrist position, focused on the question of language reform. The left attacked him as a utopian, a 'stale humanist' who isolated educational and linguistic modernization from social revolution. Glinos, a close collaborator of Venizelos since 1913 and secretary general of the Ministry of Education in 1917–20, increasingly identified with the radical positions leading the opposition from the left.[10]

The political disputes also drew attention to the pressing problem of the lack of funds for the construction of the urgently needed schools. Gondicas tried to raise a loan of 150,000,000 drachmas, but Venizelos resigned in 1924, interrupting his efforts. It was now the turn of Kalliafas to lead: he assaulted the new schoolbooks that promoted 'coeducational children' and 'corrupt romanticism'. Anastasios Orlandos, who had just been elected member of the newly founded Academy representing architecture (1926), brought to the discussions of this committee his preoccupation with the hellenistic atrium house, recommending it as the preferable type for schools, an idea that would influence the development of school architecture for years to come. He also suggested that a book to instruct teachers about the significance of architecture in education should be produced.[11]

The campaign for new school construction resumed in 1928, when Venizelos won the elections of August 1928 to become prime minister in 1929. This time the school campaign took off for good. In an important pre-election speech in Thessaloniki Venizelos declared that 'thousands of young men are incompletely educated and incapable essentially for any productive work', promising a 'radical reform of the education system', enabling 'the nation to prepare an army for the future revolution . . . of the moral and material elevation of the working classes, urban and rural'.[12]

Venizelos was undoubtedly the person to implement the aspirations of the new generation. The dream of the Great Idea had been crushed but the 1930s generation took over with a new vision. Its members had come of age in the midst of political, social and ideological decline and chaos, but they were also the best educated generation Greece had seen in its modern history, many having studied in France and Germany and having benefited from Venizelos's previous education reforms. The new generation was intellectually equipped to successfully revise legislation, establish new institutions, publish books, generate ambitious infrastructure projects and construct bold buildings. Athens, which many thought of a few years previously as merely a temporary capital astride the road to Constantinople, impressed this young generation, such as the writer George Theotokas and poet George Seferis, who would visit Syngrou Avenue (under construction in 1925–6) to watch with awe the rapid transformation of the old country road leading from the centre of Athens to the Faliro coast into a multi-lane thoroughfare divided by pepper trees for carriages, horsemen, pedestrians and speeding automobiles.[13] They were mesmerized by the traffic, appreciating 'the newborn and not-yet-expressed rhythms of a strong lyricism that calls for robust poets'.[14]

But Venizelos had to face the fact that by the end of the decade so many people were split across political lines, even his very close collaborators. Acknowledging that he was trapped between the left and the right, he declared that he had chosen the 'middle way'. In June 1929, Gondikas, once more minister of education, submitted a bill to Parliament concerning the urgent task of eliminating illiteracy. The same year the Benaki Museum, and a year later the National Theatre, were founded. A location was also identified for the University of Thessaloniki. On 4 August 1930 a decree was passed expropriating the Jewish cemetery, the space to be used for building the new University facilities that Hébrard had planned.[15] The money required for construction was finally obtained in 1930 (a loan from Sweden). Gondikas, having secured the school-building programme, resigned from his ministerial post to become the founder and first director of the Agriculture Bank that would play a major role in the modernization of Greece's countryside. George Papandreou proudly announced that during the short period they were in government, between 1928 and 1932, no less than 3,176 school buildings were constructed, a much higher figure than the 1,200 they had promised in May 1930. It also soared above 1,474, the number of school buildings built in Greece in the century that followed liberation. In January 1930 Greece began the immense operation of building 3,000 elementary and secondary schools. The list of architects involved includes almost all the key figures of that generation.[16] But there was one exception: Dimitris Pikionis.

While most of the architects in the list, fresh out of school, were beginning their professional careers, Dimitris Pikionis had been a teaching assistant in the Athens Polytechnic since 1921, and he had already built his first house. In his 'Autobiographical Notes' of 1958 he noted that he was born in 1887, the same year as Le Corbusier, in Piraeus. His family, originally from Chios, had left the island in 1822, after the infamous Massacre. As a boy he wandered over the rough rocks of Freattys, close to Piraeus, among Byzantine ruins in Kaisariani, through groves by the banks of Cephissus and Hiera Odos, below the Acropolis and on Philopappou Hill. Despite his attachment to landscape, in 1904 he entered the School of Civil Engineering. As has already been mentioned, there was then no School of Architecture; but Kaftanzoglou's complex housed the Athens Polytechnic as well as the School of Fine Arts, where Giorgio de Chirico and George Bouzianis were studying painting. Pikionis made friends with both. During his student years he also met the historian of Athens, Dimitrios Kambouroglou, and Pericles Giannopoulos, and in 1906 he visited the painter Konstantinos Parthenis and became his first student. Giannopoulos and Parthenis convinced Pikionis's father to let him study art. In 1908 Pikionis moved to Munich and then to Paris,[17] where he studied painting at the Académie de la Grande Chaumière while following courses on architecture at the Ecole des Beaux-Arts.

In 1912 Greece had declared war against the Ottoman empire and Pikionis left Paris to join the army. The day before his departure, while walking from the Place de la Concorde to the Latin Quarter, he met de

Chirico, a chance coincidence that they both agreed had a mystical significance.[18] That evening Pikionis was the first person to see de Chirico's *pittura metafisica* (paintings of stilled urban spaces involving odd perspectives and planes), to hear his theory about the cyclical nature of time and to discuss that 'the light line that separates light from shadow on moist earth is a mystery'. Pikionis's departure for Greece was delayed, and many meetings with de Chirico followed. When he finally arrived by boat at the port of Patras, his confrontation with the Greek landscape forced him to realize that he had to 'revise everything he had learned' abroad.

Pikionis served in the army in conflicts that continued into the early 1920s. Nonetheless he managed to travel several times to the island of Aegina to study its vernacular houses. In 1921–3 he built his first house in the coastal Athenian suburb of Tzitzifies. His second followed in 1925. According to Pikionis, this one was inspired by Anastasios Orlandos's reconstruction of an ancient house in Priene, yet it was less a historicist than an experimental scheme guided by the 'organic truth, sombre and simple, governed by geometry', and by the 'universal shape capable to represent our epoch' rather than a nostalgic escapade. The same year, in his essay 'Our Popular Art', Pikionis declared that in order to make buildings fit into their environment it was not enough to study them as end products; one had to investigate the design process by studying the way peasants build: 'Let us see how a peasant makes his house, the natural way he follows.' In 'Popular Art and Us', also of 1925, he remarked how observing peasant builders at work in Aegina had made him become increasingly convinced that cerebral playing with lines on paper, as the Beaux-Arts architects did, may ultimately lead only to the 'lie of civilized life'.[19]

Pikionis and the younger architects of the 1930s who adopted a regionalist direction were not alone. They were part of a broader cultural movement initiated by a circle of modern Greek writers and painters of the same generation who were similarly interested in being modern while working in continuity with tradition and in accordance with context. A key figure in the development of the movement was the painter Parthenis. A decade older than Pikionis, he is often taken as a 'symbolist' artist employing a decorative nationalist iconography. However, his approach to light, spatial composition and colour shows a twentieth-century modern mind working with the precedents of Byzantine painting, although not because of conservatism or nationalism but – like Malevich and Kandinsky at about the same time – as a rejection of post-Renaissance conventions of representation, employing chiaroscuro and perspective in order to open new ways of understanding vision, light and space. Parthenis was a major influence on Pikionis and others.

Another key initiator of the post-1922 regionalist movement was Angelos Sikelianos. At first glance his poetry appears affective, rhetorical and romantic, out of pace with the tempo of the twentieth century. But a closer reading shows that his experiments with image and language, re-using traditional precedents from popular Greek poetry fused with that of ancient Greece, run parallel to the French Surrealist explorations by Louis Aragon. Yet Sikelianos's influence in the 1930s was less in providing literary prototypes and more in terms of playing the role of a catalyst, especially in relation to the Delphic Festivals of 1927 and 1930 that he conceived and directed with his wife, Eva Palmer, an American who contributed ideas as well as her fortune to finance the events. The Festival, which took place on the ancient site of Delphi, organized independently of any commercial or government interests, succeeded in bringing together a multidisciplinary group, creating a platform that enabled the Greek regionalist modern movement of the late 1920s to become visible internationally.

Much to the shock of academic traditionalists, in Delphi Sikelianos tried to revive ancient Greek drama to create modern ritual, mixing peasants with actors, writers and artists, ancient Greek verses and costumes with folk songs and folk costume. Even nature took part in these events, in the words of Koula Pratsika, a young avant-garde dancer who was asked to work into the choreography of the event, 'the mountains, the olive trees, the eagles flying over the theatre'.[20] It may have looked as if Sikelianos was acting out a sort of nationalist programme manifesting continuity and common identity between ancient Greek culture, Byzantium and modern Greece, but far from it: Sikelianos and Palmer were attempting an agitprop event, an experimental multimedia 'happening'. The underpinnings of the Festival that fused ancient drama with folk celebration were to express the mystical idea of Greece as that of a holistic, pantheistic humanism, and a pacifist belief system in demand since the end of the traumatic First World War.

The significance of the Delphic Festivals was that the generation of the 1930s came together extemporaneously participating in the two performances as audience and as collaborators during the preparations. In addition, the younger generation joined in, as Pratsika describes in her autobiography: 'Miliades, an archaeologist, Prevelakis, a philologist and historian . . . Tsarouchis, a painter, Thanos Veloudios [a pilot, friend of the arts, in charge of instructing the chorus to dance the *pyrechios*] . . . [and] Georgios Kontoleon', a young architect who was the set designer of the first Festival in 1927. Later Kontoleon would become the architect of Pratsika's house and dance studio.

Koula Pratsika was a student of the renowned avant-garde dancer and teacher Mary Wigman, who, like Sikelianos, espoused a holistic approach

Georgios Kontoleon, set design for Delphic Festival, Delphi, 1930.

to the arts, bringing together spatial and rhythmical expression. She and her collaborators turned to non-Western musical instruments – bells, gongs and other traditional percussive instruments from Africa, China and India – to express modern ideas about abstract movement, the body and the collective, and for the same reasons (again like Sikelianos) was a passionate proponent of a 'return to Greece'. In 1932 she decided to build a studio to teach modern dance in Athens. She dreamed of a glass structure on the top of an existing building (indeed during that time she lived in a small storage room on an Athens rooftop), from which she and her students could be in direct contact with the landscape of Attica. In search of an architect, she was reintroduced to Georgios Kontoleon, who had close links with dance having himself joined during his stay in Paris the 'Academia', a commune founded by Raymond Duncan, a dancer and artist, brother of the famous dancer Isadora Duncan and married to Sikelianos's sister.

Instead of an addition to an existing building, Kontoleon convinced Pratsika to build a new school on an inexpensive site at 55 Omirou Street on the slope of Lycabettus with a view of the Acropolis. Pratsika was enthusiastic, although the project proceeded with some difficulty, all materials having to be carried up the hill, a very costly affair. But the end results were stunning. Pratsika described the school as 'simple, solid, glowing and beautiful, shining in the sun as if swimming in the light, suspended and surrounded by hills and mountains' of Attica. Building and school were inaugurated on 1 November 1934. What Kontoleon and Pratsika constructed, however, was beyond a mere facility. The syncopated classical composition of the openings of the facade are reminiscent of the facade of Adolf Loos's Villa Müller in Prague (1928–30).[21] More important, however, was the way Kontoleon related the street to the entrance court, the court to the steps leading to the entrance hall, the hall to the interior, the interior to the stair guiding to the roof, and the view opening up from the roof: these were a material manifestation of a modern idea of the relationship between the senses, body and landscape, movement and space. Again, several of these spatial arrangements can be easily traced to Loos and Mallet-Stevens. But the end product was born out of

Georgios Kontoleon, Koula Pratsika Residence and Dance School, Omirou Street, Athens, 1932–4.

the reality of the site and the region, and out of the precedents of the regional architecture.

The regionalist aspects of the scheme by Kontoleon were subtle, they were not a pastiche of familiar local details. Kontoleon's study of Greek vernacular architecture was not like that of Pikionis, which was systematic and undertaken over long periods. With the return of peace and the growing availability of modern transportation, short frequent visits to the Greek countryside and the islands became effortless, inexpensive, and did not take much time away from work in the city. In fact the lives of many 1930s architects, painters, writers and even dancers like Pratsika, devoted many hours to outings and excursions to sites, ancient and contemporary, to monasteries, villages, towns, often reaching these places on foot. Apart from the classic sites – Delos, Delphi, Epidaurus, Mycenae and Olympia – the destinations for these trips were contemporary settlements rich in vernacular architecture: Poros, Mykonos, Hydra, Santorini, Nafplion and Mt Athos. And if there was not enough time free for travelling for more than few hours they would visit small medieval buildings in Attica, or climb the Acropolis or Lycabettus, like curious tourists in their own country, eager to find something they had been wanting to see for a long time.

Most of the architects of the modern school buildings as well as the architects of the new hospitals, apartments and residences designed and built around the end of the 1920s and the early 1930s had studied in France, almost all at the Ecole Spéciale in Paris, or in Germany at various universities. They developed lasting international networks that were useful at the outset of their challenging careers and precious in the hard years that followed. Those who studied in Greece had also developed their networks, characterized as we saw by bridging disciplines and means of expression.

Interestingly, the architect who contributed one of the most international-looking modern school buildings in the Venizelos programme was one of the first graduates of the School of Architecture at Athens Polytechnic, which he entered in 1917, and who had never travelled outside Greece. Nikolaos Mitsakis was born in Pyrgos in 1899 of Cretan and French descent. He was to teach briefly at the Polytechnic in 1931–33, but it was through his buildings that he became most influential in the development of modern Greek architecture. In 1926 he was hired by the Ministry of Education to work as an architect in the design section. His first two school projects (both 1926) are typical of the transitory and superficial neoclassical regionalist character of the period; they were followed by two further school designs for Thessaloniki with Byzantine window openings, while his schools in Tinos (1927) and Naxos (1930)

Nikolaos Mitsakis, Secondary School, Dimitsana, Peloponnese, 1927–8.

featured elements of local Aegean architecture. None of these rather mediocre schemes were built. In 1927–8 he designed a school in Dimitsana in the Peloponnese, his first built project, which displayed a remarkable colonnade, a modern version of the ancient stoa.

The introduction of the covered colonnade, a space for gymnastic activities, as part of the complex was an innovation for the school programme at that time, a response to the demand for an 'outdoor' architecture adapted to particular regional constraints, what Mitsakis called the 'special conditions' of Greece. It was a modern structure using new materials while at the same time relying on traditional solutions. Its post-and-beam format is timber proto-Doric cast in modern materials, similar to a much later project by Kenzo Tange at Kagawa in 1958, where traditional Japanese construction was revitalized by means of contemporary technology and rules of spatial composition. Mitsakis continued applying the portico theme to his schools in the years that followed, experimenting with the role it could play in relation to the rest of the composition. While it is attached as an appendix to the rest of the school complex at Dimitsana, in later projects it becomes an integral part of the whole, the

Nikolaos Mitsakis, Annexe to the Marasleion Academy, Athens, 1929–30.

Nikolaos Mitsakis, Aristotelis' Girls' School, Athens, 1921–41, indoor staircase.

Marasleion Academy of 1929 being a project in transition. This independent teachers' academy was part of an existing complex – the original neoclassical building (1905) designed by Kallias, later modified by I. Antoniadis – subsequently modified by Mitsakis. His contribution was to experiment with colour, using a pallet drawn from Greek traditional buildings, to give depth and structural meaning to the openings. Integration of colour with architecture remained one of Mitsakis's preoccupations throughout his career.

In the elementary school at Kolonos (1931) the portico motif is used twice, for the open-door gymnastics facility and for a kind of raised gateway to the complex. Through this device the composition assumes a remarkable unity, and with the use of an external corridor system gives the school an original 'outdoor regional architecture' character. His complex on Koletti Street (1932) was Mitsakis's most mature – and most regional in character – school design. Given the narrow configuration of the site, he developed an informal plan driven by the requirements of the programme and the setting, breaking the complex into two parts. The classrooms were placed in the main U-shape building. The assembly hall and the handicrafts workshop were placed in the second smaller building, located in such a way as to create a closed atrium for outdoor activities. The large openings flooded the rooms with light, as the poet Palamas had envisioned, but protected them from glare and direct sunlight through projecting cantilevered balconies. On 3 August 1933, during the Fourth International Congress of Modern Architecture (CIAM) held in Athens, a group of admiring foreign architects visited the project. In 1971 Pierre Vago included the building in the list in the journal *Architecture d'aujourd'hui* of the most noteworthy international buildings constructed between 1889 and 1970. Mitsakis's school in Ambelokipoi, Athens, is by contrast a quiet scheme in which classrooms form an atrium with one side open to the neighbourhood.

A church attached to the 'Nomikos' School (1934) was a small project, but the most original design by Mitsakis and one of modern architecture's most striking schemes. To serve the school's 2,000 students, rather than designing a closed volume, Mitsakis placed in the middle of the schoolyard a plain box with an asymmetrically positioned bell-post; the west side of the box was left open to permit students gathered in the yard to participate in the service. Once more Mitsakis used colours for the interior, for frescoes would have been prohibitively expensive. But there was more than economy that dictated the design. The use of colour, rather than expressing construction functions, as Mitsakis had in Marasleion, functioned according to the principles of the painter Spyros Papaloukas, whom Mitsakis brought onto the project. They were drawn from his studies on Byzantine interiors

Nikolaos Mitsakis, Ambelokipoi, Lyceum, Athens, 1930–31, northeast elevation.

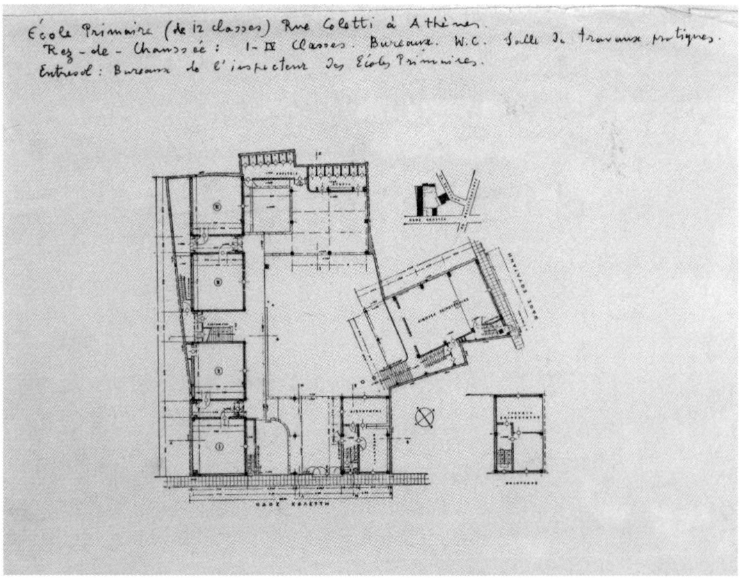

Nikolaos Mitsakis, Primary school, Koletti Street, Athens, 1932, ground-floor plan.

opposite: Nikolaos Mitsakis, Primary School, Koletti Street, Athens, 1932.

Nikolaos Mitsakis, Church attached to 'Nomikos' School, Athens, 1934.

Nikolaos Mitsakis, Church attached to 'Nomikos' School, Athens, 1934.

and Greek vernacular outdoor sites, and indicated the structure of space: ochre for the side walls, terracotta for the back wall, and blue for the ceiling.

Patroklos Karantinos was another significant contributor to the architecture of the period. Born in Constantinople to Cephalenian parents, Karantinos had also studied at Athens Polytechnic and was close to Pikionis, with whom, together with Kyriakos Panayiotakos, he went on the legendary 1921 study trip to Aegina. In 1927–8 he lived in Paris, briefly employed there in Auguste Perret's office. In addition to designing, Karantinos wrote polemical articles in support of modern architecture. Christian Zervos published an article of his on new school buildings in Greece in the French review *Cahiers d' Art* in 1934, which was followed by a book in 1938.

Karantinos's first educational facility was the elementary school (1930) in Kallithea, a garden city in Athens for middle-class Asia Minor refugees. Venizelos placed the foundation stone himself. Folding wooden divisions across the narrow side of the prismatic volume of the building produced a highly flexible plan. The most interesting aspects of the work, however, were the site arrangement, the configuration of the outdoor spaces, the rhythmic stepping up of terraces, and volumes juxtaposed

Patroklos Karantinos, Primary School, Kalisperi and Karyatidon streets, Athens, 1931.

under 'the great sun of the South', the 'Greek light', to quote the young writer Theotokas, that 'neither Goths nor Skyths' have.[22] Karantinos's most important project was the public school on Kalisperi Street in Athens, located almost beneath the Acropolis. Using the same system as in the Kallithea school, Karantinos offered a flexible plan. Despite the differences in materials and the articulation of the elements, he established a fascinating dialogue between his simple functional building and its monumental neighbour, the Parthenon. Nine concrete columns divide the facade into eight rectangular parts whose proportions, counting from the summit of the building to the ground, are very close to those of the

Patroklos Karantinos, School complex, Marousi, Attica, 1932, sanitary facilities and gymnastics shelter area.

Thucydides Valentis, School, Syros, 1931–2.

rectangular parts formed by the Parthenon's columns. The eight parts of the facade are grouped by three long, foregrounded gutters that overlay an additional 2, 3, 3 rhythm offsetting the austerity of the structure. The facade is further animated through the eccentric placement of the entrance unit at the corner of the building.

Important places for instruction were also designed by Thucydides Valentis, such as the school on the island of Syros (1931–2), and Kyriakos Panayiotakos. Like Mitsakis, Panayiotakos was one of the first students of the School of Architecture of Athens. After his graduation in 1923 he collaborated as a private architect with Mitsakis and after 1930 in the Ministry of Education, where among other projects he designed the

Kyriakos Panayiotakos, Elementary school, Liosion Street, Athens, 1931–2.

Dimitris Pikionis, Elementary school at Pefkakia, Lycabettus Hill, Athens, 1933.

Gymnasium of Sparta and the elementary school in Liosion Street Athens (visited and admired by Le Corbusier during the CIAM conference), and in Gouva, Pangrati, Athens. Pikionis himself was commissioned to design two schools in 1933, a medium-size high school building in Thessaloniki and an elementary school in the heart of Athens at the foot of Mt Lycabettus. In contrast to most modern buildings at that time, which with few exceptions, such as the Allgemeiner Deutscher Gewerkschaftsbund (1928–30) in Germany by Hannes Meyer, or Alvar Aalto's Paimio Sanatorium in Finland (1929–33), connect poorly to their surroundings, the Pikionis schools relate to their site in a remarkable way. In the Athens school Pikionis appears to have broken down the complex into elementary individual classroom units, each opening to its own open court for outdoor teaching and social activities; they are staggered as they ascend the slope of Lycabettus. In the Thessaloniki school Pikionis tried several versions, two of which give a clear picture of his dilemma: one is similar to the Athens school, the

Kyriakos Panayiotakos, Elementary School in Gouva, Athens, 1933.

other emphasizes regionalist elements in a Romantic-era picturesque manner. The second one was built. In Thessaloniki also, Mitsakis designed the Agias Sofias school (1928–33) using superficial local details to demonstrate Byzantine identity and assert its Greekness. While this was done at the expense of the city's rich and diverse history it was also reflective of the reaction against the growing trend of imported modern formulas.

In addition to regular school buildings, to promote the modernization of education as well as change attitudes and behaviour in everyday life, Venizelos and his team introduced the institution of children's summer camps, their architecture part of the architectural programme of the Ministry of Education. Of these the most fascinating are the camps in Penteli (1936–7) and Voula (in 1933–4, 1936–9), both designed by Panos Djelepy.

While school buildings were becoming the focus of architectural attention towards the end of the 1920s, at the same time a considerable amount of residential buildings were undertaken, almost all modern. In addition to producing a significant number of innovative buildings, the young generation of new architects also managed a major intellectual and public relations coup in 1933 by bringing to Greece the most prominent international group of avant-garde architects and planners of the time, the CIAM, and to elicit from its members enthusiastic responses for their work. Up until then, as we have seen, there were very few examples of apartment houses in Athens and very little attention was paid to

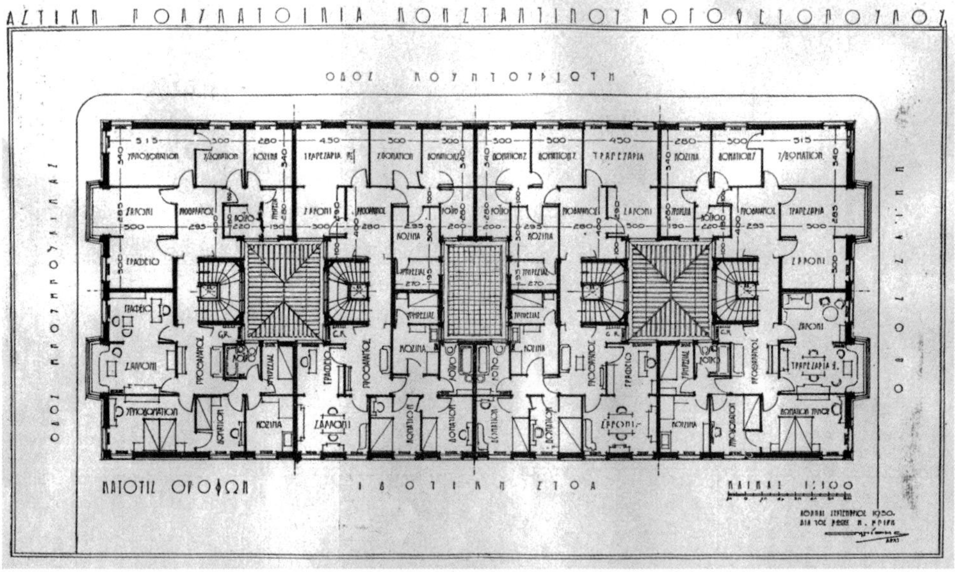

Kyprianos Biris, Logothetopoulos Apartment house, Athens, 1930.

housing. An exception was an article published in the journal *Archimedes* by Emmanuel Kriezis, in which he argued for the need to introduce apartment construction to Greece, referring of course to developments in Western Europe. Twenty years later, Kyprianos Biris, a graduate of Athens Polytechnic and just back from advanced studies in Germany, gave a landmark lecture in April 1932 (published soon after in *Technika Chronika* on 1 June). Biris had recently completed the Logothetopoulos apartment house (1930), a high-density, four-storey building that included 40 three- or four-room apartments. It occupied almost a whole Athens block, a relatively large project for Greece at that time. Biris maintained that 'today, most top architects and pioneers of modern architecture are preoccupied with apartment houses and housing, considering these topics as the most important'.[23] He criticized the capital's small-scale individual dwellings, with a density of 166 people per hectare, in the periphery and 250 to 280 people in the centre, as inefficient, creating a low-quality urban environment. He argued that for Athens to achieve the necessary high densities that modern life required, the development and adoption of the apartment house as a building type was a priority.

Contributing to this shift in residential architecture was the improvement of reinforced concrete construction that permitted both higher buildings and flexibility in the plan. But given the limitations of the Greek economy, the unavailability of bank capital for development of large-scale housing, the existing small urban plots relatively close to the centre, the new legislation permitting horizontal property, and the accompanying zoning that encouraged it, a special system of providing homes within collectively owned apartment houses emerged after the 1920s known as *antiparoche*. This was an exchange arrangement between landowners, contractors and apartment buyers, who would pay an advance of the amount for purchasing. The system was profit-based, flexible and adapted to given urban and economic requirements. Horizontal ownership was possible because of a new law of 1927 permitting horizontal ownership explicitly aimed at refugee housing.[24] It had significant consequences in the development of urban areas in Greece and in particular in Athens and Thessaloniki. In a newspaper article published only four years later Biris remarked that more than 70 apartments had already mushroomed in the upscale Kolonaki district alone.

The most significant work by Kyriakos Panayiotakos was a building in Athens on Exarcheia Square, known as the 'Blue' apartment building. The commission was given to the architect when he was only 28 years old by K. Antonopoulos, a developer and contractor in whose office Panayiotakos worked soon after graduating. The project is divided into two parts, with separate main and service entrances, and interior courts,

Kyriakos Panayiotakos, The Blue apartment building, Exarcheia Square, Athens, 1932–3.

with communication between both roof and basement. It has 40 apartments of different sizes, including a duplex. A peculiarity of the plan is the addition of a communal water-closet in the corridor on each floor. As in most apartment houses of the period, Panayiotakos employed the so-called *erker* (bay window) system that provided niche-like places and more intimate side views for each apartment.[25]

All apartments were provided with a plethora of built-in closets, drawers and bookcases that, together with the interior doors, are exquisitely minimally detailed. With equal care Panayiotakos designed the built-in furniture of the lobbies and exterior doors down to the smallest detail. Artists, theatre people and writers lived in the building, enhancing its community spirit. Indeed, one provision was a large (500 square metres) communal living- and play-room at the top of the building, which, Leonidas Kyrkos, a politician who lived in the building, remarked, served as a cementing factor between the inhabitants of the building throughout the 1930s and '40s, a period of political divisions and turmoil in Greece. But the most unique aspect of the project was its unique, daring ultramarine blue painted over the whole facade. This was conceived by the painter Spyros Papaloukas, who Panayiotakos met during his field studies of vernacular architecture with Pikionis and Mitsakis in Aegina. The Blue apartment building was visited by Le Corbusier during the CIAM conference, who

The Blue apartment building, floor plan.

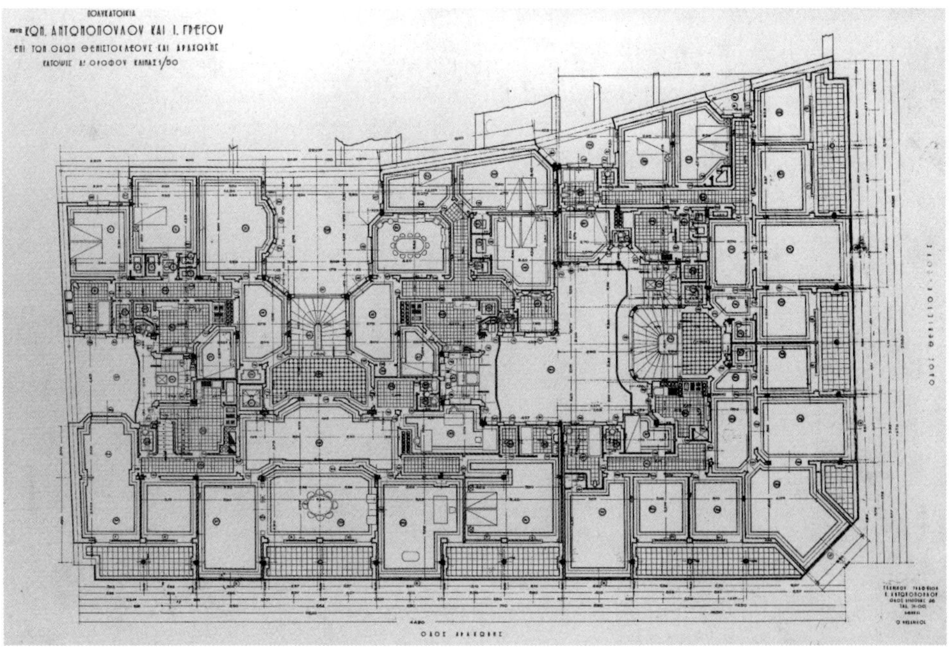

canonized it, writing on the entrance 'c'est très beau'.

While most writing of the period focused on the introduction of the modern apartment in Greece from the technical, economic or aesthetic point of view, a unique commentary on the modern way of living in apartment houses in Greece was contributed by Semni Papaspyridi-Karouzou, a prominent archaeologist, early in her career.[26] In her text on the new, urban high-density collective housing – which she characteristically called 'housing without smells of burnt food' – Karouzou discussed its impact on the social relations of the inhabitants of the city, mostly peasants who had recently arrived there as immigrants. She observed that certain domestic spaces that brought together members of extended families and neighbours, such as the 'saloni', the ceremonial room reserved by traditional families to celebrate religious holidays or other special occasions, were eliminated in modern apartment buildings, and that this affected human relations. Though not critical about these changes, she pointed out that such intangible transformations had to be taken into account because of their possible drastic influence on the quality of social life.

The Blue apartment building, staircase.

With few exceptions, the architecture of individual residences at this time was not as creative as that of the apartment houses. One of the exceptions is the Fakidis residence (1932–3) in Glyfada, Attica, by Stamo Papadakis. Here Papadakis achieved a striking spatial composition, contrasting cylindrical and orthogonal prismatic volumes, skilfully demonstrating the structural potential of cantilevering in reinforced concrete. (As in most cases of this purist architecture, from Paris to Rotterdam to Tel Aviv, the all-white skin covered a new brick-and-concrete construction.) The variety of open-air places that Papadakis provided in his scheme were the result of an exquisite formalist exercise that ignored aspects of livability. It was, however, a powerful icon of the new, open way of life to which those of the time aspired.

By contrast, the deep veranda scheme of the Gennimata residence by Isaac Saporta in Philothei offered a more prosaic deep-shaded niche fit for the open-air Mediterranean way of living, its poetic detail provided

opposite (clockwise from top left): Georgios Kontoleon, Manetas apartment building, Athens, 1932–4.

Vassilios Douras, Tsimpoukis apartment building, Athens, 1936.

Polyvios Michaelides and Thucydides Valentis, Michaelides Bros apartment house, Athens, 1933–4.

Rennos Koutsouris, first multi-storey car park, Athens, 1936.

270

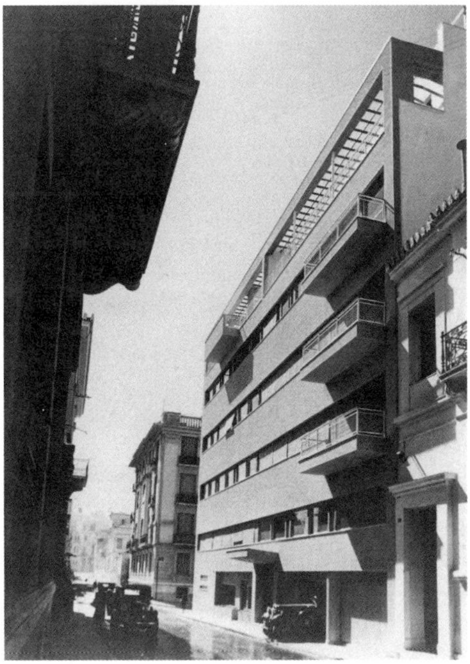

Stamo Papadakis, Fakidis residence, Glyfada, Attica, 1932–3.

by the attachment on the top of the building of an ocean liner-like, or perhaps airport-like, observation tower. By contrast, the Argyropoulos residence (1933–5), designed by Dimitris Fotiadis in collaboration with the architect Ioannis Chalepas, is an almost scenographic set sitting on a steep side of Lycabettus. Nevertheless it remains one of the most striking buildings in Athens due to its Orientalist character and the pleasant sculptural effect it achieves. Adjacent to it is another equally elaborate building, the four-storey Pallis House (1928) by Aristotelis Zachos.

Stamo Papadakis, Fakidis residence, Glyfada.

Dimitris Fotiadis in collaboration with Ioannis Chalepas, Argyropoulos residence, Athens, 1933–5.

In high contrast to these two flamboyant cases are two studio-residences by Vassilios Douras, one for the writer Nikos Kazantzakis in Aegina (1936–7), the other in Athens, next to the Acropolis, for and by the artist Parthenis. Both were austere, ascetic, prismatic, materialist but unworldly. In the biography of Kazantzakis published in 1968 by his wife, Eleni Kazantzakis, she describes various interesting incidents that occurred during construction of the building in Aegina, an experimental modern design put together by traditional builders. Both Kazantzakis and she wanted a

Vassilios Douras, Nikos Kazantzakis house and studio, Aegina, 1936–7.

'little peasant house' that was in 'harmony' with the houses of the island: 'no roof, nothing but broad terraces . . . and an outdoor stone staircase, the steps carved out of a single block'. Douras delivered a volume 'out of carved unplastered stone' shaped like the letter gamma, providing 'a patio sheltered from the winds'. The scheme included long windows, as in most modern buildings at that time. The builders, who would test the quality of the stones by 'biting' them, thought the architect was 'crazy' and refused to construct the windows.

Parthenis's house and studio in Athens, designed by the artist himself, was similarly minimalist. The site was donated in 1924 by Alexandros Papanastasiou, who was prime minister at that time. A drawing (likely by Parthenis) for a planned extension for his studio shows how the openings are proportioned according to strict harmonic geometry, and reveals a richness of formal thinking behind the poverty of the materials used in the building.

An ambitious programme of large-scale institutional construction was also carried out. One of the most interesting young architects of such buildings was Ioannis Despotopoulos. Born in Chios, he had studied in Germany and worked for Erich Mendelsohn in Berlin. Returning to Greece, and holding socialist views, like so many of his generation, he focused on the study of the relation between socio-economic structures and the modern city, and began to write and lecture on the subject. His institutional buildings include hospitals, among them Sotiria in Cholargos, Attica (1932–5), and others in Tripolis (1936–40), in Chios and Asvestochori near Thessaloniki (1937–40). Close to the Sotiria hospital, for the same complex, Pericles Georgakopoulos designed a very interesting laundry and kitchen facility, a machine-like scheme dominated by an overgrown reinforced concrete automobile ramp (1939–40).

Few structures explored the potentials of reinforced concrete as a building material during this period, but the most interesting are the dome roof for the University of Athens lecture hall in Goudi, Attica, designed by Emmanuel Kriezis (1929–35), a number of industrial structures for the company Kronos by P. Santorini (discussed on p. 115), and a large-scale tobacco depot with a concrete and glass roof designed by Isaac Saporta for the Commercial Tobacco Warehouses in Kokkinia (1935–6).

Young Greek architects were eager to show their work to a wider circle of colleagues. The opportunity arrived when the 4th International Congress of Modern Architecture (CIAM) was held in Greece in 1933. CIAM was an institution that attracted the most prominent international avant-garde architects and urbanists. Here the Greek modernists could be part of their discussions and show them their own work. Sigfried Giedion had written to Stamo Papadakis in April 1933 to inform him about the possibility of holding the event in Greece, and the official decision to do so was made in June. Papadakis had already been in contact with Giedion, having sent to him copies of his urban design projects for Athens, and Giedion responded by encouraging him to put together a group of Greek architects to participate in the Moscow Congress. Papadakis formed a small group consisting of architects who, like him, had

House and studio (at left) built by the painter Konstantinos Parthenis in the vicinity of the Acropolis, 1924.

Ioannis Despotopoulos, Sotiria Sanatorium, Cholargos, Attica, 1932–5, axonometric.

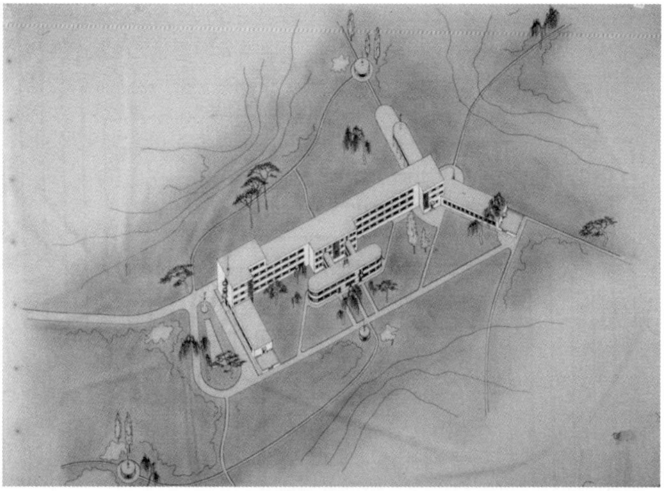

Pericles Georgakopoulos, Sotiria Sanatorium laundry and kitchen facility, Cholargos, Attica, 1939–40.

opposite:
Paul Santorini, pioneering 'mushroom', flat-slab industrial structure for the company Kronos, Eleusis, Attica, 1923.

Emmanuel Kriezis in collaboration with Kyprianos Biris and Panayotis Marthas, Interior of anatomy amphitheatre, Medical Laboratory complex, University of Athens, Goudi, Athens, 1929–35.

Isaac Saporta, Tobacco storage warehouses for Commercial Tobacco, Kokkinia, Attica, 1935–6.

graduated from the Ecole Spéciale, including G. Kalyvas (who graduated in 1929), V. Douras and D. Michalitsianos (who graduated a year later), and a few others who were linked with the German avant-garde, including I. Despotopoulos, A. Dragoumis and Gustav Eglau, with Isaac Saporta and P. Karantinos representing Athens Polytechnic.[27]

Pikionis, who was not on the list, had more in common with an architect like Mendelsohn than he did with the members of CIAM. Like Mendelsohn he was interested in exploring the unique spatial structure of the landscape and the region rather than what he saw as CIAM's concern with the development of universal rules for improving future cities. Mendelsohn in fact visited the Acropolis with Pikionis. The tour so impressed Mendelsohn that on his return to Berlin he wrote and illustrated two articles in May 1931 for the *Berliner Tageblatt* stressing the importance of the serpentine pathway up the hill.[28]

One of the most significant factors that contributed to the favourable reception of CIAM in Greece was the support it received from the newly founded review of technology, *Technika Chronika*, the first issue of which was published on 1 January 1932 under the direction of Nikolaos Kitsikis. This brilliant and ambitious civil engineer, professor, Senator and President of the Greek Chamber of Engineering sensed that the moment of modern architecture had arrived in Greece. He decided to wholeheartedly support it, welcoming a number of articles in his periodical by young Greek architects and prominent foreign ones. At the same time the Technical Chamber of Greece (or TEE) not only aligned itself with CIAM, it also took over organization of the Congress. Thus, *Technika*

Chronika on 1 March 1932 published an article by A. Sartoris on 'The New Spirit in Architecture'. Kitsikis also organized lectures, inviting Mendelsohn to speak in Athens and I. Despotopoulos, whose lecture he published.[29] Despotopoulos declared that 'the private initiative of contemporary individualistic society has brought Athens to the edge of chaos'. Papadakis also rushed into print a short article announcing the forthcoming Congress in Moscow, to examine the condition of 28 different cities in 20 countries, one of which was going to be Greece, 'for the first time' gathered among other nations.[30]

Not since the Revolution a century before had Greece attracted such a large number of forward thinking architects, engineers and planners as those who gathered on the *Patris II*, the ship that carried the participants of CIAM IV to Greece. *Patris II* left Marseille on 29 July, Papadakis travelling with them. The same day the members of the Congress begun work, with Cornelis van Eesteren opening the first session, followed by Giedion and Le Corbusier. The work continued the next day with some case studies of individual cities.

Le Corbusier, Issac Saporta, Gino Pollini and Giuseppe Terragni on the deck of *Patris II*, 1933.

On 2 August the members of the Congress visited Athens, and Balanos, the director of the Acropolis restoration works, gave them a tour of the Acropolis. They spent the afternoon in Marathon. In the evening there was an official dinner, with the ministers of External Affairs, National Economy, and Transportation, the mayors of Athens and Piraeus, a large number of ambassadors and members of the Academy all present. Kitsikis gave the key address,[31] declaring that 'the idols are abolished in Greece by the avant-garde of education'. He praised the school-building programme, stressing the role of the state for giving the opportunity to young architects to carry out daring experiments and for adopting Modernism as its official design approach. A toast followed by Constantinos Tsaldaris, Deputy Minister of Transport, who praised the principle of the 'organic city, to achieve the maximum benefit with the minimum cost', wishing it would become 'the foundation of the

future evolution of Athens'. His talk was followed by a lecture by Dragoumis in support of regionalism. Dragoumis polemically opposed the idea of an international style, arguing that 'modern architecture is created by the culture of each place, each race, according to individual customs, needs, and climate . . . and . . . for this reason there will never be an architectural "Esperanto".'

Anastasios Orlandos, Dean of the School of Architecture, gave a provocative talk responding to the speeches by the CIAM leaders. 'The School is only fifteen years old', he said, 'and it had already killed "academicism" before Le Corbusier declared it dead'. The reason for that was the existence of a Greek regional, vernacular architecture, especially the architecture of the islands, whose roots went back to antiquity, and which remained untouched by the post-Renaissance academic tradition. Referring to the tour of the islands that Papadakis had planned for the Congress he added:

> When you visit our smiling islands of the Aegean . . . these white visions that float between sea and sky, I am sure you will be surprised not only by the perfect simplicity and rationality of their layout, the purity of the contour of the ancient houses of Delos, but also by the gripping spectacle of the houses of the islands around Delos with their austere geometrical volumes . . . you will discern in these humble houses the combinations the outlines, projections and depressions of volumes, successful relations that a contemporary architect would have wished to have used in his work.

These were the result of a perfect match between form and function achieved by the 'peasant' designer. 'These humble, small island houses are "archetypes" of the new architecture.'[32]

Isaac Saporta, the youngest participant of the Congress, just 23 years of age, addressed the Congress on behalf of the Greek delegation. 'Dear friends', he said, 'we [young Greek architects] are here, few, weak, and exposed to many attacks . . . not clear about the direction to follow'. 'Whither young architect?' he asked dramatically, stressing the challenges of introducing modern architecture to Greece. Refusing to imitate that which modern architects did 'beyond the Alps', Saporta stressed the significance of the regional characteristics of Greece and, further, the understanding that 'new architecture without the understanding of a new way of life is impossible'.[33]

Very little attention was paid to technology during the Congress, which focused on urban problems, with two exceptions, one a lecture by the Polish architect-engineer Szymon Syrkus on the new techniques of exterior walls for buildings, and one by the Greek engineer Paul Santorini. Santorini (real name Papadopoulos) was born in Russia. A child prodigy, he had graduated from ETH in Zurich at a record early age, having gained a reputation for his computation skills (he was hired by Albert Einstein to assist in his calculations). Santorini discussed the 'structural possibilities offered by new developments in reinforced concrete'. The first reinforced concrete buildings were the Hotel Ritz (1920) on Eleusis Square in Thessaloniki and the Giannaros apartment (1917) in Athens. Neither were technically innovative. In Eleusis, however, Santorini had constructed industrial facilities for the factory company Kronos using a pioneering technique of vaults or domes directly supported by mushroom capitals (known as *flachdecke*).[34] The original morphology of these structures had emerged out of functional needs rather than through more typically formal experiments as practised by other Greek architects.

For Greek architecture the CIAM Congress seemed to open the way to the future. The visibility the work of young architects received was exceptional and deserved. The Greek group continued to work together in Athens with increased confidence and, more importantly, with a sense of experimentation and collegiality. Nonetheless the impact of the Congress on Greek architecture was limited. Despite the significant and enthusiastic participation of government officials and institutions, no major commissions to young architects followed, neither were the architectural and planning policies of the government much changed, especially those related to housing and to the city, the declared focus of the Congress.

As opposed to residences and apartment houses, housing, whether for the middle classes, the poor or refugees, was almost non-existent in Greece up to the end of the First World War. The disasters of the Thessaloniki fire and the arrival of the refugees were shocks that, as we have seen, accelerated modernization of building and zoning legislation and introduced the question of housing. Early projects in the Thessaloniki area were the Vardari Workers Housing for the victims of the fire by Hébrard and Kitsikis (1919), and the garden suburb Chortiatis by Jean Pleyber (1934). The need for *housing* in the form of urban apartments as opposed to *houses* was stressed also by Biris, as mentioned earlier, and of course there were the desperate struggles of Morgenthau and his collaborators of the Relief Fund to acommodate refugees in the framework of the Refugee Rehabilitation Committee of the League of Nations. The fund succeeded in undertaking 125 housing projects in urban and rural areas, but these were emergency undertakings free from architectural ambition and were seen as transitional shelters only.[35]

A new law aimed at helping refugees introduced suburban development consisting of detached individual houses; but instead of helping those in need it merely assisted the development of middle- and upper-middle-class garden suburbs not far from the centre of Athens, such as Psychico and Philothei. Between 1929 and 1931 the Philothei scheme was restarted as a low-density single-house cooperative development for employees of the National Bank. To avoid a chaotic or anarchic explosion of construction work, Angelos Siagas, the key consultant for the development, invited a number of architects to submit a house type, compiling an album that was offered to the owners of the lots.

In 1933 Papadakis published an article attacking the choice of a low-density individual housing type and the lack of an overall urban plan, and counter-proposed a solution close to CIAM formulas.[36] Soon after, Despotopoulos intensified the attack against such suburban developments, which he considered private initiatives coming from the 'contemporary individualistic class' and which was bringing Athens to the edge of chaos. He suggested an alternative architecture, but he also invited an alternative socialist society to come together and take control.[37]

The economics of the newly established horizontal ownership in combination with the introduction of new concrete technology at the end of the 1920s generated a building boom of apartment houses for the middle classes and for hotels in Thessaloniki. In contrast to their Athenian colleagues, the focus of the Thessalonikian architects was pragmatic, technical and utilitarian rather than iconic, and they looked more to bourgeois Vienna than to avant-garde Paris for lessons. The most interesting results included Max Rubens's Aaron Mois apartment house (1931), Alexandros Tzonis's Eratyra apartment house (1929) and the hotels Astoria (1929) and Lux Palace (1929).

With the return of Venizelos, in 1930 the Ministry of Social Welfare established a Technical Department that undertook construction of most of the refugee housing previously carried out by the fund. The most successful example of this was designed by Kimon Laskaris in Alexandras Avenue, Athens, and built between 1933 and 1935. It consists of a series of eight plain, stern, three-storey walk-up blocks in parallel made out of stone-bearing walls and reinforced concrete slabs. The apartments were minimal but functional. Windows and balconies were well-proportioned and rhythmically laid out in a manner strongly reminiscent of Bauhaus buildings. There was no effort, however, to control the glare of the southern sun, neither was any sun or rain protection applied so as to make the mini-balconies practical. The outside spaces between blocks were bare, unpaved, and no playgrounds or social or green spaces were provided. It resulted in a rather dramatic and photogenic scheme, but

Alexandros Tzonis, Eratyra Apartment House, Salonica, 1929.

one that was ultimately unfriendly and unfit for a residential building, particularly one for refugees who had been forced to flee their ancestral homes. The low budget constraints notwithstanding, it seems the architects were indifferent to adapting Bauhaus prototypes to fit the regional and social identity of the project.

The period during which the schools were constructed was a unique economic, social, cultural and architectural moment of modernization for Greece. The unprecedented destruction and pain of 1922 had rejuvenated rather than crushed the new state. What made this period even more idiosyncratic was that for most Western countries the years 1929–32 were a phase of severe economic depression, even 'agony', as the historian Mark Mazower has suggested.[38] Among the most important concurring factors that contributed to this paradox was that Greece, after a decade of wars, was finally enjoying a period of diplomatic and military calm. Soon after Venizelos became Prime Minister of Greece once more (on 30 August 1928), he proposed to the Turkish government a normalization of relations between the two countries, friendship and a non-aggression pact. In addition, the generation that had experienced the horror of 1922 and the frustrations of political instability between 1924 and 1928 was now mature, ready to assume professional and institutional responsibilities, and even leadership. Thus, a long series of economic, political and intellectual struggles to modernize the country, initiated and pursued by Venizelos and his colleagues since 1909, appeared justified by the end of the 1930s.[39]

One more factor contributing to the modernization of the Greek state and Greek society was the influx of the refugees of 1922 who, in contrast to the local population of Greece, were mostly literate and trained in urban professions. Furthermore, a hardship appeared to be an enabling one: with the United States having closed it doors to immigrants, the refugees became a valuable local resource, ready to work for lower wages, thus making the Greek economy highly competitive. Finally, and most important, as a result of the world economic crisis, being unable to export its few but significant foodstuffs, Greece was obliged to reorient and restructure its economy. From an underdeveloped economy, exporting unprocessed agricultural goods, it became one by exploiting its own regional resources, employing its local labour and using new technology to generate goods intended for local consumers. To quote Mazower once again, the 'new Greek miracle' occurred – an economy growing faster than any country in the world at that time, with the exception of the USSR and Japan.[40]

For a moment it appeared that, despite the economic and political difficulties that started to mount in the first part of the 1930s, Greece would continue to progress. Some, however, doubted that the path to modernization that Greece was taking was the right one. The newspaper *To Vima* showed in a series of articles under the title 'Athens an endless garbage-land' by Stefanos Stefanou (14, 15 and 18 July 1931), that the unquestionable economic progress made in many domains over the past few years was at the expense of the quality of life. The first article contained even a 'Garbageological' map of the capital that documented the open-air sites where rubbish was accumulated, the outdoor sewage freely flowing in the middle of residential areas, and the widespread use of trash as fertilizer in small farms within the city.

From a different perspective, Theotokas in his novel *Argo* (1933) wrote of Athens as a place without 'institutions, state organization, ideologies', where they were 'building everywhere heavy concrete houses', a place where 'immediately after the Catastrophe the cars started to multiply with great speed to the degree that in some avenues the trees had to be cut to widen the passage for the cars'. Cars were bringing people to places to listen to 'jazz conquering Athens and its calm suburbs' and to 'new luxurious suburbs growing in the most deserted corners of Attica that few Athenians visited before and most knew of them only by name'.[41]

Criticism about the path modernization was taking was also voiced in a unique small book documenting a single vernacular structure built in 1880, *The House of Rodakis in Aegina*. It was written by two artists, Klaus Vrieslander and Julio Kaimi, who were neither architects nor Greek, but were passionate about folk art and Greek regionalist culture. *The House of Rodakis* contained a few remarks about 'the system of the art of Rodakis', referred to by the authors but never written down in detail. It was a manifesto published 'in the midst of the sea of ugliness and superstition, in the midst of the waves of materialism of an artificial and hasty epoch such as ours'. Addressed to young Greek architects (we can't tell whether Kaimi and Vrieslander were planning to promote Rodakis internationally, as Kaimi was already trying to do with Pikionis), the work of Rodakis – an 'architect but the same time juggler of matter' as Vrieslander called him – was put forth as a polemic against the 'poverty of the modern apartment house of Athens', the 'false fantasies of the mechanized apartments', 'spiritually poorer than the poorest Bedouin of the desert', the 'life-hating' art and architecture as publicized by the books and magazines crowding the table of the author of the book (the text does not specify to which of the two authors the table belonged), the 'chaos of modernism', in Christian Zervos's journal *Cahiers d' art*, in 'the journalistic screams of Le Corbusier' – the star of the CIAM Congress – 'heard all over the place'. Kaimi and Vrieslander believed that the Rodakis house was 'great art', offering an alternative, being grounded in the region, in folk-art

Alexandros Rodakis, Rodakis House, Aegina, c. 1880.

Rodakis House, Aegina, c. 1880.

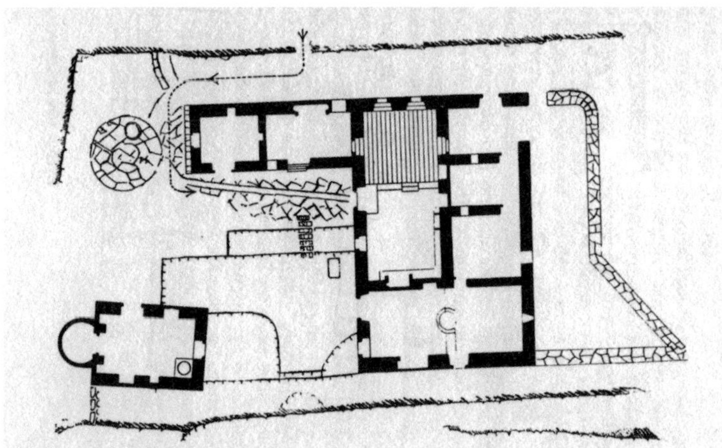

precedents, in the landscape – the natural environment. Built on the top of a hill near the village of Messagros, as Vrieslander describes it, the house 'follows the Cycladic tradition' of folk architecture. It is functional, simple and works as a whole, integrating architecture, furniture and sculpture in 'total architecture', a *Gesamtkunstwerk* that also includes the landscape. One of the most important observations by Kaimi and Vrieslander concerns the quality, or *raumgefühl*, of the Rodakis complex: 'The plan with its little L-shape court is based on a spatial principle', as they explained; we 'never reach straightaway the door . . . but . . . follow a circuitous path or a crooked way, and this in order to give an expression of the spatial sensitivity of the Greek landscape, a simple but difficult rule, to serve an aesthetic but also practical need'. 'While the houses of the West are closed to nature the Rodakis house opens to nature'; the scheme emerged 'like plants grow out of the earth', it 'acquires its form out of the character of the Greek landscape'.[42]

In 1935 Pikionis tried to reweave together all Greek artists and architects who had similar views about region, tradition and modern culture by creating a new review, *The Third Eye* (*To Trito Mati*) with Doukas his friend as editor, and with the painters N. Hadjikiriakos and Spyros Papaloukas and the architect Karantinos on board. The review succeeded *Frangelio* (first published in 1927), a less sophisticated publication edited by Nikos Velmos. Pikionis's publication, on the other hand, was academic and included a collage of modern texts by foreigners and Greeks together with medieval, Byzantine and popular art and architecture. Apart from its excellent visual quality, due to a great extent to Pikionis's talents, and the strong commitment to bringing together Greek folk culture with modern art, there was no real originality in the enterprise. It was unique in Greece, but came too late and contributed too little to the debate of modern culture, unlike the forward-thinking reviews in the Balkans, such as the Serbian *Zenit* (1924).

During the first one hundred years of its independent existence, Greece went through periods of enviable modernization and development. But progress was always short-lived. Unfinished, irregular and temporary architectural interventions could not solve severe large-scale urban problems or create long-term social harmony. At the beginning of the 1930s, with the preparations of the CIAM Congress, the government welcomed the initiatives by young modern architects and new urbanist ideas were received with great interest. But by 1934 the climate was significantly different.

The ups and downs of the provision of shelters for the war refugees and the urban immigrants in Athens and Thessaloniki were more tortuous than the progress of the school-building programme. While in the case of schools, the state performed energetically and in most cases effectively, in that of refugee housing the state intervened sporadically, so that refugees were left to the mercy of land speculators. This was one of the reasons that the late 1920s was not only the moment of a Greek modern renaissance but also of mounting conflict, protest and urban unrest. In 1927 a fascist organization, EEE, had published the notorious and fraudulent anti-semitic text *The Protocols of the Elders of Zion*. On 29 June 1931, war refugees in collaboration with the Venizelist newspaper *Macedonia* incited a riot. A crowd of about 2,000 marched to the Camp

Campel housing project where 300 Jewish families were sheltered following the 1917 fire, and burned it down. Sikelianos reacted immediately, protesting the aggression.[43] In April 1932 the rioters were brought to court and almost all acquitted.[44] The event led to thousands of Jewish families leaving the city, many, like the municipal councillor, Abraham Recanati, to settle in Palestine. Even more damaging were the economic conflicts. On 11 June 1928 a general strike by tobacco workers left six dead and 60 wounded.

In the process of debating how to solve these problems, Venizelos's party was split in two. On one side was the group that had searched for solutions through social reforms, housing policies and the introduction of a social security law to protect the unemployed. Between May and August 1932 this was discussed in Parliament with support from all parties. However, the political crisis that followed prohibited its implementation and it was only later during the dictatorship that it became law. On the other side was the group that had sought for solutions via 'law and order'. Although not opposed to social reforms that group ignored housing and planning policies. Given the Bolshevik revolution in Russia, a country not so very far from Greece, for some people the danger appeared imminent and the only way to contain it was through police action rather than welfare policies. On 16 July 1929 the *idionimon* law (4229/1929) was passed with the aim of controlling not only actions against the state but also 'thoughts' against public order. An additional law was passed in 1931 that prohibited civil servants from striking or associating with groups that 'believed in the existence of class struggle'. The severe punishment provided by the law – vague and confrontational in its content – was paradoxical in a country where the tradition of toppling kings and governments was endemic and the resort to *coups d'état* was seen as a legitimate way to solve problems.[45]

The new law did not yield the expected political results for Venizelos. As the Greek economy declined deeply during the second half of 1932, so did his political power in the September elections. Among other groups, Venizelos lost the support of the refugees who were angry with his negligence of their needs and the 'friendship agreement' he had arranged with Turkey. Those who gained were both the conservative Popular Party and the Communist Party. Neither did the *idionimon* law protect Venizelos's followers from being called 'Venizelocommunists' due to his policy of economic modernization, even if the policy was promoted by the governor of the National Bank of Greece. For them these anti-laissez-faire policies suggested that 'private enterprise was not enough for this purpose', which was 'a job that the state had to take over'.[46]

By December 1932 the drachma had devalued by 75 per cent, Venizelos was out of office, and *Technika Chronika,* the champion of CIAM, published an article representing the views of the Technical Chamber of Greece that recommended not hiring foreign architects or engineers. The climate worsened with the assassination attempt on Venizelos on 6 July 1933. The opposition headed by Tsaldaris now accused Venizelos of supporting the interests of big capital. Venizelos continued to work to promote his programme of modernization, introducing elements of governmental economic intervention and planning, which the Popular Party criticized as promoting 'state socialism' and the 'sovietization' of Greece (a characterization given also to Herbert Hoover's 1932 RFC Act and to F. D. Roosevelt's New Deal programme). Interestingly, Lincoln MacVeagh, a committed anti-communist, appointed by Roosevelt as Envoy Extraordinary and Minister Plenipotentiary to Greece – and famous for having given a speech in ancient Greek when he presented his credentials as envoy – having the New Deal in mind, commented on the negative remarks made about planning that politicians in Greece were completely ignorant about what a planned economy had achieved and what it could bring about.[47]

But Venizelos was not Roosevelt – if anything his proposals resembled, very remotely, Hoover's and his federally funded projects. Venizelos's collaborators, with the exception of Papanastasiou, were not only 'liberals' by definition, Liberal being the name of their party, they had very little knowledge about how a directed economy, or perhaps any modern economy, worked. The unprecedented transformations the economy needed were seen with awe. Mark Mazower quotes the old minister of finance, the banker and patron of Zachos, Spyros Loverdos, feeling pity for 'the minister who, eager for renewal and radical changes, will worsen this chaos'.[48]

Distrustful of the welfare projects Venizelos insisted he would carry out, Theotokas added his voice: 'the Greeks are very lucky that they are not the proletarians one wishes they will never become . . . the proletariat is a disease and socialism is the therapy . . . it is absurd to try to get sick just to have the opportunity to get treated well'.[49]

Given all these pressures, the reforms Venizelos tried at the end of his political career were too improvised, too narrow and too late. Public works were very limited, and urban and housing construction projects scanty; the opposition to Venizelos meanwhile was dreaming of a small and traditional Greece. They circulated nostalgic visions of decentralized local communities,[50] and even sought to establish a national socialist party as an alternative. In March 1935, in a last desperate attempt, Venizelos gambled and tried once more to carry out a *coup d'état*. He lost. The following year he died in France; his close collaborators in the reform programmes, Papanastasiou and Papandreou, were exiled. Mussolini became for many

Dimitrios Kyriakos and Kimon Laskaris, Refugee Housing, Alexandras Avenue, Athens, 1933–6.

a popular figure in Greece and for some an exemplar to be emulated. It was the end of an era.

The situation was no better internationally. Apart from the mounting economic crisis, the 1 February 1935 issue of *Technika Chronika* stated that it was 'happy to publish' a text written by Stamo Papadakis, submitted on behalf of the Greek section of CIAM, protesting 'The closing of the School of Dessau' (the Bauhaus) 'last October', for 'chauvinistic' reasons, the school not being thought 'German' enough. Papadakis had already left Greece for the USA when the letter was printed. Saporta was in Germany and visited Mies in the 'new' Bauhaus in Berlin to find it attacked by the Sturm Abteilung, Hitler's 'brownshirts'. Mies appeared not to be worried about it, but Saporta was. He returned to Greece still expecting the situation to improve and prepared to team up with Dragoumis, who was working under the mayor of Athens, Konstantinos Kotzias, at that time. Part of the plan was to bring to Greece Gropius's collaborator, Martin Wagner, City Architect of Berlin, who was under pressure from the Nazis for his socialist leanings, and with him start a genuine branch of modern urban planning within the Greek government. They succeeded in bringing Wagner to lecture at the Polytechnic in December 1935. He gave an impressive talk, revealing how modern cities function, what their economic basis was, their technological nature and their morphological character. The lecture gave indications that perhaps, despite many unfavourable conditions, there was still a possibility to practice urban design creatively in Greece.

Indeed, a small number of refugee housing projects were built even after the death of Venizelos by the Technical Department of the Ministry of Social Welfare: in Stegi Patridos, designed by K. Laskaris and constructed by S. Dimitriadis, and in Dourgouti, which included four blocks designed by D. Kyriakos (1933–6) and two by Laskaris constructed as late as 1938 and 1940. They were the most interesting experiments in social housing carried out by Greek architects since the time of Kapodistrias, but they were hardly enough for the thousands of refugees stuck in the same conditions as they were when they first arrived. Even more so, the projects were unfinished, random and isolated in an increasingly chaotic urban environment.[51]

CHOCOLATES

chapter four

Hard Times: The Third Hellenic Civilization, War and Reconstruction

Ioannis Metaxas declared the 'Third Hellenic Civilization' at 8:00 p.m. on 4 August 1936. Pretentiously named, the 'Civilization' lasted just four years, with no distinctive 'civilized' cultural output. Yet it was a historical episode that marked the development of Greek architecture. Metaxas, a brilliant military officer, though a rather unsuccessful politician (only a few months before August 1936 his party had received just under 4 per cent of the vote), did not hesitate in appointing himself leader (*Arhighos*, when widespread industrial unrest and Parliament's lack of credibility made the country appear ungovernable. Metaxas defined his regime as the 'Third Hellenic Civilization' by claiming ancient Greece as the first and Byzantine as the second. He justified taking over the government by claiming that Greece was threatened by communists, an opinion shared by many conservative as well as centrist politicians in the mid-1930s. Yet, as historians today tend to agree, in reality communism in Greece was a raucous but small movement at that time.

The politicians' support of regime change came in the context of the political instability that much of Europe was facing at that moment, and an 'epidemic of strikes' in Greece, the worst happening on 8 May 1936 in Thessaloniki, which left the city without transportation or electricity, and with twelve dead strikers and 200 injured. Bert Birtles, an Australian, arriving at Piraeus from Haifa in 1936, said the port resembled a 'zoo with all the animals free', the 'lions' being the taxi drivers; Athens, he observed, was a place where 'there are as many rules as there are people'.[1]

The Third Hellenic Civilization was not a universally welcomed alternative to this chaos. As the poet George Seferis reacted in his diaries: 'We are no more in Greece . . . this . . . is not our place, it is a nightmare. Nothing more bitter than to be nostalgic of your own place while living in your place.'[2] Like Seferis, Metaxas was an obsessive diarist, but in the hundreds of fascinating pages in which he recorded his thoughts, which contain many shrewd as well as paranoid observations about political events and personal details, there are few references to buildings. Perhaps there was not much to say about architecture in those days: the golden

Vassilios Kassandras and Leonidas Bonis, Army Share Fund (ASF) building, Athens, 1927–38.

era of building schools, apartments and hospitals was almost over, and in 1936 Greece faced severe economic difficulties as well as, like the rest of Europe, the cost of intensive military preparations. Metaxas increased the state's defence expenses threefold from it had been in 1931. During the same period, with the exception of road building (which doubled), public works decreased three times.[3]

Although construction had shrunk, and Metaxas appeared alienated from his public (he often referred to them in his diary as 'those people'), one of his most important preoccupations was the physical planning of the capital. During the four years of his regime, he spent time, though very little money, trying to establish some administrative order over the city and organize urban life. Some of these interventions were pathetically ineffective; others lasted until the late 1950s. In addition, being a fascist leader, he was also concerned with the possibilities the city could offer as a platform supporting public spectacles to hammer home the regime's legitimacy and collective identity.

To satisfy these needs, on 15 September 1936 Metaxas founded a new ministry for the administration of 'the region of the capital', a centralized post with broad responsibilities covering the whole of Attica. He housed the new ministry in the prestigious Old Palace, and having already appointed Konstantinos Kotzias mayor of Athens in April 1934, made him Minister Governor of the Capital. Kotzias was to be assisted by a Director General, the architect Kostas Biris, and a Director of Technical Projects, the civil engineer Elias Krimbas. The appointment appeared successful: as mayor, Kotzias had proven to be a zealous organizer and passionate showman. Metaxas also established a new Supreme Planning Organization of the Capital with two branches, architecture and city planning. Echoing the urban ambitions of Kemal, Mussolini and Hitler – the three leaders Metaxas admired – he appointed himself President of the Ministry's Supreme City Planning Council. Kotzias was a charismatic figure with a totalitarian mindset, but at the same time he tolerated, and even understood, radically opposing views as long as they did not infringe directly on his projects. His great passion for the theatre also transcended his political views. As Minister Governor of the Capital he saw buildings and squares as potential theatrical stage sets for state spectacles glorifying the Third Civilization. By temperament an activist-impresario rather than a planner, most of his urban schemes did not materialize into concrete projects, although his work as chief image maker of the regime produced tangible results, including numerous theatrical-political performances in Athens, in Thessaloniki, and across the country.[4]

Paradoxically, Kotzias's hyperactivity could mean destruction for architecture and the theatre: the original Demotiko Theatre of Athens, a neoclassical building designed by Ziller, was demolished in 1937 for no serious reason other than a desire for renewal. The daily newspaper *Acropolis* had warned on 9 July 1936 that 'Athens is losing its beautiful mansions. This evil must stop'. These actions were indicative of the regime's general lack of appreciation of the nation's architectural heritage and the vacuum of a broader and deeper cultural vision. Likewise, the propaganda shows, rallies and festivals, where plot and decor celebrated the 'Third Hellenic Civilization', amounted to shallow populist happenings accompanied by collaged ornaments from antiquity, Byzantium and folk art, usurping pieces from Sikelianos' Delphic festival that fused ancient drama with peasant folk arts and crafts, turning them into a popular variety show. K. Pratsika, who had earlier collaborated with Sikelianos in his Delphic Idea festival, produced such events, conceiving the melodramatic ceremony for lighting the flame for the 1936 Olympic Games held in Berlin, which was filmed by Leni Riefenstahl and used to promote the Nazi regime. Pratsika also organized the celebration for the first anniversary of the Dictatorship in 'Third Hellenic Civilization' style. Even the Polytechnic was co-opted: the three-day celebration of its centenary (1837–1937) included pantomimes, decor and costumes in 'Three Civilizations' style.

The disapproval by intellectuals was widespread but silent. In his diary entry of 24 October 1939, Seferis called the performance of *The Persians,* 'awful', the 'power of stupidity, the power of ugliness'. To make things worse, the 4th of August regime, like all totalitarian governments, in its 'unbearable and stupid effort . . . to erase, bury and deform history, present and ancient' did not hesitate to censor, among many other texts, Sophocles' *Antigone*, works by Aristophanes, Pericles' Funeral Oration by Thucydides, and writings by the super-nationalist P. Giannopoulos; and the regime twice included among its 'urban shows' the public burning of 445 censored books, in Piraeus and in Sparta.[5]

Naturally, support for the theatre involved commissions for the design of new venues; these, however, were few and somewhat limited in scope. In a meeting on 11 February 1939 that included Metaxas and Kostis Bastias (the first Director of the newly founded division of Letters and Fine Arts at the Ministry of Education), Kotzias asked the young architect Constantinos Doxiadis to design open-air facilities for 8,000 to 10,000 people for the Royal Theatre on Philopappou Hill, Athens. The previous year (May 1938) Bastias, in close collaboration with Doxiadis, had been busy putting together a long proposal to the government for an ambitious national programme of theatre-building. In the same month Metaxas responded in *I Kathimerini*, officially approving the proposals. Following developments in Italy, France and Germany, Kotzias studied the possibility of developing outdoor theatres, using open urban spaces, as well as restoring and reusing ancient Greek theatres. At Bastias's request, Doxiadis also designed a complex temporary structure, metal-framed with wood and red canvas, that held an audience of 1,000 people for the *Chariots of Thespis* (a programme for promoting theatre in the provinces), for the Summer Royal Theatre of Thessaloniki.[6]

The son of the Venizelist Minister Apostolos Doxiadis, he had studied architecture at the Athens Polytechnic, where he was influenced by Pikionis's teachings, and undertook postgraduate research at Berlin's Technical University. Writing to Pikionis from Berlin, he reported on the dramatic shift by students away from teachers of modern architecture (such as Hans Scharoun) and towards the traditionalists (for example Tessenow). Doxiadis himself concentrated on investigating the spatial arrangement of ancient Greek complexes, earning his doctorate in record time, in 1936. While it was not firmly grounded in archaeological fact, his thesis presented a daring, stimulating and influential hypothesis that argued that behind the seemingly chaotic pattern of ancient Greek sites there was a rigorous optical system common to all.[7] Doxiadis returned to Greece, where Pikionis published an article on the findings in his revue *To Trito Mati* in 1936. Panayiotis Michelis, a young architect and writer, was the antithesis of Doxiadis's energetic fast-thinking. Just back from studying in Munich, whereupon he was made a professor in the Polytechnic, this important theoretician of Greek architecture responded with an elaborate negative critique in the review *Technika Chronika* in July 1938, doubting the methodological and epistemological correctness of Doxiadis's conclusions. It was the beginning of a major theoretical debate of international interest hosted by the review for Greece, unsurpassed in quality to this day.

Nikolaos Mitsakis and Dimitris Pikionis, Apartment House, Heyden Street, Athens, 1934.

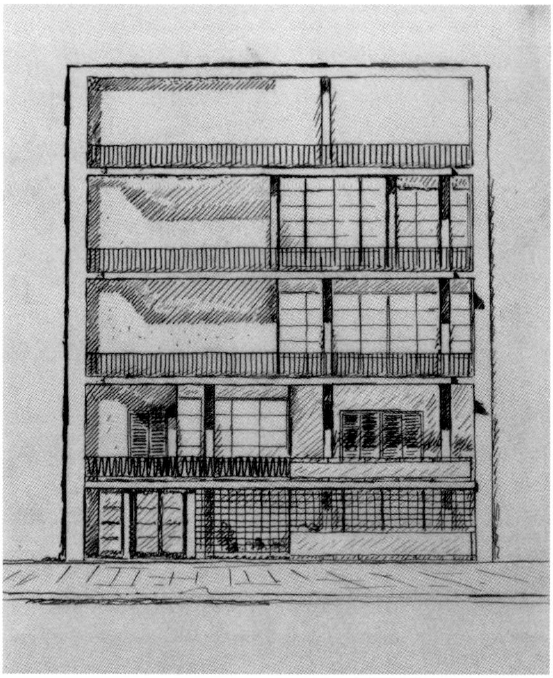

Pikionis's collaborator, Nikolaos Mitsakis, commissioned by the regime to design the Greek Pavilion for the 1937 Exposition Universelle in Paris, declared that in designing the project he refused to mimic 'any current forms' of the French or

German school' and that he sought to convey the 'real manifestations of the Greek in architecture'. Criticizing his own first sketches of the pavilion, where he had tried elements of Macedonian domestic architecture and collaged on a modern structure to give to the design project a Greek identity, Mitsakis called them 'foreign, pretentious, and picturesque', having no relation to the rationality of the load-bearing structure. Such reuses of traditional architecture, he argued, lacked any consideration of the potential precedents offered for providing old solutions to new problems. In the final design of the pavilion Mitsakis applied wooden beams and load-bearing stone walls, recombining elements from Greek folk art and ancient temple architecture to create an effective scheme that avoided expressing a nationalist credo. While the project cannot compete in freshness with Mitsakis's highly innovative previous work, such as the little church of 1934 for the Nomikos School, Mitsakis came closer to achieving it in another project that same year, an apartment house on 26 Heyden Street, Athens, designed in collaboration with Pikionis. The scheme emerged after a critical evaluation of the current fashionable use of the *erker* (bay window) system discussed in chapter Three. The Heyden Street commission differed significantly from other projects of the early 1930s by Mitsakis, but this was not the result of an ideological shift. While modern, the building reused elements of regional architecture (as his early sketches reveal particularly well) taken from Macedonia, Zagoria and Mt Pelion, and from the nineteenth-century vernacular Athenian house, such as the projected roof and the continuous balconies. In fact, the use of the *erker* on apartment buildings was finally eliminated that year, following new regulations by the Ministry for the Administration of the Capital, which banned any further enclosed porches overlooking streets.

A similar regionalist strategy was followed in his project for a retreat for students of the University of Thessaloniki. Like Pikionis had for his Experimental School in Thessaloniki, Mitsakis re-employed the Macedonian projected roof, a tried solution to inclement weather and blinding sunlight. Local timber and stone were used for this load-bearing structure.

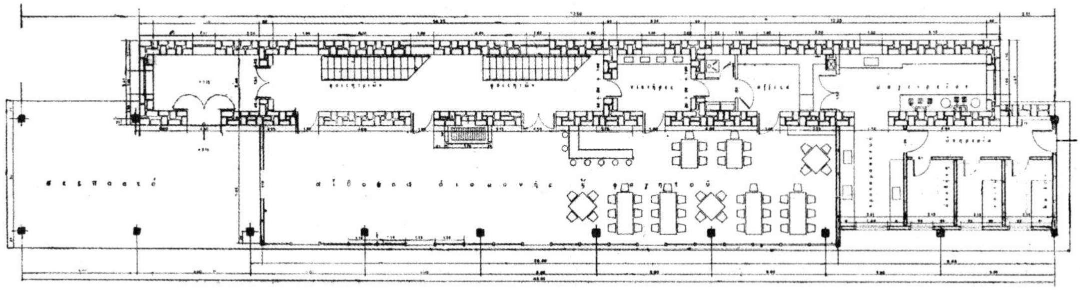

Nikolaos Mitsakis, Student Retreat, Salonica University, Pertouli Forest, Thessaly, 1939–41, ground-floor plan.

Dimitris Pikionis, Experimental School, Salonica, 1935.

But the spatial arrangement had a modern analytical thinking behind its composition, similar to Mies's elementalist schemes of the time.

Closer to the Metaxas regime's historicist or regionalist strategy to create sentimental nationalist settings were a small number of conformist residences of the period not very different from similar residences of the republican era. The Levides (1938–40), an all-white, red-tile-roofed country house in Pallene, a project by Pericles Sakellarios (1905–1985), is a collection of clichés of Greek 'Aegeanist', 'Mediterraneanist' architecture. The same can be said for the 'ranch-style' residence in Athens for Ioannis Lydes (1937), which strongly resembled Spanish architecture of the early Franco years (now the residence of the U.S. ambassador). The local site, the materials and the historical or regional precedents were taken to represent Greekness, as the author Theotokas describes it in equally gaudy words: 'the sweetness of the island atmosphere of the Aegean', 'playful and easy-going', 'perfumed with the smells of the Greek sea, the Greek mountains, Greek wine'.[8] The spirit of creative exploration and rigorous experimentation of modern architecture was sacrificed in favour of conformism, escapism and schmaltziness.

Most of the very few public buildings constructed during the Metaxas era had been conceived and commissioned before he took over power, and thus they cannot be seen as products of the spirit of the regime: they include Trapeza tis Ellados (Bank of Greece, 1933–8), by N. Zoumboulides, D. Tripodakis, and K. Papadakis, and the Agios Savas Cancer Hospital (1936), a modern building in all respects albeit with a monumental axial entrance designed by Angelos Siagas. Similarly, the glass, steel and grey Kokkinaras marble Ford Show Room and Service Station (1936–7) by Kontoleon – indeed from a compositional point of view the most conservative and formalist of his buildings – cannot be blamed on the conservatism of the regime but on the global anti-modern mood of the time, which reached from Michigan to Moscow. However, in about 1933 Kontoleon designed the Kyriakides residence, a highly modern scheme reminiscent of the Casa Malaparte in Italy.[9]

There is no indication that the regime disapproved of such buildings. Indeed, Metaxas, at a meeting of the City Planning Council, declared that 'the Greek State will support art, whatever its style'. And while he

Georgios Kontoleon, Ford Show Room and Service Station, Athens, 1934–5.

Georgios Kontoleon, Kyriakides residence, Kavouri, Attica, c. 1933.

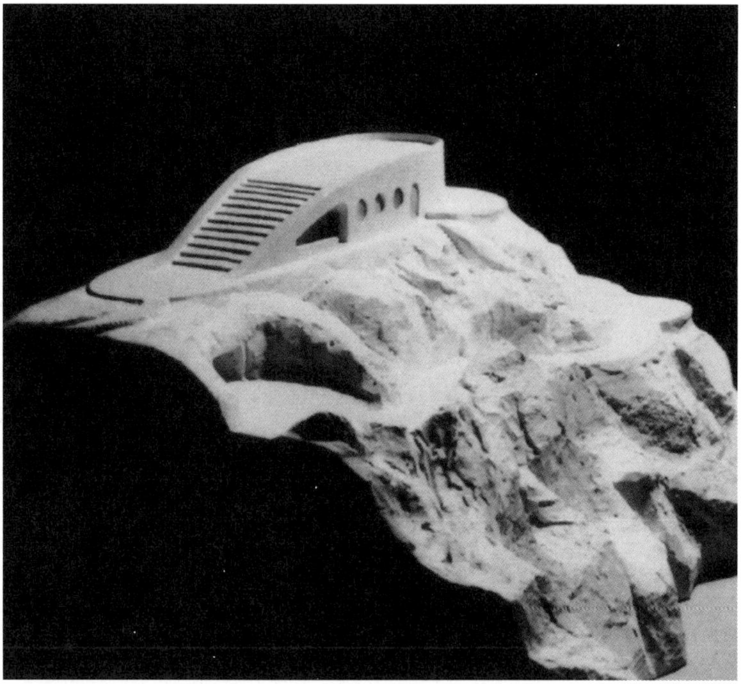

recommended that Greek artists be inspired by 'those things that the land of the whole of Greece supplies', on another occasion (August 1937) he argued that it was not the business of the government to 'put constraints on art'.[10] It appears that Metaxas was sincere in this, for the same opinion is to be found in his private diary.

Two of the most important modernist undertakings completed during the Metaxas period were the Army Share Fund Building and the Rex movie house and theatre complex. The original scheme of the Share Fund Building was submitted by Vassilios Kassandras and Leonidas Bonis as an entry to a competition in 1924 that had a prominent but conservative international jury, one of whom was Sir Reginald Blomfield. The background of the two architects is interesting. Kassandras was born in Athens in 1896 and went on to study at the Ecole des Beaux-Arts in Paris, graduating in 1927. He worked with Leonidas Bonis, who had also studied in Paris, at the Ecole Spéciale d'Architecture, graduating in 1928. Like the mature buildings of Nikoloudes, their Share Fund Building scheme skilfully packaged multiple heterogeneous uses – offices, an arcade, shops and restaurants on the ground floor, parking, and two theatres. The expression is monumental. The facades are ordered spatially according to the classical canon but decorative elements are virtually absent; the

opposite: Vassilios Kassandras and Leonidas Bonis, Rex Cinema and Theatre Complex, Athens, 1935–7.

Rex

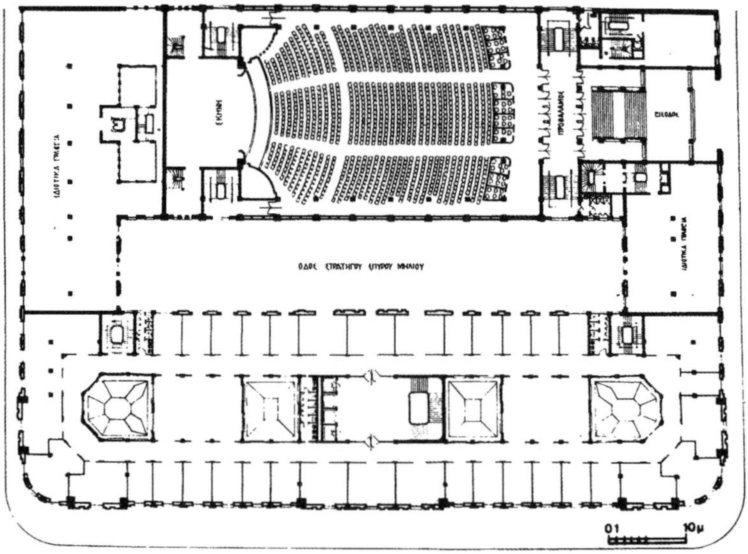

Vassilios Kassandras and Leonidas Bonis, Army Share Fund (ASF) building, Athens, 1927–38, plan at parquet level.

Army Share Fund (ASF) building, interior of Pallas theatre.

massive volumes work well on the site (formerly used for the royal stables) and the scale of the various elements, the rhythm and proportions of the openings, the locations of entrances, are appropriate to the street. Provocatively, Bonis and Kassandras did not paint the building white, but in a warm, sombre, pale red 'urban' colour. Much the same colour had been chosen for the pseudo-Byzantine arcaded facade of Marika Eliades maternity hospital (1936). Designed by G. Epitaux, this building effectively distanced itself from the purest white of the hospitals of the Venizelos era. It is notable in this context that polychromy combined with decorative elements characterize the buildings of both Vassilios Kouremenos, such as the elegant apartment house facing the hill of the Acropolis, and Emmanuel Lazarides.

The shift away from the values and beliefs the modern movement stood for, otherwise known as the *retour à l'ordre* anti-modern movement, was an international phenomenon of the 1930s. The historicism and regressive regionalism of that decade in Fascist Italy and Nazi Germany were also present in countries not dominated by racist or chauvinistic dogmas. British, and even American, architects followed a similar approach, as they did too in Russia.

The approach of Aris Konstantinidis was different. Konstantinidis had studied architecture at the Polytechnic in Munich between 1931 and 1936. Soon after his return from Germany he was appointed to the Planning Department of Greater Athens but in a minor post; he also had a commission from a well-to-do client who abhorred modern architecture and wanted something 'Greek'.[11] The house Konstantinidis created consists of two parallel areas on two levels which form a pair of outdoor 'nests'. The interior is comfortable, informal and flexible, with the spatial organization carefully calculated to make use of all available room and to avoid crowding. Furthermore, this was a design that could 'stand well in the landscape' and make an 'open-air way of life' possible. The spacious porch and terraces can be used in various seasons.[12]

From a photograph taken at the time the project appears to be landscaped like a typical Mediterranean farm, on falling ground from hilltop to sea. Konstantinidis sculpted the sloping site into small, step-down platforms supported by retaining walls, framed on the side by non-bearing, free-standing stone walls running parallel to the built volumes, and a bamboo-and-wood canopy. He placed the building on a platform at the top of the site and terminated the space in front of it with a row of five pillars on which rested a steel-section pergola. The two porticoes dominate the scheme, one temple-like, the other shed-like, the latter made from stone and timber put together in a manner no different from the way Mediterranean peasants build their huts and shelters. The

Aris Konstantinidis, Eftaxias Weekend House, Eleusis, Attica, 1938–40.

clear spacing between vertical and horizontal components, the contrasting solid and void elements, the white plastered volumes of the house and the orthogonal structure of the scheme gave the barren site a 'mathematical purity', a display of a way of life free from the pretensions of the Third Hellenic Civilization.

The defence of modern architecture, not as a formal style but as a means enabling a way of life, was further undertaken by the lawyer and future politician Ilias Iliou in his essay 'In Praise of Boxes'.[13] Although Iliou had not trained as an architect, his essay is one of the most important critical texts concerning modern architecture in Greece. Subtitled, with ironic modesty, 'Letters from a Provincial', his article rounded on widespread philistine accusations that modern buildings were nothing more than boxes. Pragmatic, yet with an excellent sense of the absurd, and without using obscure technical or ideological arguments, it pushed architectural discussion beyond the Third Hellenic's abstract, sterile and vacuous debates. Calling modern buildings 'boxes', Iliou wrote, was not an insult. The Greek phrase 'it comes like a box' means it fits perfectly; consequently, he reasoned, a building that is a box is one that fits people. Implied in Iliou's thinking was the idea that everything that satisfies a purpose is a 'box' and 'everything is architecture', that is, not only buildings displaying a specific style. People should be freed from their biases and accept the broader definition of architecture brought about by the modern movement. Modern architecture, Iliou argued, paid attention to the inhabitant of the building rather than a preconceived idea of the building as such. It is characterized by 'the joy of the house and the joy of the user of the house'. Referring to the production of architecture of the beginning of the 1930s, Iliou concluded: 'For the first time . . . since the

Eftaxias Weekend House, Eleusis, Attica, 1938–40.

times of the ancient temple . . . (and) the Byzantine basilica . . . there is such blooming of architecture in our country, in quantity and quality . . . I am a child of my times . . . I understand the Parthenon, Gothic cathedrals, Byzantine basilicas, Arab masterpieces, and I side with the modern apartment house . . . I am for the boxes.'

Iliou's commonsense approach also broke away from the confines of the elusive rhetoric of 'authentic Greekness'. For him, 'Greekness' was to be found in the everyday 'terrace, the hanging garden, the pergolas' circumscribed by modern architecture. Like Iliou, Konstantinidis was a realist. He made 'boxes' that were able to accommodate people in their everyday life as circumscribed in terms of the limits and possibilities of the region. After the war Konstantinidis would introduce a more organic term than Ilious boxes – 'life vessels'.

Metaxas's Supreme Planning Organization of the Capital had no clear urban or planning ideas traditional or modern. Its attention was scattered over specific problems without advancing Athens as a modern city. In 1938 Metaxas, Kotzias and Doxiadis met to address a major and urgent problem, the establishment of an Industrial Zone for Athens. Industry was gradually becoming a major factor in the development of Greece, for most factories were placed close to where labour was easily available, i.e., in the middle of residential districts. None of Metaxas's planners were in any way knowledgeable about planning. The outcome of the 1938 meeting was to place industry opportunistically in whatever under-used sites existed or in sites close to refugee settlements: the area behind the port of Piraeus, the western periphery of Athens, the Botanical Garden, and various dispersed locations in Patissia and Ilissos. Indeed the regime was accused of paving over the bank of the

Ilissos river paved over, Athens, photograph c. 1950.

Ilissos river, destroying irreparably one of the most significant world cultural heritage sites.[14]

As for city growth, Metaxas, much like his predecessors, even as prime minister-dictator, was not potent enough to manipulate the multiple mighty forces controlling the city legally or illegally. The privately initiated settlements in greater Athens of Psychico, Kypriadou, Ilioupolis, Cholargos, Vrilissia, Nea Alexandria (Philothei) and Ekali continued to expand as middle-class suburban developments. Building inside the city, a new phenomenon for Athens, required demolition of the nineteenth-century buildings. The newspaper *Akropolis* announced on 9 July 1936 that 'Athens is losing its beautiful mansions. This evil must stop.' But it took more than four decades for that to happen.

In addition there were also the areas given over as refugee settlements, as mentioned in chapter Three, in which, despite the establishment of a national organization for housing, the refugees continued to live under the same temporary conditions as when they had first arrived.[15] Bert Birtles wrote that he found people living in one settlement in Tambouria, Piraeus, in 'mud brick whitewashed two room sheds, with no water connection and no toilets'. There were also pockets of land inside the city where buildings appeared without any plan or regulation. In 1940 the architect Patroklos Karantinos published his plan for the capital. It contained some fragmented suggestions and marginal improvements but contributed very little to the future development of Athens with the exception of the establishment of a site near the Acropolis for folk-dance performances. Such plans are reminiscent of the remark made by the architect Vassilios Tsagris back in 1918: 'New Athens was built and it continues being built, left at the mercy of God, without the help of the people.'[16]

Doxiadis moved to the Ministry of Transportation and Public Works, leaving Karantinos in his place and retaining his personal association with Kotzias. It was a shrewd move by an ambitious young man: it was becoming clear by then that the new-founded Ministry of the Capital did not have much of a future. In addition, parallel to his successful civil service activities, Doxiadis started preparing for a different kind of future endeavour. He began to plan a vast research project, a multi-volume publication on the cities of Greece, intended to present Greek architecture juxtaposed to the International style, combined with guidelines for a regionalist architecture that reflected the Greek way of life as determined by economic, social and environmental conditions, similar to studies he claimed were happening at that time in other countries, such as Great Britain, Germany and Russia. The project never materialized, but the process of its gestation yielded results, as we will see later, in other unexpected domains.

By 1940 the regime had no time or energy to think about New Athens, the big question being not if, but when, the cataclysm that was the Second World War looked to engulf Greece. Further fueling general anxiety was a second, related question: with whom was Greece going to side? Greece had a strong left-wing movement by then but also a mass of supporters of Western liberal democracies. Adding to the ambiguity and to the bewilderment of the police was the presence, towards the end of the 1930s, of a flock of Germans, Italians, Britons and Americans, including the cosmopolitan writer Henry Miller, all demonstrating their love for the country, its history, its landscapes and its architectural heritage, including its vernacular tradition, which was becoming increasingly fashionable following the CIAM Congress. Herbert List photographed classical landscapes and vernacular buildings during the 1930s. Miller visited ancient and vernacular sites. Vrieslander studied the architecture of Hydra. They all met in and around Ziller's Grand Bretagne Hotel. By the middle of June 1940 many were leaving, some having been told to depart by the authorities.

The uncertainty was finally over when Metaxas was woken up in the early hours of 28 October and, still wearing his night robe, rejected an ultimatum from Italy demanding the right for its forces to occupy strategic locations on Greek soil.

The Greco-Italian War began well for the Greeks. They managed to halt and reverse the Italian armies that invaded from Albania, but this Axis setback brought Nazi Germany directly into the conflict. Unexpectedly, in the middle of the tense winter months, Metaxas died on 29 January 1941. On 6 April his successor, Alexandros Koryzis, spurned a German ultimatum and Germany immediately invaded both Greece and Yugoslavia. Less than two weeks later, 18 April, Koryzis was found dead. It was suicide. He had served as Prime Minister for exactly 80 days. Kotzias was asked to form a new government. But the Germans penetrated Thessaloniki on 9 April and it was clear that the king and part of the administration were going to be forced to leave Greece. On 21 April Seferis noted in his diary that there was a sudden change of decor in the streets of Athens: the posters with Hitler caricatures were covered over by images of the Virgin Mary. The German army entered Athens six days later. In the meantime the king, his court, most of his government and a few civil servants and military chiefs embarked for Egypt via Crete.

A large number of architects as well as academics at the Polytechnic, including its School of Architecture, joined the emerging movement against the Occupation as Greece replaced an era of construction with its opposite, which had a major impact on the modernization of the country and its architecture. The economist Stavros Thomadakis summed up the framework of the Occupation economy as comprising three 'mechanisms': inflation, the black market, and force.[17]

Given Greece's low level of industrialization, the occupying forces, chiefly Germans, applied an 'extractive' rather than 'reproductive economic policy', recruiting all 'public and private . . . stocks of food (including much of the olive oil), apparel . . . and means of transport'. This, Thomadakis remarks, 'must have been the first contributing factor to the great famine in the winter of 1941–2', which resulted in the deaths of 'one thousand persons a day just in the Athens–Piraeus area'. The 'burden of occupation expenses was five times higher per capita in occupied Greece than in occupied France'. Parallel to this enforced plunder, the economy became a free market operating through a black-market system that led to record inflation. 'Average city property traded at 30 to 100 times its prewar cash value', and 'select property' at 150 times. Exploiting the situation, black-marketeers hoarded immense amounts of food, thus worsening the crisis. Without rationing and International Red Cross aid, most of the capital's population would have perished. The emerging resistance movement, the National Liberation Front and the Political Committee of National Liberation, reacted by creating new small-scale economic structures, taking the entry of commodities into the urban economy from the control of the black-marketeers. Despite these undertakings the wealthy merchants continued to accumulate spectacular profits until the end of the Occupation, with the largest part of these profits invested in construction (39 per cent versus 27 per cent in industry), making such entrepreneurs architecture's new patrons.

Reacting to this situation Konstantinidis published a confrontational article in the conservative – and at that time enthusiastic supporter of the occupation forces – newspaper *I Kathimerini* (7 May 1942), touching on fundamental moral professional issues and attacking the upcoming 'new class of landowners', the 'new class of the rich'. The article was risky under the circumstances because it directly assailed those who profited from the Occupation by collaborating with its forces. That same year he entered the Ministry of Public Works as a civil servant, like Doxiadis, where he would remain for eleven years. Life there was not easy: his diary for 9 October 1941 records that 'It is terrible to feel alone. A stranger among others with whom you have nothing to say.'

Unlike Seferis, who, diplomat as he was, concealed his private views throughout his public life, Konstantinidis had frequent public outbursts concerning issues of quality and integrity in architecture that threatened to jeopardize his career. He was also opportunistic. To some degree he had to be: since he was an architect rather than a writer, his ideas had to be built rather than remain confined to notebooks. He was able to take advantage of the chaos of Greek bureaucracy and have his projects undertaken without anyone bothering him. Konstantinidis was fortunate in having had the experience of the nature of Greek administration before the war while working for the Minister Governor of the Capital, Kotzias. In July 1940 Konstantinidis jotted down the following thoughts in his diary: 'In a state so disorganized how can an architect work correctly?' Yet, he went on, 'it is inside this disorganization that you have the possibility to escape from many mindless regulations'. And as if advising himself he added: 'you must do (your) work properly without being noticed. Because the responsible agencies . . . pretend they do not see and are indifferent, out of lethargy and laziness'. And he concludes (rather surprisingly for an architect dedicated to the idea of order in architecture): 'long live therefore disorder that lets you dare and materialize things outside what is common . . . and wrong.' He would follow this strategy after the war working for the Greek Organization for Tourism (EOT).

While working for the Ministry of Public Works during the Occupation, Doxiadis convinced the government of the need of a large-scale collection of data covering war damages, putting together a group of trusted assistants, relatives and old classmates to work for it. By May 1941 they began gathering information related to the damage caused by bombing by Allied forces, sabotage by guerrillas and destruction by the occupying forces. The data was passed to the National Resistance Group known as Hephaestus (headed by Doxiadis) and from there via Turkey to the Allies in the Middle East. In the meantime Doxiadis cultivated the aura of a leading technocrat that proved to be an excellent cover for his clandestine activities. He worked towards an ambitious project of total mapping that would include the landscape in its entirety, the cultural, historical, production-based and commercial buildings. He also included data about building regulations for each parcel of land, statistics of free spaces, changes of the built tissue over time, public versus private services, and transportation patterns for every city. In addition, with an eye on Greece's post-war development, he compared the administrative structures of both Axis and Allied countries 'to open the way for any future effort' in rationally planning the country. A similar activity was the publication of a semi-clandestine periodical *Chorotaxia* (regional planning). It contained texts that were originally delivered as talks within the Circle of Technical Experts, a kind of continuous education project, whose aim was to prepare technical people for post-war reconstruction. Several of the articles were written by Doxiadis himself, introducing current problems of regional planning and social housing. The articles were non-ideological, biased toward traditional and practical, rather than experimental or utopian, solutions, and included detailed references to social-democratic planning in Austria; even communist approaches were included, as well as references to kibbutz collective housing in Palestine. In addition to these more technical topics there was a lengthy presentation of the cities of ancient Greece and an extensive article by Angeliki Hadjimichali on 'Folk Art and Art', emphasizing the value of self-help construction and the creative role of the non-professional peasant-technician; this would be picked up after the war by Pikionis.

Chorotaxia, which rarely published articles on architectural criticism, also included a controversial and somewhat prophetic article by Konstantinidis on the 'problem of architecture'. It was a polemical text in which he argued against the shallowness of the new photogenic formalism of modernist architecture (Konstantinidis being a superb photographer of architecture himself) that made use of publicity and media, undercutting the significance of authentic traditional architecture and destroying the 'feeling deep inside us of the *Mediterranean* value of our country' and quality in architecture in general.

In addition to more focused professional discussions, such as those in the Circle of Technical Experts, intellectual life began to pick up after the first traumatic year. In his 'Chronicle of a Decade', the poet Odysseus Elytis sketched an idealistic, lively but intimate and politically naive interaction between writers during the years of the occupation – some actively engaged with resistance movements, some only so in their imagination, their preoccupation being Greek heritage and identity, and their place within European culture.[18]

The public funeral of Kostis Palamas on 27 February 1943, during which Sikelianos read an inspired poem, was one act of resistance that ended in a spontaneous demonstration, bringing together huge crowds, including writers, artists and scientists as well as the general public. There were also the organized multidisciplinary resistance groups of the National Liberation Front, to which architects Karantinos and Djelepy were attached, and the most important planning 'think tank' of the left, the Political Committee of National Liberation (PEEA), which was preparing plans for reorganizing the overall territory of Greece in relation to the organization of the professional services and the education system.[19] 'The Liberation was nearing', Elytis wrote in his 'Chronicle of a Decade'. 'The Germans will not be able to last more than one year . . . after that everybody has to be ready to spell out what they believe'.[20]

On 12 October 1944 the Germans withdrew from Athens.[21] Soon after the whole country was free, although German troops remained in a garrison in Crete and in a few other islands. Greece by then was the poorest country in Europe: its income was only 72 per cent of Bulgaria and only 16 per cent of Great Britain, with land resources at 1.19 hectares per cultivator in contrast to Turkey's 2.27 and Bulgaria's 1.73. But even as the country lay in ruins, Greece was preparing not for reconstruction, but for a new war.

The 'devious days' (Elytis in the *Chronicle*[22]) that followed the Occupation began on 4 December 1944 with a bloody battle in Syntagma Square. A new war would follow, transforming Athens and the rest of the country into a real battleground: full-scale guerrilla war broke out in 1946 with Greek communists among those fighting government forces. It would last until 1949. Bullet-scarred walls are still visible today. Even Anafiotika and the Acropolis were battle zones, in violation of the law Klenze had secured during Otto's time that prohibited military use of the Acropolis. Seferis

Drapetsona district, Attica, in flames, 1944.

returned to Greece, to his old home in 'idyllic Plaka', and wondered in his diary (7 December 1944) 'who could imagine' that this place will become the first battleground between the West and East'. The horror mounted as the leftist insurgents in retreat took with them 'bourgeois' hostages, that is middle-class people, some according to a 'plan', some to settle old accounts, some randomly; among the hostages was the great dramatic actress Eleni Papadaki, who was brutally executed, and the Surrealist poet Andreas Embirikos, who returned home safely. A few months after this initial tragic conflict and before the beginning of the main part of the bloody Civil War, the government started making moves to raise funds for reconstruction.

The Sacrifices of Greece in the Second World War, published in Athens in 1946, was a report compiled during the Occupation by the Office of Town and Country Planning attached to the Ministry of Public Works using data 'collected by public services or by private individuals . . . composed by the architect C. A. Doxiadis'. In its pages the report documented that of a total of 1,730,000 houses, 401,000 (23 per cent), were destroyed, leaving Greece with 1,200,000 people homeless, some 18 per cent of the population. About 65,000 Greek villages had been set on fire by German troops, 1,200 of which burned down completely, amounting to 165,000 buildings. The population had decreased from 7,335,000 in 1940 to 6,805,000 by 1944; about 6 per cent of the population had died. Doxiadis claimed that 1,250 people were collecting these data during the withdrawal of the German army in 1944, a rather overestimated figure. The publication was associated with an exhibition that after Athens travelled to London and Paris.

The report said little about the loss of 56,000 Greek Jews living in Thessaloniki, 87 per cent of the city's 79,950 population, and did not mention the annihilation of the centuries' old historical Jewish cemetery. Following orders by the Greek administration of the municipality, a massive team of workers entered the 550,000 square-metres site of the Jewish cemetery on 6 December 1942, destroying many graves, even ignoring German orders to protect certain tombs of archaeological significance. The material was immediately employed for the construction of roads and buildings or sold in construction yards. Historian Rena Molho has written that one can still find fragments of such tombstones 'decorating children's playgrounds, bars, and restaurants in modern hotels in the summer resorts of Cassandra, in Chalkidiki' a few kilometres outside Thessaloniki. The cemetery site was given to the University to build its extension.[23]

The first step towards reconstruction was taken on 24 February 1945 with the publication in the *Government Gazette* of a law signed by the

Constantinos Doxiadis with Paul Hoffman, of Studebaker Corp., head of the American organization the Economic Cooperation Agency (ECA), 1950.

The U.S. Congress passed the Economic Cooperation Act that authorized the Marshall Plan on 2 April 1948 and President Truman signed it the next day. The aid the Plan provided was to be administrated by a temporary American organization, the Economic Cooperation Agency (ECA), based in Washington and headed by Paul Hoffman of Studebaker Corp., with Averill Harriman special representative in Europe. Harriman announced (3 September) that Greece was authorized to receive supplies of a value of $5,100,000 from European nations and their colonies out of the Marshall Plan's total budget for Europe of $101,400,000. Doxiadis was appointed as the 'Coordinator' on 15 November. On 24 November Greece, together with the other European countries participating in the Marshall Plan, submitted to the CEEC a Four Year Program of Reconstruction. It included proposals for infrastructure, tourism and housing projects, the revival of the countryside, and a cutback on Greek immigration to foreign countries.

By 1951 the Ministry of Reconstruction had designed 150 communities and 200,000 houses, improved and extended the road system generally and the highway linking Athens with Thessaloniki in particular. However, the problem of housing the Asia Minor refugees remained unsolved. In 1940 the Metaxas regime had estimated that 16,000 houses for refugees were needed. It was an underestimation. During the war the situation had worsened, with bombing in the Piraeus area destroying a large number of refugee settlements. In 1952 the Urban Refugee Housing programme was established, which recognized the urgent needs of over 32,000 people still living in substandard shelters and 7,000 in temporary sheds. It took seven years to reduce this figure to 26,000. As Renée Hirschon wrote, this ongoing situation 'played a significant role in the perpetuation of the refugees' sense of 'separate identity', an identity that passed from parents to children, thus the children who were born years after in Greece were asserting 'we are also refugees', which had lead to both social and political problems.[26]

The approach to reconstruction was criticized by several people from different points of view. In the September 1946 issue of the periodical *Eklogi*, Pikionis, in an article titled 'Reconstruction and the Spirit of Tradition', stressed the spiritual nature of the problem and the relation between tradition and innovation in the design of new accommodation. The 'old', he argued, should not result from 'memorization', meaning imitation of old forms, while the new should not be produced 'without memory'. Then Pikionis put forward an unusual idea for the time but one that was seriously considered a decade later, a new approach to the process of creating architecture rather than new forms of architectural products. Pointing to the exemplary refugee self-help shelters designed and built by the inhabitants themselves, he recommended mobilizing folk builders for the reconstruction instead of using labourers executing plans produced by experts.[27]

Despotopoulos, whose work during the 1930s was discussed in chapter Three, and who by this time was a professor of architecture at the Polytechnic, criticized the approach to reconstruction taken by the government. His 'Reconstruction' was published in the 2 June 1945 issue of *Antaios*, a left-wing multidisciplinary review published by D. Batsis, author of the much discussed *Heavy Industry in Greece*, in which Batsis favoured a Soviet model of development for Greece. Similarly, Despotopoulos promoted the idea of breaking away from the ideas of the past. For him, the question was not how to reconstruct the buildings, cities and infrastructure that Greece had never had; it was to construct the modern environment Greece did not yet possess: 'Reconstruction cannot become an enterprise of whatever kind . . . especially a capitalist enterprise'. In the end Despotopoulos was optimistic about the future of Europe, for through reconstruction it 'is put together like an enormous factory and is left free to work . . . the result will be more gigantic and speedy than destruction has been' during the war. The same point was also made by Konstantinidis, who objected to the use of the term 'reconstruction', which implied a return to the past while 'we are different from those people of the past, even from ourselves as we were before the war'.[28]

On the one hand Despotopoulos was misguided, since framing the challenge of construction after the war as a problem of development rather than one of reconstruction made no sense in the context of post-war international negotiations that were taking place at that time, whose exclusive subject was reconstruction. On the other hand he was justified in as much as when Greece demanded compensation for damage it wished to use for building its infrastructure and settlements (during a meeting on German compensation in Paris, 12–15 November 1945), it received a humiliatingly small amount, with the excuse that she was poor, meaning having lost very little during the war. When 'a bomb fell in Belgium', the argument went, 'there was a high probability that it fell on a factory', 'while if it fell in Greece the probability was that it fell on Olympus', thus causing no economic damage.[29]

Of course by giving pre-eminence to the broader issue of development, socialists and communists appeared to be promoting their centralist, stateist planning agenda as exemplified by the Soviet prototype. However, as the programme for reconstruction was coming to a quick end, due to the worsening situation with the Korean War, and the outcome of the programme started to become visible, similar criticisms were voiced by people within aid administration, including Xenophon Zolotas, an important liberal Greek economist, who worked during this period for the Greek government as a technocrat and American advisor. In a long article in the daily newspaper *To Vima* on 10 August 1950, Zolotas criticized the office of reconstruction and especially its head, Doxiadis, accusing him of being unable to put together any serious plan for the productive domain of the country, and thus could not utilize the budget he was given by American aid. The civil war, Zolotas continued, could not be used as an excuse for the failures of reconstruction, because by definition it was impossible for reconstruction to be carried out, since no plans existed for it. The money was spent mainly on ill-constructed projects: 30 per cent of the roads were worn out as soon as they were built and a very large number of the houses had already collapsed.

An even more severe critique of the way the Greek government was handling the reconstruction programme can be found in the official reports to the U.S. government by Paul R. Porter, Chief of the U.S. Economic Cooperation Administration (ECA) Mission to Greece (September 1949 and November 1950) in charge of the Marshall Plan, written after his visit to Greece.[30] Porter was a lawyer devoted to the principles of the New Deal; he expected the Greek government to take the major lead in normalizing the situation and turning around the country towards development. This was evidently not happening despite the money forwarded by the U.S. Porter was after numbers and statistics in order to find out the truth about the situation in Greece; at the same time he thought it was important to come into close contact with the people he was writing about.[31] Porter was shocked when he visited Kalavrita, the 'Lidice of Greece', as he called it, to find the 'locals' inactive, still living in ruins and blaming the partisans who had attacked the Germans as those responsible for the destruction. Similarly he was critical of the use of U.S. aid by the Greek government to fight the Civil War while raising every kind of obstacle and bureaucratic interference, using the Civil War as an excuse for doing a bad job and failing to exploit the opportunities the country was offering. Although disappointed by the fact that more than a year after the Second World War was over, out of the 150,000 destroyed houses only 1,300 had been rebuilt, he did not criticize Doxiadis, whom he met and found to be 'one of the best technocrats' (26 February), a typical city planner in his thinking. He praised the Archbishop and commended the evaluation of the economic condition of Greece by the socialist economist Angelopoulos. In his search to identify the root of the failure of the Reconstruction Programme in Greece and warn the American Mission about the causes, he singled out the Greek establishment, 'the existing local ruling classes', which he found 'repulsive and opposed to American values'. Porter was worried about Soviet penetration in Greece but also about the establishment's 'psychological paralysis' in handling the American aid. Porter identified a clique hidden behind the government, a group of high society Greeks, 'elegant cosmopolitans', with their base in 'Cannes, St Moritz, and Kolonaki Square in Athens', 'charming people' speaking excellent English and honest in helping the job of the American Mission but only to secure their own 'financial privileges', whatever 'the cost of the financial health of the country'. These people were not willing to 'invest their profits' anywhere in Greece for the 'recovery of the country', preferring to let them find their way 'to the banks of Cairo and Argentina'.

Equally critical were three articles published in *The Reporter*, Max Ascoli's well-respected, liberal, intensely anti-communist magazine.[32] They argued that despite the $711,600,000 of American money spent between April 1947 and June 1949 in Greece, and the military defeat of the communists, there was still no assurance that the communist threat was over. Quoting Doxiadis, it was pointed out that the 'problem starts at the moment of demobilization' of the nationalist forces, when the pressure for shelter facilities will be greater (13 September). For Ascoli, the Greek political leadership was inept, undemocratic and avaricious, 'considering Washington as an artesian well gushing dollars'. Coming to the same conclusion with Porter, the author wondered if 'Greek rulers, the product of forced elections, genuinely want peace', since they took for granted that America will continue pouring money in to keep the war going. 'Never had so few asked for so much and done so little with it', said one of the members of the AMAG to the journalist. Finally, Ascoli argued that the most important issue was that Greece was underdeveloped not only economically but also politically. This 'structural' deficiency had led to an economy that produces highly priced goods that few can buy and to big infrastructure projects – 'the little TVA' he called them – that are not to benefit 'the greatest possible number of Greek citizens' but only a handful of 'well connected' monopolists.

It is interesting that while these critical comments were circulating widely, the American government was uncritically supporting Greece financially, while in Greece itself a nationalist, anti-Western spirit was on the rise. In two articles in the conservative newspaper *I Kathimerini* (13 and 15 June 1948) titled 'Greece and the West', Kleon Paraschos argued that since the mid-nineteenth century, after the 'intrusion of the Western spirit in all areas of intellectual life', Greeks felt a 'deeper racial hate' against 'Western man' more intense than that against 'Easterner, Persian, or Turk'; they were against the 'new yoke'.

A liberal government won the elections and on 13 December 1950 a Parliamentary Committee convened that led to the elimination of the permanent post Doxiadis held, thus practically firing him despite the fact that he was one of the very few who functioned properly in implementing the reconstruction programme. Finally, it authorized the new Minister of Coordination to establish a new organization and create a new position of vice-minister.[33] It was the end of an era but not of a career.

On the last day of 1951 the European Recovery Program (the Marshall Plan) ended six months before its original planned date, with very few of the proclaimed goals of development and modernization made by the Greek government having materialized. Urban crises mounted, as did the number of *authaireta*, the self-help illegal houses. According to the *Statistical Yearbook of Greece* for 1955, between 1945 and 1950 no fewer than 17,491 unauthorized new houses were built in Athens, half of the total of new houses in the capital.

The problem of housing the refugees – still unsolved since the time of the 1922 Catastrophe – resurfaced in 1950 in political debates. The refugees voted consistently for the left, leading to official recognition of the urgent needs of 32,000 people by the government (7,000 people were still living in temporary shelters) and to the establishment of an Urban Refugee Housing programme in 1952. By then, the problem had worsened, the Civil War having generated new refugees, thus escalating the numbers of homeless people. In 1947 the number of Civil War refugees was already 700,000 and growing.[34]

The Greek government turned to emigration as a way of solving the problem of unemployment and homelessness. In addition to those who emigrated in search of economic opportunities there were those

Flooded 1922 refugee settlements, 1961.

who left Greece for political reasons – a major loss of precious intellectual capital for the country. Of the architects of the generation of 1922, Stamo Papadakis had been the first to leave in 1934, before Greece entered its long period of crisis, becoming a leading architectural critic in the United States. In New York he taught at Brooklyn College and after the war he joined Giedion, Gropius, Neutra, Sert and others forming the CIAM Chapter for Relief and Post-War Planning. Isaac Saporta became a professor of architecture at Georgia Tech, and was actively involved in the civil rights movement there as well as nature conservation. Ioannis Despotopoulos, who lost his position in the Polytechnic as a result of his political views, left to become guest professor in Göteborg, Sweden, and later in Germany.

More painful, however, was the departure of a younger generation of architects who had finished their studies at the Athens Polytechnic soon after the liberation and in the early years of the Civil War. They risked being trapped by the conflict and being destroyed before having the chance to develop their talents and to contribute as architects. Writing in 1945 on 'Technical Education in the Framework of Reconstruction' in the journal *Antaios*, Nikolaos Kitsikis evaluated its School of Architecture, 'justifying the opinion that Greece can soon become the centre of a serious architectural movement'. But Octave Merlier, a French scholar who arrived in Greece before the Second World War to work at the French Institute in Athens, thought differently. He took measures to facilitate the exodus of several highly talented architects straight out of the Polytechnic, together with other young Greek intellectuals. Merlier asked the French government to offer scholarships for Greeks to study in France and succeeded in obtaining funding for 200 individuals. Sixteen architects were among them, including Aristomenis Provelengios, Georges Candilis, Manolis Kindynis, G. Focas, Theodoros Gatos, Panos Tsolakis, Elli Iliadou, Nikos Hadjimichalis and Emmanuel Lazarides. The head of the group was the oldest member, the 52-year-old Panos

Djelepy. Iannis Xenakis left later. Provelengios, Candilis, Kindynis and Hadjimichalis went to work for Le Corbusier.

Slowly, at beginning of the 1950s, some kind of normalcy returned to Greece. A period of 'peace more demanding than war' began, to quote Elytis.[35] Yet very little progress was made to deal with the lack of housing created by the Second World War, and a large number of buildings were still in a state of wretchedness. Very few could afford to pay for a new luxury, or rather luxury-looking, apartment or a single house, aside from those who belonged to what Konstantinidis called the 'New Class', the nouveau riche, emulators of the wealthy international set of the 1930s, who celebrated their recent affluence.

Among those who practiced during this period were Pericles Sakellarios (1905–1985), who designed Levidis country house (1939–85), Emmanuel Vourekas (1905–1992), responsible for the Athenée Palace Hotel (1950) and the revamped lobby of the Splendid Hotel, and Pavlos Michaleas (1904–1990). The most prolific were Kostas Kapsambelis (1909–1984) and Kostas Kitsikis, who identified the new type of client of architecture that had emerged from the entrepreneurial underground of the Second World War, and who argued with Konstantinidis in defence of the 'New Class'.

A radically different position was presented in 1950 by Konstantinidis, once more in a small book with the title *Old Athenian Houses*, a part-critical, part-documentary manifesto dedicated to the vernacular Athenian houses constructed in great numbers by builders during the nineteenth century. It might appear strange today that Konstantinidis was so polemical in his text, defending regional Greek architecture by using categories of the modern movement. After all, it was only a little more than a decade since Greece had hosted CIAM, and many of the architects who took part in the meetings would have agreed with almost all the points Konstantinidis raised: the need for understanding the conditions or the region, the constraints of the climate, the potentials of local materials, and even the errors committed by the 'German educated' architects (who of course were not so much products of Germany, as discussed earlier). If we situate the text, however, in the context of the post-war nouveau-riche kitsch architecture for the 'new class of landowners' imitating Western European fashions, we can see that what Konstantinidis wrote about was a vehicle, or rather a parable, by which to voice his opposition to mainstream architecture in Greece at that moment and to suggest an alternative.

'Every true architectural form', Konstantinidis argued, 'is the fruit of liberation' from the slavery of intellectual subordination. Quoting Ion Dragoumis he blamed the 'king brought from abroad' and 'his

Kostas Kapsambelis, Kalligas Apartment building, Athens, 1951.

organizers, the fat Bavarians' and the 'German educated architects who brought from Europe samples of houses' and the 'monkeying' Greeks 'struggling in a lagoon of old and new ideas', 'neither advancing nor regressing', 'suspended', 'trapped in the spirit of romantic antiquarianism'. The alternative Konstantinidis offered was 'realism'. 'Look at these houses I want you to love and understand', he exclaims pointing to the houses he documented and published in the book. Their traditional atrium-type closed gardens, their 'glass-covered internal verandas', the 'union of the inside with the outside', fit perfectly with the climate and the 'Greek way of life'. Despite the strong emotional tone of the writing, there is no chauvinism or patriotism in his argument. His suggestions to 'search for memory' and his declaration that 'popular work' is the 'prime material' the 'dough' to be used to make new architecture are grounded on empirical, physical facts.[36]

Konstantinidis was pragmatic, arguing for the specific qualities of these old Athenian buildings as precedents: the urban atrium space with an enclosed mini-garden, the glass-covered internal arcade, the 'union of the inside with the outside'. The world he was enamoured with, struggling to celebrate and construct within the adverse conditions of his time becomes clearer in the second important building of his career, the house in Sykia (1951). In contrast to the white plastered volumes composing the scheme of the pre-war villa in Eleusis, here there is no trace of plaster or indeed of any covering material. The bare structure is the driving force shaping the work, an exposed load-bearing stone wall

Aris Konstantinidis, Kakrides House, Sykia, 1951.

aided by horizontal structural zones of concrete, and a concrete flat roof. The structure recalls the shift Le Corbusier or Egon Eiermann in Germany made at around the same time towards a realistic, 'brutal', kind of architecture. Yet, if one looks at Konstantinidis's diaries, studies and photographs it is clear that if there is a precedent to this 'new realism' he had arrived at, it was the bare stone buildings he admired and sketched as a soldier in the Albanian front that used horizontal wood elements to reinforce the stone structure. Here, his love for the Greek landscape and its buildings, the wind, the waves, the walls, the sensual happiness of outdoor life, emerges from the claustrophobia of the Civil War, leaving behind the memory of the shallowness of the Third Civilization, and stripped of the oppressive cosmetic plastered paraphernalia of the 'villas' and apartment houses of Greece under reconstruction. The work may

bring to mind a bygone way of life, that of the peasant or the Aegean fisherman, the houses of 'the simple people', 'under a tree and . . . under the starry sky, in Greece', yet was unmistakably modern in its means of construction and layout.

chapter five

Halcyon Days

The mid-1950s began a period of cultural creativity. Although architecture during this time made less of an international impact than did Greek music (with the work of composers Manos Hadjidakis and Mikis Theodorakis) or literature (as with the poet George Seferis and the novelist Nikos Kazantzakis, for example), it was none the less characterized by a commitment to innovation and change combined with a dedication to regionalism. The architecture that emerged in Greece was part of a broader movement of Critical Regionalism,[1] an approach that enhanced the cultural diversity and local identity of regionalism, but which was opposed to the commercially kitsch and nationalist aspects that dominated regionalism under conservative or totalitarian regimes (as seen in late nineteenth- and early twentieth-century architecture). More reflective than adversarial, Critical Regionalism was opposed to the post-Second World War corporate International Style that ignored the early modern movement's environmental and social goals; yet it was committed to modernization when new thinking or technology offered sustainable improvements over traditional, local practices.

For post-war Greece to overcome the devastation of the Second World War and the Civil War that had followed, construction was key. Between 1958 and 1961 Greece devoted 5.4 per cent of its GNP to the construction of new homes, which was a good deal more than the United Kingdom's 3 per cent, West Germany's 4.9 per cent or the 4.6 per cent spent in the Netherlands. Given the ongoing destruction caused by the Civil War and the poor performance of construction immediately thereafter, as we have already seen, one might argue that the true period of reconstruction in Greece did not begin in 1945 but in the mid-1950s. Why did this happen?

To a great extent, the reasons were economic, but they were also social, political and cultural. During the second part of the 1950s, Greece, together with Spain, joined the rapidly growing countries of Western Europe. By the end of the Civil War, and after joining the Atlantic Alliance in 1952, Greece appeared secure, gradually becoming for the first time in

Nicos Valsamakis, Apartment building, Semitelou Street, Athens, 1951–3 (civil engineer P. Stamatiades).

its history a 'normal' country. Italy, Turkey and Yugoslavia, all of whom had either seriously threatened the integrity or the very existence of Greece in the past, were now allies. Despite the rhetoric, provoked by the Cold War, no serious menace seemed to be lurking in Bulgaria or Albania, the latter a country with which Greece was still in a state of armed conflict. Finally, despite low health standards, persisting poverty, continuing imprisonment for political reasons for certain people – which included numerous architects, engineers and artists – no serious obstacle seemed to lie in the way of a promising career and a good quality of life for ambitious professionals.

The normalization process began to be put in motion with the elections of March 1950; the process unfolded gradually, unevenly and painfully, but with no serious setbacks. The 1952 elections brought to the government the conservative 'Greek Rally' party and its leader, Alexandros Papagos, the former head of the army during the campaign against the Italian occupation and Civil War. Papagos pledged that his government would turn the inertia of the past into 'action' and 'production'. Indeed, on 9 April 1953 his highly sophisticated Minister of Coordination, Spyros Markezinis, devalued the drachma, thus stabilizing the economy, making it more competitive internationally, and initiating a trend of private savings. He also initiated a tourist development programme, the only short-term source of immediate income that did not require sophisticated new technology or major capital investment. Despite the continuing repressive political measures dividing the country after the Civil War, Papagos's government ushered in forms of stability and development unknown in Greece other than sporadically during the Venizelos era. Konstantinos Karamanlis, who served in Papagos's government as a successful Minister of Public Works, and who succeeded him as Prime Minister in October 1955 following Papagos's death, continued in the same direction and with new confidence. The figures were impressive: the economy began to grow at the rate of around 7 per cent annually.[2]

The country also succeeded in establishing a new architectural tradition through the Polytechnic and a number of thoughtful practitioners. For these architects, construction technology had to embrace local materials and traditional design precedents, trusting that in many cases they offered better solutions to carry forward the much delayed modernization of the country. The city became the focus of their activities.

After the Second World War there was a major increase in urbanization. In 1940, 33 per cent of Greeks lived in towns with a population of more than 10,000; by 1951 this had increased to 39 per cent, and by 1961 to 44 per cent. Cities, mainly Athens, but with Thessaloniki and other provincial towns not far behind, had to become more densely occupied, more intense and diverse in their activities; the goal was to accommodate more people and to be more open and diverse, both socially and culturally. It was also becoming clear to many business people (though not to large-scale investors, for there were too few at that time in Greece) that constructing new apartment buildings could drive the economy as a whole, with the city the icon of economic growth.

With the city now becoming the point of focus, the apartment building (in Greek the *polykatoikia*) began to embody the desires and aspirations of the post-war generation. It was understandable: after the two catastrophic wars, despite the rhetoric produced by nationalist literature prolonging the myth of the happy freedom-loving Klephts in the Greek mountains, life in the countryside continued to be one of deprivation, the impact of the Civil War's oppression, terror and dislocation of community ties, still painful.[3]

Among the artists who focused on the urban way of life and its environment was Yannis Tsarouchis. He brought working-class 'city' people into his paintings, including scenes of the gay subculture, featuring interiors of dilapidated urban houses typical of Athens at that time, or the facades of neoclassical buildings. Tsarouchis's idealization of neoclassical Athens and Piraeus may have seemed conservative at the time, but it was to be a farsighted critical comment about the enthusiastic but also naive and unsustainable ways of the 1950s and early '60s generation who were intoxicated by new building and ignored the impact of construction

Yannis Tsarouchis, Coffeehouse Parthenon in Chauteia, Athens, 1957.

on the city's physical and social environment. Indeed, he helped to raise awareness of the value of the neoclassical urban heritage in anticipation of the conservation movement of the 1970s.

For those who had secured a job and possessed modest capital, Greece, and Athens in particular, offered unique opportunities for acquiring a basic apartment residence. The building code allowed dense occupancy of the urban sites, the legal framework permitted horizontal ownership (set in place by the late 1920s, as described earlier), and a system of financing was based on an exchange arrangement (known in Greek as *antiparoche*).[4] Even the well-heeled centre of the capital was built through such an alliance between small-scale contractors, small-scale landowners and small-scale investors. The availability of a simple, inexpensive and flexible, reinforced concrete-construction technology – reminiscent of Le Corbusier's Domino system – helped. Such apartments satisfied the immediate needs for the upcoming class of middle-income people. They supplied minimal interior space (in fact substandard, according to Western European norms), but this shortcoming was compensated for by the amenities of vibrant outdoor life. Despite tight economic conditions, a significant number of these new apartments were designed by architects of the new post-war generation. Nicos Valsamakis and Takis Zenetos were the most notable practitioners, while Konstantinidis and Pikionis, discussed earlier, and now part of the older generation, both produced the best work of their career in this era.

The six-storey apartment building on 5 Semitelou Street in Athens was Nicos Valsamakis's first work after graduation with P. Stamatiades the civil engineer. No Athenian architect had demonstrated such warmth and conviviality since Ziller, and indeed these distinctions are to be found in most of Valsamakis's later work. He designed an exposed structural frame, set back the apartments from the street line, and cantilevered from each floor a long continuous balcony, rather than many small ones. Further, he linked his balconies by slender shafts to form an orthogonal concrete grid frame. Finally, he applied stone and wood, and added warm colours and canvas awnings, creating deep welcoming shadows on every floor.

Without doubt this apartment building is indebted to the scheme developed by Mitsakis and Pikionis for Heyden Street back in the 1930s. Some also thought it was influenced by Giuseppe Terragni's apartment buildings. But rather than being compelled by formal considerations, Valsamakis was instead inspired by the life-style aspirations of a new post-war generation of clients, and he was driven by the still unexploited regional possibilities of materials, technology and culture – the unfulfilled agenda of the generation of 1922.

Thucydides Valentis, Antzaklis apartment building, Athens, 1947–8.

Valsamakis was not the first architect in Greece to eschew white, off-white or cream-coloured prewar 'boxes'. Thucydides Valentis also exhibited the same structural organization (concrete-bearing pillars and horizontal slabs) in his pioneering Antzaklis apartment building (1947–8), which stood a few metres from Valsamakis's. Valentis applied the same idea in the Air Force Share Fund Office Building in Athens (1947–9). The entrance also was set back behind a protective colonnade that gave an air of monumentality to the building.

Valsamakis's Semitelou Street building also allowed for generous verandas, a reinterpretation of the Mediterranean loggia that worked well with the local climate. The loggia carried a social meaning: leisure and community in post-war Athens were beautiful and possible. The building fits remarkably well into the context of its site, time and circumstances. It influenced enormously the future development of modern Greek architecture for decades and it is still seen by many as a viable solution to urban living.

Two years after the building's completion Valsamakis was busy designing in the same vicinity a larger, six-storey residential building, 129 Vassilissis Sofias Avenue (1955–6). Again, the facade of the enclosed block stands back, for the apartments' fenestration supply the back walls of the balconies. The balconies are cantilevered to the front edge of the building, unified once again by an elegant grid frame, this time even more emphatically stated. The top floor is set back, the building terminating with a long railing. Here too Valsamakis used colour and texture to achieve an agreeable sensual result. It is not only the building's hedonistic character that is reminiscent of Ziller. It is also the subtle classical elements underlying the organization of the scheme in addition to the rigorous clarity of its orthogonal frame. The emphasis is on the vertical, a tripartite schema that directs attention to the coronal element at the summit. There are enough elements in this early work to suggest that Valsamakis was a classicist manqué long before his repeated allusions to classicism in the 1970s.

Thucydides Valentis, Air Force Share Fund building, Athens, 1947–9.

Valsamakis's Hotel Amalia on Amalias Avenue (1957–9) overlooking the National Garden uses glass and white marble in the carefully crafted facade, giving the building a more formal appearance than his earlier apartments, one suited to a central hotel standing near the Parliament.

Valsamakis also introduced the curtain wall to Greece in an office building on Hermou Street (1958–9) next to the Byzantine church known

Nicos Valsamakis, Apartment building, Vassilissis Sofias Avenue, Athens, 1955–6.

Nicos Valsamakis, Hotel Amalia, Athens, 1957–9.

as Kapnikarea. Despite the incongruity between the industrial materials of the office building and the handcrafted medieval stone and ceramics of the church, the glass facade is skilfully proportioned.

Other architects contributed to the evolution of the Athenian apartment building, offering resourceful solutions within the rigid zoning regulations and the complex constraints of the city's small and hilly sites. The apartment building on Deinokratous Street in the heart of Athens, close to Lycabettus, by Constantin Decavalla and Thales Argyropoulos (1960–62) is an intriguing scheme, eight storeys high at the front and four at the back facing Lycabettus, a format dictated by the site's steep incline. Not all upper-income apartments were so inventive, but most

Nicos Valsamakis, Office building, Hermou St and Kapnikareas Square, Athens, 1958–9.

of them were comfortable, intelligently proportioned, and with simple but well-crafted details, as in the case of the apartment house on Neophytou Douka Street by Alexandros Kalligas (1960–62).

The office was another important urban building type of the period, although fewer innovative solutions were introduced than was the case for apartments. One exception to this general rule was the Doxiadis Associates Office Building, Athens (1957–8). Doxiadis had emigrated to Australia in the early 1950s, but returned to Greece in 1954 to establish a private consulting and design practice, Doxiadis Associates, in the capital. Soon the firm employed about 400 staff, engaged on various massive projects all over the world, including the Middle East, Asia Africa and the United States. Doxiadis later established a number of organizations associated with the firm, a research centre, a design school and a scholarly review, *Ekistics*, dedicated to planning.[5]

For the Doxiadis Associates headquarters, he selected a 950 square metres site at the foot of Mt Lycabettus. Officially the project was the work of Doxiadis himself, with T. Kouravelos and A. Scheepers, but in fact the team included an additional four architects, eight civil engineers, two mechanical and electrical engineers and a large number of technical staff, for Greece an unprecedented number of professionals dedicated to working on a single building. Design and construction began in the spring of 1957, and by the end of 1958 the whole complex was completed. The Athens Technological Institute, the research and teaching branch of Doxiadis's empire, was added later. The complex comprised office space, a meeting hall, a library, an auditorium, and a small theatre with an independent entrance. It was one of

Constantinos A. Doxiadis, Titos Kouravelos and Arthouros Scheepers, Doxiadis Associates office building, Lycabettus, Athens, 1957–8.

the first organizations internationally to include major communication and computation electronic facilities.

Criticism was levelled at the project for blocking views of Lycabettus from elsewhere in Athens. Indeed, the building is far too large for the historic hill, and its prominent horizontal lines are in conflict with Lycabettus's poised summit, though the character of the landscape is now long gone. Even so, the designers had made every effort to reduce the negative impact of the complex, breaking up its 15,000 cubic metres into smaller volumes – three wings of different heights. Doxiadis himself was anxious to make the project fit for its location: the idea of integrating buildings within landscape was after all the subject of his PhD thesis, of his dialogues with Pikionis, and the very core of his planning theory, known as 'ekistics', which underlay his projects around the world. This way of thinking about planning theory was followed by the generation of architects he recruited as staff, most of them Pikionis's former students, and which of course influenced the 'critical regionalist generation' of the 1950s.

The building was conceived as a large atrium, with built volumes clustered around a large interior courtyard, which doubled the facade surfaces and provided all areas with direct natural lighting and ventilation. It also gave the organization a physical heart and a sense of communal identity. (The idea was later repeated by Doxiadis Associates in a watered-down version, though with less inspiration and success, the former Royal – now National – Research Foundation in Athens.) The designers also

Constantinos Decavalla and Thales Argyropoulos, Apartment building on Deinokratous Street, Athens, 1960–62.

tried to maximize the views of Lycabettus and the Acropolis. The site's steep incline required the removal of 4,400 cubic metres of rock in order to provide car parking and storage – a substantial figure for the standards of the time. An open-plan arrangement was adopted for the office floors, with space and structural organization controlled via a square-grid module of 75 cm. Both methods and materials were chosen to prioritize local resources, although this decision meant constraints as well as potential. Wood, glass and aluminium (manufactured in Greece) were employed for the exterior. Most of the interior surfaces were of exposed painted concrete with wood partitions. The building functioned without air-conditioning, although this was installed later.

By the mid-1960s the *polykatoikia* had spread further into Attica, though there were variations too: one of the most elegant examples was designed by Nikos Kalogeras, Panos Koulermos and Spyros Amourgis – the Vacation Apartments in Vouliagmeni (1965–7), a small two-rooms apartments complex in the form of row houses for summer use, whose stepped-down whitewashed volumes are reminiscent of the regionalist architecture of the 1930s generation.

Given the economic conditions, the lack of substantial private capital and the overall indifference of the state regarding housing responsibilities, while it was possible to build apartment blocks, larger-scale

Nikos Kalogeras, Panos Koulermos and Spyros Amourgis, Vacation Apartments, Vouliagmeni, Attica, 1965–7.

I. Papailiopoulos and A. Spanos, Hara apartment complex, Athens, 1959–61.

housing was rare. A few exceptions include the 'Chara' (Joy) apartment complex by I. Papailiopoulos and A. Spanos in Athens (1959–61). Its ground floor included nine shops, apartments with small private yards and separate entrances, and a central area occupied by green communal space, a swimming pool and playground. Another large housing scheme with a less complex programme was the skilfully sited Asyrmatos apartment complex for workers (1967), close to Philopappou Hill, designed by Elli Vassilikioti.

A significant scheme of the period was on the island of Santorini by the Ministry of Public Works to accommodate victims of the 1956 earthquake. Carried out between 1956 and 1959, the project was designed by

Elli Vassilikioti, Workers' apartment complex, Athens, 1967.

the Department of Housing.[6] It involved the restoration of old houses, eleven new settlements, ten of them extensions of existing villages, and the new village of Kamari. This emergency project faced major difficulties: a shortage of skilled labour, inadequate building materials and poor transportation. Despite these challenges, the architects developed an interesting complex adapted to regional constraints. The plan provided a circulation system separating pedestrian and vehicular traffic. It included a network of narrow stepped footpaths, small squares and, drawing on traditional island settlements, an ingenious arrangement of built volumes for the protection of open spaces from strong winds. The scheme supplied two standard house types, which could be extended and individually varied. In addition to residential units it included administration offices, shops, a church and a school. The architects developed an efficient and highly effective construction system, a simple vault made of a standard block of pumice set up on a removable formwork. The units, the configuration of open spaces and construction methods were heavily influenced by regional architecture.

A little later, in 1959, a programme was established to house the earthquake victims in Santorini as well as those of the Ionian islands earthquake in 1953, and Thessaly in 1955. Furthermore, a law was passed for settling the housing issue for the refugees of 1922, leading to the initiation of projects in several areas of Attica.[7] However, political criteria continued to

Department of Housing (directors P. Vassiliades and A. Spanos), architects Constantin N. Decavalla, Savvas Condaratos, Vassilis Bogakos, Nikos Sapountzis, Vassilis Grigoriades, Reconstruction of the island of Santorini, 1956–9. Post-earthquake housing development by the Ministry of Public Works to accommodate victims of the 1956 earthquake.

play a role with regard to those who were to benefit from the settlement programme, and many decisions were never actually implemented.

Another rare case of large-scale housing during this period was the Aspra Spitia Housing Development project in Antikyra (1961–5) for workers employed by the fledgling aluminium industry. The 1,100 dwellings were intended for a projected population of about 5,000 employees of the French company Aluminium de Grèce, close to its plant. The design by Doxiadis Associates (with George Argyropoulos as chief designer) included the site plan, the landscaping, the units (twelve different housing types to be constructed in stages). The brief described the site 'as L-shaped (the short leg of which is bordered by the sea, while the long one is flanked by two hills)', inside which 'four neighbourhoods were created, each surrounded by a peripheral road and penetrated by culs-de-sac in selected locations'. The plan included shops, business premises and a community centre. Recreational and tourist facilities were also built along the waterfront. Every effort was made to develop a design and construction system adapted to take advantage of regional opportunities. The materials of the houses comprised stone, concrete and wood. Walls were either whitewashed, colour-painted or left untouched, with stone and concrete used for the outdoor spaces. The designers also integrated existing olive trees within the piazzas, streets and front yards. The project is a rare example of large collective housing in Greece.

A new decree established an 'Autonomous Organization for Workers Housing'. Its size was small compared to West European social housing standards, but it was relatively important for Greece, whose housing

Doxiadis Associates (chief designer George Argyropoulos), Aspra Spitia, housing development, Antikyra, 1961–5.

Aris Konstantinidis, Low Income Housing for the Workers' Housing Organization (OEK), Nea Philadelphia, Athens, 1955–7.

situation, despite the self-congratulatory claims of its governments, lagged behind most European countries.[8] Responsible for the design and construction of the public social housing was the Low Income Housing Department (OEK), the Design Section, starting March 1955, headed by Aris Konstantinidis. Though he was only in charge for two years (he resigned in March 1957 in protest against the exclusion of playgrounds from one of his projects), he completed a considerable number of projects, more or less as he wanted them. Among these is the low-income housing scheme in Nea Philadelphia, Athens (1955–7). The site plan is clearly indebted to Bauhaus precedents, as are several building features, while the details of the balconies bring to mind contemporary solutions by Egon Eiermann in Germany. Among other important projects are Konstantinidis's two-storey low-income housing in Herakleion on Crete, which have minimal concrete frames with an interesting system of two-part windows, and his single-storey individual units in Serres, northern Greece, where Konstantinidis experimented with sloping tile-covered roofs and, closer to traditional Greek architecture, small, tile-covered porticos.

Soon after his resignation from the OEK, Konstantinidis was appointed to the design section of the Technical Department of the National Organization of Tourism (EOT), a new institution. Ever since Greece had hosted CIAM, efforts had been made to exploit the beauty of the Greek landscape and coastline and its cultural heritage. However very little was accomplished until Karamanlis headed the Greek government. Many of the ideas he guided towards actuality, such as the development of a hotel system serving the most important cultural sites of the country and the integration of tourist targets together with the overall development of Athens, were conceived before his era, but it was only during the intial period of his premiership that the tourist programme and its architectural component truly took off.

The first important project Konstantinidis designed in his new post was the Triton Hotel (1958) on Andros, close to the island's capital. All rooms looked out over the sea, forming a gigantic lattice structure. The Triton was followed by the Xenia Hotel in Mykonos, the Cycladic island admired for its famous whitewashed houses. Konstantinidis designed a series of long, single- and two-storey pavilions, arranged around a central administration and communal block, their load-bearing stone walls quarried from local stone, the same colour as both the ground on which they stood and the rocky coastline. By contrast, the roofs, made from concrete, were white, as were the concrete lintels over the windows, echoing to the island's traditional buildings. As opposed to the small scale of the traditional Cycladic houses and churches, the roofs of the hotel were long and oversized in height, their vigour emphasized by bringing the inverted exposed concrete beams to the edge of the building. The lintels were similarly overscaled, and, inserted between the small individual room units, were equal size gaps, atrium-like protected outdoor spaces. Konstantinidis placed the units irregularly on the site, the single-storey on the lower part of the site, the two-storey examples closer to the sea front. Thus, while the stone walls punctuated by the large orthogonal openings of the 'atria' appeared as the continuation of the very ground, albeit ordered according to a strict geometrical pattern, the concrete roofs and

Aris Konstantinidis, Xenia Hotel, Mykonos, 1959.

lintels appeared to levitate. Indeed, the architect likened the buildings to animated Greek dances.

Conservative Greek intellectuals sentimentally attached to Mykonos's cutely picturesque houses and churches reacted to the Xenia Hotel complex with horror, a response that Konstantinidis simply disregarded. A year later (1958) he was busy designing for the same Tourist Organization dressing rooms for the renowned ancient open air theatre of Epidauros, its reconstruction finished just in time to stage large-scale performances of classical Greek drama. Soon after, a second phase – guests' quarters: 1960, 1962 – followed. As in the case of Mykonos, Konstantinidis used an unadorned local stone for his walling system combined with robust concrete flat roofs. And as in Mykonos, the scheme was driven by his love of 'life in Greece . . . in the open'. Access to these units is directly from outside, and all individual rooms have verandas.

As in the case of the Mykonos Hotel, the layout of the units in the Epidauros landscape appears highly informal, the buildings seemingly scattered across the landscape, in actuality arranged by Konstantinidis in accordance to the geometry of the sloping site. The scheme of the individual units is partly reminiscent of Le Corbusier's Maisons Jaoul in Neuilly-sur-Seine (1952–4), and there is no doubt that in the design of the site plan, Konstantinidis drew from Le Corbusier's mid-1940s experiments situating repetitive stone-wall structures on sloping Mediterranean sites, as in Roq et Rob at Roquebrune-Cap-Martin (1948–50). In contrast to Le Corbusier's placement of the long volumes parallel to the direction of the slope, Konstantinidis arranged the walls of his units perpendicular to it, after the manner in which Mediterranean peasants set up retaining walls on slopes to create terraces for cultivation, or the way shepherds formed settlements for themselves and their animals in Mediterranean countries. As in such peasant structures, the stone walls in the Epidaurus buildings are interrupted by wide, floor-to-ceiling openings, leaving dark gaps. Between the units the ground was left rough, allowing the olive trees to grow freely.

Almost contemporary is the two-storey, 22-room Xenia Motel in Kalambaka (1960), sited next to the Byzantine Meteora monasteries amid prominent rocks, one of the most dramatic landscapes and older monuments in the world. Once more a masterpiece of site arrangement, the Xenia is one of the very few cases for which Konstantinidis applied a slightly sloping roof in response to the steepness of the site and in contrast to the upwardly thrusting rock formations.[9]

More hotel projects followed in the 1960s, following the similar principles of a robust skeletal structure and ingenious interpretations of site conditions, which include the Xenia Motel, Olympia (1963), the

Aris Konstantinidis, Tourist Organization, Dressing Rooms and Guests' Quarters for the ancient theatre of Epidaurus, 1960 and 1962.

Xenia Hotel, Herakleion (1963–6), and the Xenia Hotel, Poros (1964). In 1965–6 Konstantinidis designed the Ioannina Archaeological Museum. It is remarkable how this architect-civil servant managed to construct so much in such a brief time and of such a high standard within the context of a Greece still struggling to become a developed modern state. Reflecting on his years on the Xenia buildings with the National Organization of Tourism (EOT) he noted how EOT 'let me free . . . to do my own thing' (*to kefi mou*).[10]

Even more impressive is that parallel to his work in the Ministry he succeeded in designing a number of remarkable private residences. The house on Archimedes and Kleitomachou Streets (1961) is one of the best examples of an urban private home in Europe built in the second half of the twentieth century. It served as residence and study for Alexander Xydis, a diplomat and art critic. Located in the centre of Athens, not far

Τάφος ένας τοίχος ύψος 1.70 [illegible] [illegible] ... Οι πέτρες [illegible] ... Κάθε [illegible] [illegible] σχήματα!

[illegible]

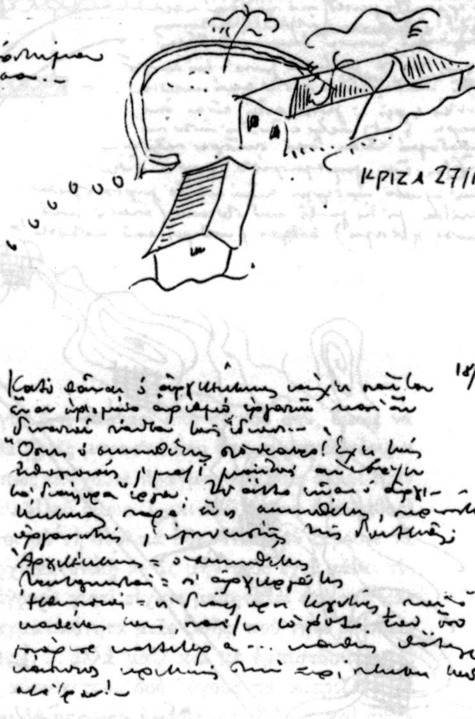

Ich selber habe nicht die Erbschaft eines anderen angetreten, sondern nur das genommen, was niemand gehörte!
Napoleon

18/2/41

[illegible] ο αρχιτέκτων [illegible] ...

Αρχιτέκτων = ο [illegible]

[illegible] = οι αρχιεργάτες

[illegible]

[illegible] ??? 18/2/41

opposite: Aris Konstantinidis, Epiros houses, sketches from his notebook, end of 1940.

Aris Konstantinidis, Xenia Motel, Kalambaka, Thessaly, 1960.

from the ancient Stadium, it provides a modest residential plan with small interior spaces of high functional quality. The post-and-beam reinforced concrete structure is exposed, as in Konstantinidis's other buildings. But what makes the building particularly exciting is the intricate manner with which it occupies a corner setting masterfully adapted to the peculiarities of a unique hilly site.

Konstantinidis's Weekend House (1961–2), not far from Athens on the way to Cape Sounion in Anavyssos, was placed on a bare shore and in isolated surroundings. As if designed not to disturb the stillness or even the few shrubs and cactuses growing there, the Weekend House is itself a silent sentinel, just as much as any ancient Doric temple lying abandoned in a forgotten site. The scheme – stone walls, like gigantic brute

Aris Konstantinidis's photo of animal shelters made by Greek shepherds.

Aris Konstantinidis, Xydis House, Athens, 1961.

pillars, and one corner feature, a right-angled wall supporting a flat concrete roof, was a Mediterranean answer to Mies van der Rohe's minimalist American shed-like residences of the second part of the 1940s. But Konstantinidis's shoreline shed is not only very different from Mies's structures in terms of materials – Mies's being elegant high-tech glass and steel, Konstantinidis's no more than primitive stone and concrete – it is also distinct in terms of the way the weekend retreat and its setting suggests a life lived outdoors, Konstantinidis's beloved theme. (Responding to exactly the same location and landscape, Valsamakis opted for large cantilevered planes discreetly supported by massive stone pillars or slender metal columns or boldly projecting directly from the ground over the cliff in his two masterful houses in Anavyssos, both of 1962–3.

Aris Konstantinidis, Papapanayiotou Weekend House, Anavyssos, Attica, 1961–2.

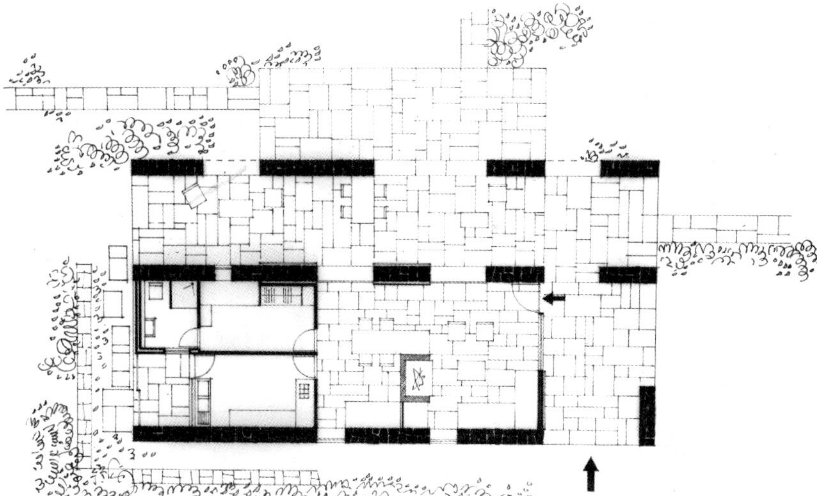

Papapanayiotou Weekend House, Anavyssos, plan.

These were versions of his ideal housing type that was finally applied in his own house in Philothei, Athens, of 1963.)

By 1966 Konstantinidis's reputation was known beyond Greece. In 1965 he spent time lecturing in Vienna on 'Architecture and Rationalism', and in Munich, Zurich and Stuttgart on the 'Principles of Modern Architecture'. He was then 53, and, despite these public appearances in front of large audiences, was still very much an architects' architect rather than a media celebrity. When Mies's eightieth birthday was celebrated around the world, two major German architectural journals – *Baumeister* (3/1966) and *Bauen +Wohnen* (5/1966) – asked Konstantinidis to comment on Mies's contribution to architecture, a major recognition of Konstantinidis and of the deeper values he stood for, beyond the reductive 'tectonic' post-and-beam structure schema and the orthogonal regulatory grid he shared with Mies. Konstantinidis responded by saying that 'architecture is not concerned with problems of aesthetics but problems of life and existence'. He found Mies's buildings 'somehow monotonous and too much tied to the present', enclosing all functions always 'under the same roof, within the same structural frame, and always looking the same'. However, Mies's motto – 'less is more' – indicated 'one of the most correct directions for the future of contemporary architecture'. Konstantinidis also took the opportunity to criticize Philip Johnson, Saarinen and Skidmore, Owings & Merrill for having produced Mies-like buildings as mere 'decorative eccentricities'.

Despite Konstantinidis's growing international reputation, the influence he had on the design of the numerous tourist facilities built in Greece during that time was rather limited. One of the priorities of Prime Minister Karamanlis was to develop the Saronic coast of Attica, landscaping the waterfront and adding tourist structures. Most of these projects were carefully designed, minimal and functional, such as the Mont Parnès Hotel (1958–61) by Paul Mylonas, the Astir Beach in Glyfada designed by P. Vassiliades (1955–60), E. Vourekas, P. Sakellarios and collaborating architects A. Georgiadis and C. Decavalla, which consisted of light wooden structures – changing rooms, bungalows, a restaurant and a cafeteria. However, overall the Saronikos projects did not relate well to the natural topography of the area, completely ignoring the unique scale, morphology, materials and natural planting of the place, and as a result one of the most beautiful sites on the Mediterranean was destroyed. The decision to remove all pre-existing picturesque seafront buildings, leaving no trace of the history of the sites, was also unwise.

Even more disruptive was the Athens Hilton Hotel (1958–60). It was the first large-scale international hotel to be built in Greece, and although it was a multinational project it was heavily subsidized by public money.

Prokopios Vassiliades, Emmanuel Vourekas, Pericles Sakellarios, Astir Beach and Resort Complex, Glyfada, Attica, 1955–60.

Designed by P. Vassiliades, E. Vourekas, A. Georgiades and S. Staikos with heavy input by Hilton experts, its exceptional height and placement in relation to the city block depended on the granting of a royal decree.[11] Previous regulation permitted a building of 24 metres maximum height and only seven floors above the ground floor. The new regulation was arranged by Vassiliades, who next to being the key designer of the project was also a high-ranking employee of the Ministry of Public Works in charge of building regulations. It was the first time that such an exemption was granted in Athens, and it opened the way for more tall buildings to appear, such as the Telecommunications Centre (1961–5) by Kostas Kitsikis, a nondescript public sector office tower for OTE. Vassiliades later removed his name as the Hilton designer consultant, but the original contract signed 5 December 1958 still bears his signature.

An influential journalist writing for the paper *I Kathimerini* and signing her articles simply as 'E', celebrated the building with the words 'Yes, here is good taste, daring prodigality, and imagination', 'the most perfect American product, the shining Cadillac . . . coupled with the added luxury of European taste and Greek marble', adding that 'with the moonlight, a little music, the evening breeze, a glass of wine, and the terrace of the Athens Hilton, you have the best romantic materials in the world'. (The same journalist tried hard to denigrate and even stop the work of

Prokopios Vassiliades, Emmanuel Vourekas, Antonis Georgiadis and Spyros Staikos, Hilton Hotel, Athens, 1958–60.

Konstantinidis for EOT in the name of 'tradition' and 'Greek' values.) E's remarks quoted here were cited by Yale University's Vincent Scully when the Hilton was finished. His critical appraisal, 'The Athens Hilton: A Study in Vandalism', was published in the *Architectural Forum* in 1963.[12] Scully focused on the pernicious impact the building had on the cityscape of Athens and the landscape of Attica, and on the absence of any consideration of the urban context either by the American commercial designers or by their Greek co-designers, or by the city authorities, or by most of the Greek press, which he considered a shocking dereliction of responsibility and care.

Scully did not fail to mention the scandalous situation whereby 'the architect in charge of the Town Planning Directorate, Mr P. Vassiliades' was at the same time pronounced to be 'one of the associated architects who designed the building', and in this dual capacity 'managed, under existing laws relative to building of public utility and tourism, to procure a waiver' from his own ministry and from the administration he headed, 'permitting the violation of the Athenian building code . . . relative to height'. Scully's outrage was justified not just because of the moral political scandal but also because passing this law initiated the undoing of the minimal spatial order the city had succeeded in establishing with much effort by that time. He pointed to the Telephone Company (OTE) building, 'which sticks up like a monstrous sore thumb on the other side of the town'. Joining Scully's criticism, Doxiadis remarked that from a symbolic point of view, if the neighbouring site was to become a cultural centre, as Karamanlis was planning (in fact, the National Gallery by Dimitris Fatouros and Pavlos Mylonas was built on it in 1976), it was most unfitting to be overlooked by a hotel.

As Scully noted, 'this is really the way to tear the city apart at its heart – flood it in an asphalt sea', turning the vicinity into a 'shopping centre or used car lot environment', 'a conspicuous example of what can happen when men build on the earth without intelligence, reverence, or love', leading ultimately to nothing but 'the destruction of the earth by men.' He also drew attention to the fact that the high air-conditioning volume was going to add to the 'smog that now hangs over Athens', the long-term implications of which only a few then perceived. He remarked finally that those who would profit most from the arrangement would be those lodged in the hotel: they will be 'among the favored Athenian few . . . not seeing' the monstrous building itself.

By contrast, the U.S. Embassy (1959–61), another project built in Greece around the same time to designs by a foreign architect (Walter Gropius / TAC, with P. A. Sakellarios as consulting architect) created no controversy. Gropius, following the soft-regionalist direction he and Belluschi had developed in the 1950s, designed a quietly modern scheme sheathed in the marble of the region and drawing from the typology of classical architecture: a square, 'peripteral', atrium building. Like the Doxiadis design headquarters, it contained an interior court, encircled by columns that bore the structure. Most importantly, it was relatively low, just two storeys on pilotis, in an originally unfenced landscape, and open on all sides, suggesting that the institution was highly accessible, yet at the same time making it hard to discern where exactly the entrance was. The overhanging roof and the ceramic curtain wall at ground level were responses to the intense local light. Old olive trees were carefully transported and

A Walter Gropius/TAC (Consultant Architect, Pericles A. Sakellarios), U.S. Embassy Athens, 1959–61.

planted next to the building. However, its references to classical architecture were too forced, too literal, and too rigidly applied; moreover the rigid square symmetrical scheme did not respond to the particularities of the sloping, asymmetrical site.

While a few Greek texts protested against the rapid deterioration of the Athenian cultural and physical environment, a major project stood up as a powerful non-verbal critical statement. Pikionis's complex of paths (1950–57) linking the Acropolis with the summit of a neighbouring hill, Philopappou, was also arguably his most significant work. The idea of the 'path' had already been developed theoretically in his essay 'Sentimental Topography' published in *To Trito Mati* in 1935.[13] Its origins, the idea of wandering in the landscape and 'promenading without an end in mind', as well as the notion of *sentimental* has roots back in eighteenth-century France, notably Jean-Jacques Rousseau's *Rêveries d'un promeneur solitaire* (1782). Rousseau's ideas about this aesthetic and sensual experience also contained a deeply critical message against absolutism as a political system and the Western drive for amoral efficiency. Similarly Pikionis saw in his work a message beyond aesthetics – one about the 'good life': 'This lonely trail is infinitely superior to the avenues of the metropolises.'[14] Twenty years after publication of his essay, Pikionis, in a letter of 1955 to Karamanlis, Minister of Public Works, presented the 'path' as a critical expression of professional and moral responsibility that countered the 'banalities' of fashion and the commercial exploitation of Greece as a tourist resource,[15] but also opposed 'streets, alleys, road junctions, car parks'.

The fact that the project was conceived soon after the end of the Civil War gives Pikionis's architecture of the path a social and political meaning in addition to its phenomenological significance: the path can be seen as a memorial to the conflict, and as a mechanism for national reconciliation, enabling interaction and community, local and universal. In the words of the Greek intellectual Zissimos Lorentzatos, when Pikionis spoke 'he was talking about us but at the same time talking in the name of the people of the whole earth'.[16] Despite the citations from mythology and the mystical tone of the texts, the lecturing and the presence of so much antiquity, history and ruins surrounding the Paths project, in the end walking through it one experiences the sensual reality of the surfaces, the rhythm of climbing and descending, the topology, the aromas, the close-up view of grouped rocks and ruins, the distant landscape views; but beyond these phenomenological experiences of a *promenade solitaire*, there is an overpowering sense of social vitality.

The project quickly gained international recognition. Pikionis's idiom may have been local limestone and shrubs typical of the Attica region, but the message was global, in tune with the efforts of a younger post-war generation of architects: Louis Kahn, Ernesto Rogers, James Stirling and the members of Team Ten, in particular Aldo van Eyck and Shadrach Woods, who, much like Pikionis, shifted their attention away from formal spatial qualities of architecture to focus on buildings as containers of movement and human interaction. Like Pikionis, Woods, one of the most lucid spokesmen of his generation, thought that 'the approach' to architecture 'can no longer be only visual'. What Woods proposed in his 'web', or 'stem' system was 'the creation of environment at every scale of human association' appropriate for a 'society . . . entirely new . . . , a completely 'open', 'non-hierarchical' 'co-operative', shared by all on a basis of 'total participation and complete confidence'. In fact what Pikionis had designed was a stem, not a built one but one embedded in the landscape that was intended to enhance the quality of the 'environment of human association' as dreamed by many young architects of that time. Indicative of Pikionis's appreciation by the younger generation of architects was the publication of an article by the leading Japanese 'metabolist' architect and critic, Kisho Kurokawa, in an issue of *Kinshiku Bunka* in January 1963. Kurokawa celebrated Pikionis's Paths as appealing to 'crowds of people', declaring it as prototypal architecture of the future, 'an architecture for human movement'. Kurokawa compared it to the new town devised by Candilis, Josic and Woods and to his own work. Pikionis's Paths was also presented alongside the work of members of Team X, Bakema and van der Broek by Lewis Mumford, another critic of the direction modern architecture was then taking and a partisan of 'regionalist' design. When he visited Greece in 1960, Pikionis gave him a tour of his project for the Acropolis. Mumford was

Dimitris Pikionis, Acropolis–Philopapou Hill Paths, detail, 1950–57.

Two sections of Pikionis's Acropolis–Philopappou Hill Paths.

Dimitris Pikionis, Attica landscape, from the 'Attica' series of drawings.

so deeply moved by the experience that he included the project in *The City in History*.[17] Writing in the mid-1960s to Artur Glikson, an Israeli architect and regional planner who was searching for ways to overcome the dehumanizing architectural practices of the time, Mumford added that he was 'grateful to him for one thing', that he introduced him to Pikionis. He then recommended to Glikson to 'stop off in Athens and talk to him and see his work': 'So well' designed 'that hardly anyone realized that they were landscaped.'[18]

Pikionis shifted his focus from design to conservation. In his essay 'The Rape of the Earth' he pointed out the imminent danger of destruction of the natural-historical landscape, yoking together the two qualities as being impossible to dissociate.[19] Written in a poetic idiom in the first person, with the author impersonating Attica, and published at the peak of the take off of post-Second World War reconstruction in Greece, it was an urgent, angry appeal. Pikionis referred to the quarries of Attica and their 'cursed job', 'eating up even the Pentelic outline', and to the two historical rivers of Attica, 'Ilissos, and Kifissos, inside which 'you threw your refuse from your factories'. In the name of the earth of Attica, he addressed modern Greeks, calling them 'cowards, ignorant, and barbarians', asking them: 'what are you doing, what are you eradicating' without realizing that 'I am your mother . . . she who nourished you'.

What is remarkable about Pikionis's Paths project is that, like the hotels designed by Konstantinidis, it was built pretty much as it had been conceived, with only a few changes, and both projects were state works. There was a moment of crisis when the project – and the participation of Pikionis in its construction – was in danger, for Pikionis's reflective

Dimitris Pikionis, Playground in Philothei, Athens, 1959.

participatory practice not only did not fit into any contractor's scheduling but showed no indication of the project's time of completion. Pikionis proceeded with the project using oral instructions, trials, improvisations and revisions to construct daring large concrete forms, their complex shapes inspired by the geometry of Paul Klee's line drawings 'overcoming conventional schematization'. Several times he did not hesitate to adopt experiments carried out by his technicians, mostly inspired by the accidental constraints of the immediate site conditions or the available materials – pieces of stone or architectural elements found in demolished neoclassical buildings, polemically refusing to see his project as autonomous, or complete. In the correspondence that followed, Pikionis reacted against a decision to stop him from visiting the site and his replacement by a professional manager to supervise the construction, these so as to avoid costly daily interferences by him. Pikionis, quoting the famous ancient Greek proverb 'Hasten slowly', argued that this was not possible. His status as consultant to the Committee planning historic grounds around Acropolis was ambiguous, and according to him did not involve simply supplying drawings – if not actual participation in the construction process it did at least mean necessary supervision. Further, he argued that it was on principle impossible to separate the task of the designer from that of the supervisor, the supervisor being himself a designer;

like an orchestral conductor who interprets the musical score the architect supervisor 'interprets the drawing'.[20] Pikionis, like Konstantinidis, finally got his way and the project was constructed more or less as it was draughted in the architect's mind – very few technical drawings ever existed (the same was the case for his Playground in Philothei, Athens, of 1959, one of his most complex works).

Pikionis was also featured in a special issue of the art journal *Zygos* in 1958. Founded in 1955 *Zygos* was one of the most interesting developments of the 'halcyon days' of the 1950s, when a number of new publications presented and discussed the work of Greek artists and architects.[21] With interest in architecture growing, *Zygos* hired a special architectural editor, Orestis Doumanis, a young civil engineer who gathered around him a group of architects as advisors.[22] In 1963 Doumanis left the review after his idea of publishing student work alongside the professionals was refused by the publisher. A few days later he was invited by the founder and director of a new architectural magazine, *Architectoniki*, to become its director. Founded in 1957 by Antonis Kitsikis, son of the architect Kostas Kitsikis (and nephew of Nikolaos Kitsikis, who had contributed so much to the promotion of modern architecture in Greece in the 1930s as director of *Technika Chronika*), *Architectoniki* was the most ambitious Greek publication to be devoted exclusively to architecture.

As a non-institutional publication *Architectoniki* offered possibilities for Doumanis to present new people, ideas and projects. However, the content of the publication was mixed in terms of quality: on the one hand it published new buildings by leading architects like Konstantinidis, theoretical articles and critical texts; on the other, commercial mainstream buildings occasionally appeared with the sole aim of advertising the client. In 1964 Doumanis quit the journal to take over the post of press office for the Technical Chamber of Greece and *Technika Chronika*; his important contribution was to come three years later with the founding of the Yearbook *Architecture in Greece* (*Architectonika Themata*) in 1967.

As interest in architecture and in the future of Athens grew, more articles started appearing in cultural reviews for a broader public, such as the left-leaning monthly art review *Epitheorisi Technis*, whose director was an architect, Nikos Siapkidis. It ran from 1954 to 1967. Many of the founder-members of the magazine were architects based in Paris, including Panos Djelepy and Aristomenis Provelengios. One of the young architects involved in founding it was Takis Zenetos, who had trained at the Ecole des Beaux-Arts. On his return to Greece he was commissioned to redesign and expand the Fix Beer Factory (1957–63), one of the first modern plants in Greece, on Syngrou Avenue, Athens. At last, a truly modern structure, the kind that the author Theotokas had dreamed of in

Takis Zenetos and Margaritis Apostolides, Fix Brewery, Athens, 1957–63.

the early 1930s, had arrived. The scale was colossal for Athens. Yet, because of its height, within the limits of the Athenian code, the planarity, horizontality of elements and serenity of the facade, the building was not imposing whether viewed from the street or from a great distance. In fact, one might claim that the plainness and sobriety of its skyline enhanced the grace of the outline of the hills and mountains of Attica and made the chaotic volumes of the cityscape more tolerable. A lover of technology

Ioannis Liapis and Elias Skroumbelos, Passenger Terminal and Customs Facility, Piraeus Port Authority, Agios Nikolaos Pier, Piraeus, 1962–9.

and industrial buildings, Zenetos made parts of the interior of the factory and its machines visible to the passer-by.

In addition to the Fix factory, Zenetos designed the Vianil detergent factory in Agios Ioannis Renti, Piraeus (1964). The same characteristics of laconic architecture, emphasizing skin and planarity rather than structure and three-dimensional volume, are to be found in a much smaller project by Zenetos and Apostolides, the Single Family House on Helidonous Street, Nea Kifissia (1959–60). Planned around a central hall, it was divided into three parts: living rooms and guest area, sleeping area, and services. The architectural similarity between the two projects, so different in size and use, demonstrated Zenetos's maturity and sophistication as a designer, one able to develop a personal idiom together with a universal set of tools capable of handling a variety of architectural challenges.

In contrast to the laconic projects by Zenetos, the departure and customs facility for the Agios Nikolaos Pier in Piraeus (1962–9) by I. Liapis and E. Skroumbelos was a monumental building that included basic passenger terminal needs, a customs hall, waiting rooms, a departure hall, shops, bars and restaurants.[23] Its expressive structure and big uninterrupted spans exhibit proudly the technical achievements Greece was capable of by the early 1960s.

Soon after the Fix factory, Zenetos designed an apartment complex on Herodou Attikou Street, Athens (1959), and a villa in Kavouri, Attica (1959–61), Zenetos always employed industrial components, and his preoccupation in all these projects was the appropriation of the site by a highly agile, light and non-intrusive structure, using a plan sufficiently flexible to accommodate multiple changing functions, and to which

Takis Zenetos, Villa, Kavouri, Attica, 1959–61.

Takis Zenetos and Margaritis Apostolides, Apartment Building, Athens, 1959–60.

attention has been given to the orientation of the building. All these concerns resulted in schemes that generated a sense of intelligence rather than brute force despite the harshness of their industrial elements and the rigorous geometry of their configuration.

Zenetos's Apartment Building on Amalias Avenue and Daidalou Street Athens (1959–60) was the first residential structure in Greece to employ curtain walling. There were many innovations in the design. The architect provided a flexible space-division system enabled by means of a highly sophisticated three-dimensional grid that coordinated the building's various components. He also developed a means to establish a visual continuity of elements in facades where building code restrictions did not permit less than one metre distance between an end balcony and the property adjacent to it. He circumvented the code by extending the railing but not the floor of the balcony, which was what the code

Takis Zenetos, Cable City conceptual drawing, Rethymno, Crete 1966. Masterplan of the tourist development of Plakias, 'Liakota' showing site plan of 1,200-bed complex and view from the sea.

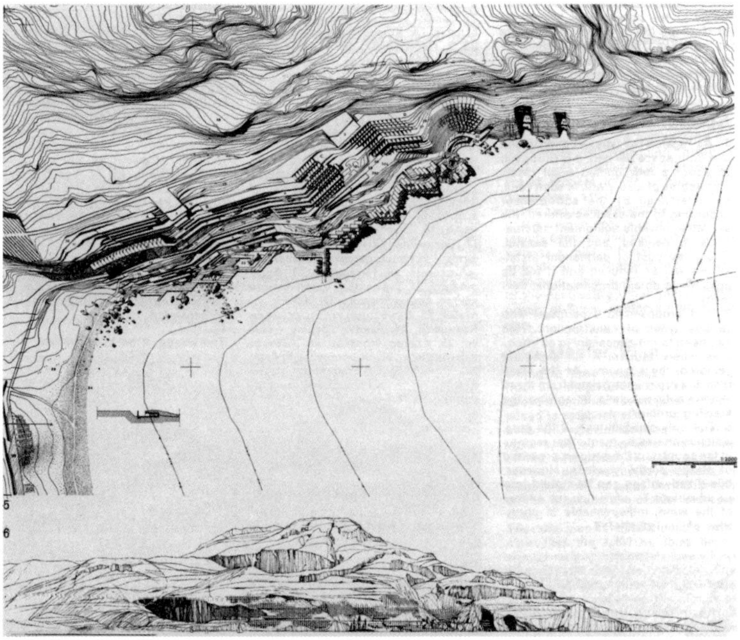

constrained. While this may seem a minor detail, it had an important visual impact on facades, a novelty that was to be widely imitated in Greece.

High density settlements paper experiments were carried out by Zenetos who tried to introduce his building-scale high-tech ideas into high density mega-structure developments such as the Turnine Gorge, the Cable City and the Hanging Hotel sculpturally integrated into the landscape. A sample of the kind of environment Zenetos was after, a combination of technological craftsmanship, lightness and sympathy with the particularities of the site and the identity of the landscape, is the Lycabettus Theatre, on Mt Lycabettus, designed and constructed between 1964 and 1967. Shaped as a parabolic cone, the facility accommodated 3,000 spectators. Zenetos located the backstage services under the auditorium, below the level of the orchestra, gracefully placing a light, minimal structural space within the void of the old abandoned quarry, leaving the natural environment intact.

On the whole, during these years there were very few medium-scale urban design ideas running alongside the numerous high-quality individual buildings, with the exception of the Doxiadis headquarters, whatever were the weaknesses of that project. A rare paper project was carried out by Panos Koulermos in collaboration with Nikos Kalogeras and Spyros Amourgis for their entry to the Panhellenic Competition for the Army

Share Fund Office building in Athens. The mass of the project was shaped to follow the building-block line accentuated by horizontal straps of the facade marking the floor levels. The facade pattern, however, is in direct contrast to the character of the mainly neoclassical buildings of the area predominant at that time, some of which survive today. Koulermos sculpted the volume skilfully, forming an interior court by setting back each floor within the block, a unique solution for Athens and one that could have been applied in many Mediterranean cities. In the end, the scheme was not built.

Understanding that urbanism had not developed as much as architecture in post-war Greece, and recognizing its significance for the country's modernization, Karamanlis realized that he had to bring in experts from abroad. To deal with the increasing air traffic he commissioned the prominent American architect Eero Saarinen to design Hellenikon airport

Takis Zenetos, Lycabettus Theatre, Athens, 1964–7.

Panos Koulermos in collaboration with Nikos Kalogeras and Spyros Amourgis, Panhellenic Army Share Fund (ASF) building in Athens, 1963, competition entry.

terminal (1959). And to confront the growth of the automobile in Athens (9,810 vehicles in Greece in 1954, but 42,139 seven years later), Karamanlis invited Wilbur Smith, an American traffic engineer based in New Haven, Connecticut, to carry out the first transportation study for greater Athens. By the time Smith reported the results of his study in 1962 there were 50,115 vehicles in Athens, and he predicted that there would be 135,142 by 1967. In the letter to George Markakis included in his report, Smith recommended a system 'consisting of 52 km of freeways and 44 km of new expressways, for conditions expected in 1980', but 'much of it needed now'. It also acknowledged that this 'system' should be complemented by 'expanding and extending mass-transport facilities so that a properly balanced transportation plan will be produced'.[24] The results of Smith's study were published in 1963, concurrently with Colin Buchanan's report on Britain, *Traffic in Towns*. Smith's study was purely behavioural, without any explicit values or visions attached to it. Although it mentioned the need for public transportation it did not include it as part of the recommended solution, promoting in the end total automobilization of Athens and Attica. (By contrast, Buchanan's *Traffic in Towns* was a normative investigation that viewed London as a system of rooms and corridors, a model intended to safeguard the environmental and social quality of the city, qualities that modern Athens was losing day by day.)

About the same time Smith was preparing his study, Karamanlis was also submitting his plans for public transportation that were criticized severely by the left as mainly benefiting the prosperous; they did not pay enough attention to those who really needed it, neither did they contribute significantly to a sustainable development and modernization of the country. While a candidate in the spring 1958 elections, Karamanlis was attacked by a 68-page pamphlet written by Nikolaos Kitsikis, the ex-president of the Chamber of Engineers, Rector of the Polytechnic, Director General of Public Works and champion of modern architecture during the 1930s, who was by now a member of the Parliament representing the left. The tone of the text was vitriolic, confrontational and narrowly 'nationalist', claiming that foreign technical advisors were, if not dangerous, useless. The attack targeted the 'myth of Karamanlis', Kitsikis claiming that he was just a showman politician who 'planted innumerable foundation stones' for 'promotion' rather than 'production', 'projects, selling Greece to the United States, Western Europe, and NATO', who, together with the 'shady people of economic oligarchy', had conspired against the industrialization of Greece. Kitsikis, who had followed technological and planning developments in Western Europe at that time, appeared narrow minded in relation to the Metro plan for Athens that Karamanlis had begun to consider at that time, claiming that it was megalomaniacal, too costly, and did not contribute to the solution of the problem of transportation. Bizarrely, Kitsikis claimed that congestion in Athens was caused by 'the circulation of pedestrians'. Equally conservative was his criticism of the modernization of Omonoia Square, which had introduced escalators and underground shopping for the first time in the capital. Despite all that, many of the points Kitsikis made in relation to the urban development of Athens were astute. The continuous expansion of the Hellenikon airport was in direct conflict with the development of the Saronikos coast – from Faliro to Sounion – a Greek Côte d'Azur zone for tourism and leisure, as Karamanlis envisaged it. The absence for a comprehensive plan for drainage and sewage even in the centre of Athens was a scandalous fact.

With relatively limited access to a broad spectrum of experts, Karamanlis tried hard to recruit the best people for his ambitious projects of urban development and tourism, inviting back left wing architects who, as mentioned in the previous chapter, had left Greece due to the Civil War. Thus, in 1960, Ioannis Despotopoulos was recalled from Sweden to his old position, professor of architecture at the Athens Polytechnic, and at the same time to undertake the study of the planned (never completed) cultural centre complex for Athens, located in a site adjacent to the Hilton. He also invited George Candilis, practising at that time in

France, to design a major outdoor international sculpture exhibition on Philopappou Hill. The exhibition included works by Degas, Mestrovic, Calder, Hepworth, Rodin, Picasso, Malliol, Matisse, Giacometti, Max Bill and Léger, and was curated by the art historian and critic Tony Spiteris. Aristomenis Provelengios, who, like Candilis, worked with Le Corbusier, also decided to return to Greece. His first project was a Studio and Residence (1956–8) on Kykladon Street for Tony Spiteris and the sculptress Ioanna Spiteris, a vibrant, multi-level open space made out of glass and a bare, brutalist reinforced-concrete structure proportioned by Le Corbusier's Modulor system.

Unique as the 'halcyon' years might have been in terms of design excellence and creativity, they were limited mostly to individual built projects. Pikionis, Konstantinidis, Valsamakis and Zenetos, as well as a number of other architects of the post-war generation, were an isolated 'miracle' group whose work did not represent the overall reality of the Greek urban and rural environment. Greece lagged behind the Netherlands or northern Italy, for example, who were modernizing in a more comprehensive way.

For those who could not benefit from the government programmes or who did not have the funds to be served by the private sector, the city permitted another alternative, the bottom-up, freewheeling, self-help solution beyond the world of law and contracts and also health standards. The percentage of unauthorized houses in greater Athens in the period 1945–50 was 48 per cent, in 1951–60 it was 28 per cent, and in 1961–9 down to 19 per cent.[25] From 1945 to 1969 a total of 206,147 illegal houses were built in Greece with 137,602 of those in Athens. Yet even these houses required sums of money not available to a large number of the population of Greece at that time.

Hence, it is not a paradox that during these years immigration increased, arriving at a peak in 1965, when 117,167 persons settled permanently, against 59,241 that went abroad to find temporary work. Karamanlis approved of it; the Centre party called it a 'curse' but had no idea how to arrest it. So couples and families continued to be broken up in Greece, communities were dissolved, and popular songs, many *rebetika* songs among them, were written that sung of the pain of departure, separation, waiting, and death abroad. And, as in the 1930s, the failure to satisfy basic needs and the difficulties of curtailing growing protest led to extreme political crises.

Indicative of the way the halcyon years were limited was the unexpected repression by the authorities of the performance of a comedy by Aristophanes *The Birds*, interpreted by the leading Greek theatre director Karolos Koun. Following the pioneering vision of Sikelianos (though eschewing his rhetorical aesthetics), Koun put together a team of leading artists of the 1930s and post-war generation, including Tsarouchis, Hadjidakis and Rallou Manou, fusing elements of antiquity and modernity. Performed in Greece and abroad during the 1960s, the government, fearing that the show mocked the church and the Atlantic Alliance, closed it down in 1967.

One historian called these days the 'short . . . unrealized spring'.[26] Indeed, most of the ideas in culture and in architecture that bloomed during the second half of the 1950s were soon to be frozen during the decade that followed, many of which remain unrealized even today.

ΤΡΑΠΕΖΑ ΠΙΣΤΕΩΣ
CREDIT BANK

chapter six

Architecture of the Junta

Greece's 'halcyon days' officially ended on the eve of 21 April 1967, when the country awoke to marches and prewar popular songs on the radio,[1] and to news that a military junta had taken over the government. Yet perhaps the uniquely optimistic and creative period in the history of modern Greece had already exhausted its course by May 1963, when Prime Minister Karamanlis had allegedly uttered 'Who is ruling this country after all?' – a reference to the 'Palace' and the plethora of overt and covert organizations which, at that time, were exercising disproportional control over the government.[2] The political crisis had already intensified by November of that year, when George Papandreou won the election; and then, on 9 December, Karamanlis resigned and left for Paris. The crisis came to a full-blown political disaster when Papandreou, having won the election again in February 1964, followed with his resignation months later in July after coming into open conflict with the Palace. A period followed of political chaos, waves of protests and unsuccessful attempts to put together a viable government by Papandreou's ex-collaborators, the so-called 'traitors'. The turmoil came to a halt on 21 April 1967, when a group of officers, often referred to as 'The Colonels', took control of Greece, establishing a dictatorial regime under the slogan of maintaining a 'Greece of Christian Greeks'. Political normalcy did not return until 1974, the year the dictatorship fell, with Karamanlis returning to Greece and becoming once more head of the government.

The junta lasted seven years, much longer than the 4th of August regime of the 1930s. Its influence on Greek architecture and the environment, both in its destruction and on the retardation of modernization, was severe: the junta years were lost years. Apart from political repression and cultural vulgarity, the colonels' regime was characterized by an unprecedented building boom. It was no accident that Patakos, one of the leaders of the coup, deputy Prime Minister of the military government, used to call Greece 'a construction site' and himself a 'builder's trowel'. Indeed, soon after the *coup d'état*, during the second trimester of 1967, there was such a surge in construction that the junta succeeded in

Yiannis Vikelas, Athens Tower on Vassilissis Sofias and Mesogion Avenues, Ampelokipi, Athens, 1967.

reversing the downward trend that had begun in the middle of 1966. The turn-around resulted from government policies: tax reduction, availability of bank loans, enforcement of 'social tranquility' and last but not least, as in Pinochet's Chile, unreserved acceptance of the 'market economy', a decrease in social welfare programmes and the shrinkage of government regulations constraining private enterprise, the last-mentioned having a direct impact on real-estate development and construction.

In 1968, a year after the military coup, the government passed a new law that allowed a more efficient use of real estate,[3] and took a number of decisions that facilitated tax exemptions and loans, allowing big enterprises to enter the housing market, opening the way for large-scale construction, unprecedented in Greek history. For the first time Greek construction companies emerged as serious enterprises. Tourist and shipping companies invested in tourism building projects. Thus, at the beginning of 1972 the regime proudly announced that the economy had expanded at around 7 per cent; the German newspaper *Die Welt am Sontag* included the leader of the economic policy of the junta, Makarezos, in its global list of top personalities who had contributed considerably to the economic development of their country during 1971. That same year, Greece, a country of chronic unemployment and a mass-exporter of economic migrants, accepted between 20,000 and 30,000 foreign workers.[4]

Inaugural Issue of *Architecture in Greece* (1967).

But the seven junta years were marked by a paucity of new architectural ideas. To a certain degree this was the result of political and ideological repression. Konstantinidis resigned from his position in July 1967 after serving seven years with the Greek National Tourist Organization, leaving the country to teach at the ETH in Zurich, where he was appointed visiting professor, a post he held until 1970. The government interfered in the schools of architecture by firing personnel who did not share its political views.

Equally characteristic of the period was the unprecedented devastation of the physical and cultural environment of the country. The year 1972, a year of spectacular economic growth in Greece, was also the one in which a high level of atmospheric pollution – the *nefos*, as it was known – was officially acknowledged to be pervading Attica. It is therefore incredible that this crisis coincided with the publication of a new architectural periodical, *Architecture in Greece*, the most ambitious and coherent ever seen there, which appeared a week before the coup of 21 April 1967. Its editor, Orestis Doumanis, the ex-editor of the defunct *Architectoniki*, had since 1965 been arguing for two years of the need for a major new architectural publication, a yearbook, to present Greek architecture to the world.[5]

In the Introduction of the first issue, Doumanis made a case about Greece falling behind 'within developing Europe' and 'becoming provincial'. Among the commentators in this first issue, Panos Koulermos pointed out that, due to the existing construction laws and the new General Building Regulation, outside spaces had shrunk, buildings were being constructed around light wells, and the famous light of the region could reach most dwellings only through shafts. Another commentator, Thales Argyropoulos, argued that the city was perceived as merely a collection of objects, abstracted from its real function and environment. The 1968 issue of *Architecture in Greece* followed the formula established by the first one and contained a commentary by the academic Dionysis Zivas on 'The Protection of National Monuments', arguing for a new approach to urbanism, beyond the standard post-Second World War 'urban reconstruction' practice, that would give priority to the preservation of historic sites. The issue also contained a text attempting for the first time to sketch a historical-critical portrait of contemporary Greek architecture. It was written by François Loyer, a young French historian who was at that time living in Greece. On a more theoretical level, in tune with the 'utopian' urban studies carried out at that time in Paris, Takis Zenetos, whose remarkable early buildings featured in chapter Five, focused on the possibility of constructing a new kind of artificial environment driven by 'tele-labour' and 'tele-contacts', what today we would call a vast virtual environment allowing for distance work. Rethinking the idea of New Towns, Zenetos's intention was to employ advanced media technology as a means of establishing a network of equally distributed settlements over a region in order to arrest the decline of small, geographically isolated rural communities.[6] Last but not least the issue included a presentation of the most recent work by Dimitris Pikionis, who would pass away within a year.

Such was the warm reception of *Architecture in Greece* that Doumanis initiated another publication, *Design in Greece* (later retitled *Design and Art in Greece*), focusing on industrial design and art as well as interiors. Doumanis succeeded in promoting his publications internationally and with that he highlighted the work of Greek architects who stood outside the vacuous nationalist ideology or the vulgar materialism of the regime. He also succeeded in securing the collaboration of foreign contributors as well as introducing new ideas. It was a unique achievement at a moment when Greece, thanks to its military regime, had become a pariah within the international intellectual community.

Within this political and economic framework, it is no surprise that, with few exceptions, the architecture of urban apartment houses during this period would boast achievements in terms of quantity rather than quality. Their unprecedented numbers helped the rising numbers of middle-class Greeks acquire homes with more square metres of private space per person than at any time before and for a reasonable price. At the same time, the environmental and social amenities of these apartments were for the most part inferior to homes of previous decades.

The Apartment Building in Benaki Street, central Athens (1972–5), by Dimitris and Suzana Antonakakis and their collective Atelier 66 opposed the mainstream architecture of the junta and the dogmas of the junta itself. The adoption of critical regionalism had direct design implications, allowing for a creative reuse of regional precedents and permitting the architects to redefine the plan of the urban apartment beyond the confines of the *polykatoikia* of the 1930s and 1950s. Thus, instead of a sealed apartment-lobby, the entrance to the Benaki Street building was a paved yard open to the sidewalk. The main stairway was also open, so that which was often a depressing gloomy service space in commercial apartments served as a semi-public area open to the street and the neighbourhood. The bedrooms and work spaces of each apartment were grouped around an open communal living area – a kind of interior courtyard – without sacrificing individual privacy. A great effort was made to accommodate what Pericles Giannopoulos in the 1930s had called the Greek attachment to an 'outdoor way of life'. Each apartment opened to outside spaces enriched with small pockets of greenery. Going beyond the mainstream approach of Greek architects at that time, Dimitris and Suzana Antonakakis ignored the practice of designing apartments by stacking together individual standardized units varied only in terms of room numbers. Instead they 'sculpted' each apartment according to the requirements of each individual family, interlocking them inside an overall urban envelope.

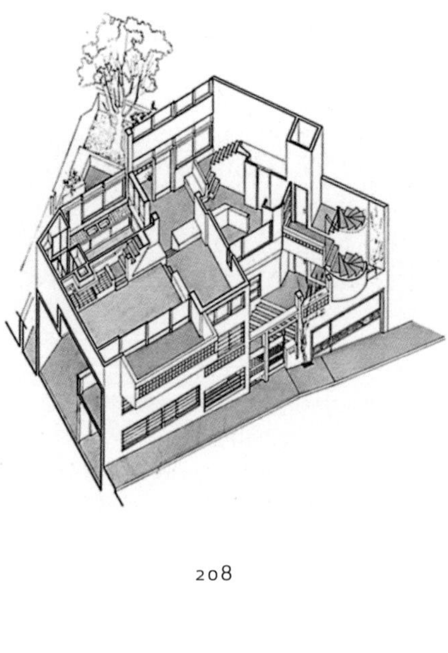

Dimitris and Suzana Antonakakis and Atelier 66, Apartment Building, Benaki Street, Athens, 1972–5.

Dimitris and Suzana Antonakakis, Apartment Building, Benaki Street, Athens, 1972–5.

Indeed, the architects chose the Benaki Street apartment house for their own home. For their interior they provided a double-height space in the heart of the unit whose interior details resembled doorsteps, passages, niches, built-in furniture and other features that one would associate with the outdoor patios of traditional houses. The court analogy redefined the indoor living room, prompting the remembrance of a 'domestic hearth'. In addition, the scheme was also laid out along a 'path', conceived not just as connecting corridor, for it 'carries within its fabric a commentary about architecture, life, and society . . . a petrified stream of passages and places which carry a moral statement. Even when empty, (it has) a voice . . . a protest against the destruction of community . . . the dissolution of human contact'.[7] In its limited dimensions, the path here appears 'as a shorthand version of the vast stream of the Philopappou hill' by Pikionis.[8]

It is remarkable how such a sophisticated scheme was built in Greece during the uninspiring years of the junta. Without doubt the fact that the project was a cooperative helped, having been undertaken by several people who together with the architects contributed their own share of capital and land, and sometimes even labour. Thus the communal and exploratory spirit manifest in the design was shared by the four families that participated in the design process as well as the use of the end product. One might suggest that this inspired original work was a shared

Dimitris and Suzana Antonakakis Archaeological Museum, Chios, 1965–72.

Dimitris and Suzana Antonakakis, Vacation House, Oxylinthos, Evia, 1973–4.

symbolic act of defiance, enabled by architects who were publicly critical of the regime, an act of faith for better days to come.

Situated on the road from Liopesi to Spata in Attica – a privileged location at that time now destroyed by the arrival of the Venizelos airport – the House at Spata (1973), also by the Antonakakises, for a family of three, demonstrates even more expressively the idea of the path applied to the small scale of a domestic organization where 'spaces are linked to each other in a . . . succession fitting into the landscape according to the requirements of the microclimate or the constraints of the site', unfolding around a central courtyard that features an olive tree. Likewise,

Alexandros Tombazis in collaboration with Dimitris Diamantopoulos, Difros Apartment Complex, Chalandri, Athens, 1971–5.

the Antonakakis Vacation House in Oxylinthos, Evia (1973–4), built on a steep slope and overlooking the sea, reuses the way space is organized in regional traditional houses to accommodate outdoor life and to provide indoor and open spaces for work, rest or conversation. At a time when air-conditioning was fast becoming fashionable among Greece's newly affluent class, the Oxylinthos property maintained high standards of environmental comfort through the arrangement of the built volumes and the materials without even being connected to electric power. Its 83 x 83 cm crisscross pattern running parallel to the slope organizes the indoor and outside semi-covered spaces in east–west zones, an arrangement that takes advantage of the course of the prevailing cool summer breezes and views of the sea.[9]

One of the most important developments during the unprecedented construction boom of the period was the decline of the central Athens as the favoured location of well-to-do Greeks and the beginning of an exodus to open areas on the periphery of the capital, primarily the northern suburbs, the traditional district for elite vacationers and weekenders. A similar phenomenon took place in Thessaloniki. The move was a consequence of the economic boom, for commuting and suburban living was more expensive than living downtown. The idea of segregation and escape attracted many affluent people, but new legislation by the junta favouring urban development permitted a higher density of construction in the green suburbs. Taking advantage of this legislation, in particular a short-lived section of the new building code that permitted excessively high towers to be built in Athens,[10] the young architect Alexandros Tombazis, in collaboration with Dimitris Diamantopoulos, designed and built the Difros Apartment Complex in Chalandri (1971–5; developers Alvertis Dimopoulos). Comprised of four towers of different heights interconnected in pairs by a circulation core, the H-shaped plan offered maximum privacy as well as – by means of verandas on three sides for

Giorgos Manetas and Eleni Komili-Maneta, Apartment Building, Palaio Psychico, Athens, 1973–4.

Dimitris and Suzana Antonakakis and Atelier 66, Residential Complex, Distomo, 1969. Housing for employees of the local bauxite mine.

every apartment – degrees of contact with the natural world that even luxury downtown residences could not match. The sculptural intricacy of the complex – influenced by the Japanese Metabolists – seemingly was not the result of a play of forms but of functional objectives, the most important being the variability of the size and layout of individual apartments.

One of the best examples of the efforts to redefine upper-middle-class collective housing in the urban periphery (again by taking advantage of that short-lived section of the building code), is the Apartment Building in Mantzarou Street in Palaio Psychico (1973–4) designed by Giorgos Manetas and Eleni Komili-Maneta. In contrast to the traditional *polykatoikia*, with short vistas and suffocating openings, the Psychico 'complex of houses' (as this kind of scheme was referred to after it became a market prototype and an object of emulation by many architects) has large verandas that work as extensions of equally large living spaces with views of the surrounding trees.

Part of the new trend towards large-scale collective housing was a Residential Complex in Distomo, Boeotia (1969) for the employees of the local bauxite mine, designed by Atelier 66. In relation to the elaborate planning of services and public spaces of Aspra Spitia also in Boeotia by Doxiadis, Distomo was poorer in design. However, the site arrangement of the scheme in relation to the landscape was successful. Moreover, it provided common facilities for social activities, integrating the various groups involved in the enterprise – supervisors, managers and manual workers, and engineers, stressing the community character of the settlement. Although uniform on the outside, internally the units differed in order to accommodate the individual needs and priorities of the inhabitants. The plan was divided into parallel private and public zones, and perpendicular to them were equal-size served and service zones, the latter for pipes and cabling. The uncovered stone facade merged the project pleasingly into the mountainous landscape.

Constantinos A. Doxiadis and Arthouros Scheepers, Apollonion Porto Rafti Vacation Development, Porto Rafti, Attica, 1970–81.

Kleon Krantonellis, Power Distribution Station for the Public Power Corporation of Greece, Athens, 1973–7.

Another first for Greek architecture was a high-density, low-rise housing development in Porto Rafti, the Apollonion Porto Rafti Vacation Development designed by C. Doxiadis and Arthouros Scheepers (1970–81), although ultimately it became a gated community and dormitory town for Athenian commuters and weekenders.

Few public buildings of architectural distinction were built during the junta years. In most cases they expressed a structural functionalist orthodoxy of the previous decade: a building had to manifest the way it was built by exposing its structural elements in a conventional and monotonous manner. Kleon Krantonellis designed an interesting scheme defined by a tight triangular site above the Metro underground line, planned but not constructed until 1973–7, a functional urban solution that accommodated an uncommon facility for a city centre: a power distribution station for the Public Power Corporation of Greece. In addition to the three colossal switchboards that control electricity distribution for the whole of Attica, the building included offices. Giving special attention to the use of materials and proportions, Krantonellis succeeded in creating a city-friendly artefact despite the mechanistic nature of its purpose.

The military government did construct a number of educational facilities including several that were designed and commissioned before its tenure. L. Kalyvitis and G. Leonardos won a competition for the School of Theology, Athens University, in 1965. Eventually built in 1973–6 during the junta period it is a monumental complex organized in parallel volumes that are stepped down a steeply sloping site; these are interspersed with open courtyards connected by corridors, thus on the one hand alluding to ideas about university prototypes developed by Shadrach Woods in the 1960s, and on the other to Eastern Orthodox monasteries.

Similarly, the Music Conservatory of Athens (1969–85) was awarded to I. Despotopoulos after winning the competition for the Athens cultural centre in 1959. Despite his earlier leftist convictions, Despotopoulos decided to work with the regime. Only part of the Conservatory was built, with the result that the central linear structure with a long frontal portico appears odd – a truncated monumental mass – without the two buildings planned to flank it. The oddity is emphasized by the fact that the building was conceived as part of the larger urban composition of his ambitious Athens cultural centre complex, an idea abandoned during the 1990s. The building now resembles an accidentally dropped form lying in the middle of an amorphous site.

Lazaros Kalyvitis and Yorgos Leonardos, School of Theology, University of Athens, Zografou Campus, Athens. Competition won in 1965; project built 1973–6.

Takis Zenetos, Secondary School, Agios Dimitrios, Athens, designed 1969–72 and constructed 1972–4.

Exceptional for its unconventional, open and daring character designed (1969–72) and constructed (1972–4) by Takis Zenetos was the Secondary School in Agios Dimitrios, a working-class district of Athens. Before beginning his design, Zenetos spent six months trying to familiarize himself with recent research on education, especially the areas concerned with information technology and learning. He decided to accept the basic typological school-building norms, such as the relation of classrooms to corridors, and try to create a spatial arrangement capable of accommodating future social and technological changes, such as combining the uses of a circulation core with a community space, a 'panopticon' pattern which, as Mariella Doumani remarked, because of its centralizing character was appreciated by educators, believing that administrative control and collective identity were essential for an ideal teaching facility.[11] Zenetos adopted a freestanding scheme approximating a cylinder that provided exposure to the outside for all classes while minimizing the peripheral surface and maximizing the interior volume of the building.

In order to achieve a building that would be adaptable to other functions, he tried to design spaces of non-specific use that could support a variety of contexts. To organize these spaces into a coherent plan he followed a standard approach adopted by his generation from pre-Second World War ideas: he developed a three-dimensional grid system (one with polar coordinates consistent with the requirement of a central circulation core) that integrated an independent fixed bearing structure – which for reasons of economy and durability he chose to be reinforced concrete – with a flexible system of light–space divisions. Innovative for Greece, it was an example of pragmatic building technology, inexpensive and easy to apply. However, predictably, the light–space divisions proved dysfunctional in terms of soundproofing, an essential requirement for an educational facility. The scheme was conceived to accommodate 1,500 students in its first phase of operation, with the long-term expectation that the number would eventually be halved.

Zenetos was also concerned with the environmental performance of his building, developing a scheme of shading devices that reduced the impact of heat and glare. Paradoxically, despite the fact that the impact of the sun on a building changes during the day and through the year, Zenetos chose to make the devices part of the 'fixed' system of the building, incorporating them with the load-bearing structure and producing them out of reinforced concrete, rather than constructing them out of light materials and making them flexible. For him this was a stepping-stone in a research process, an experiment to be revisited, monitored and re-evaluated.

As far as urbanism was concerned, the junta's record was uneven. It did try to rationalize building regulations by publishing, as already mentioned, a new law in 1968,[12] organizing the land outside the formal boundary of the city proper and developing a long-term regional plan with a fifteen-year perspective. It commissioned Doxiadis Associates to develop the National Regional Plan and a 'Regulatory Plan and Programme for Athens'. The new policies, which continued those of the Karamanlis period, succeeding in decreasing the occupancy density of the capital from 1.5 people per room to 0.94.[13] There was also a new trend that started around 1970: while the population of the capital proper remained stable, that of greater Athens increased. This trend reflected the numbers of people that were moving to the comfortable suburbs as well as those arriving at the underprivileged periphery.

Professor Dionysis Zivas was commissioned to develop a study for the Old Town of Athens, concerning the future of the nineteenth-century area of the city that contained a large number of important neoclassical buildings. With the exception of the above study on the Old Town, the historical centre, the lasting value of these studies has been questionable. They were piecemeal technocratic studies born within a vacuum, suppressing questions about the future of Greece as a society.[14] Apart from the various geopolitical priorities of his regime, Papadopoulos was very eager to be seen as championing a social agenda within which housing played an important role, especially housing for the refugees of 1922, neglected by a succession of governments. In 1972 many Greeks were still so ignorant of the problem that when an American anthropologist, Renée Hirschon, decided to carry out a field study of the refugee settlement of Kokkinia, a district of greater Athens, she was warned by her middle-class Athenian friends, who were concerned about Hirschon's safety in, as they saw it, a notorious area'.[15]

Earlier, in a state of the nation address delivered on 14 December 1968, reported by the Council of Europe,[16] in which Papadopoulos declared democracies to be in the 'midst of chaos and anarchy' and that there was a 'worldwide decline of ideas and values' with the exception of his regime, he also announced his commitment to solve the housing problem of the refugees, who were known for their left wing leanings. He pledged 'to develop prototypal multi-storey settlements with all the needed facilities . . . to provide new prototypes (and initiate) a new drive for housing policies', this in order 'to demonstrate that the problem of antisocial individuals deceived by the communist sirens was not ideological but social'. Those 'individuals' who lived in Tavros (not very far from 'notorious' Kokkinia), Papadopoulos continued, were inhabiting shacks with a density of eight people per room with one outdoor toilet per eight families, which during the winter turned into a swamp 'in the middle of the capital'. 'No wonder communism was on the increase', he concluded.[17] However, just as previous Greek politicians had not, Papadopoulos did not deliver on his promise.

Similarly, despite its absolutist police power, the regime was conspicuously ineffective, continuing the old Greek traditions of disrespect for the building code and indifference to the resulting chaos, urban sprawl and environmental cost. While it is true that the junta issued a directive in 1968 aiming to regulate urban development,[18] and passed legislation in 1973 establishing a new general building code that asked for punitive measures (not severe, but punishment none the less) against those who built without a permit,[19] at the same time it allowed for loopholes that periodically legalized, for a fee, the illegal appropriation of both public and church land and the illegal structures built on them. This guaranteed the perpetuation of the lawlessness of the system, demonstrating the contradictions of the regime, on one hand rigid and dogmatic on the other spineless and opportunistic.

Despite the many manifestations of its limited capacity to manage, by 1973 the dictatorship appeared to have become a government of the long term. Unsurprisingly, many architects, engineers and planners decided to join it, despite the fact that they did not identify completely with its dictatorial politics of violence or its kitsch intellectual world. But just as the predictions affirming the permanence of the Franco regime in Spain turned out to have been made during its final years, fate also had a different scenario in store for the Greek regime.

chapter seven

Modern Architecture Comes of Age

Following the student occupation of the Polytechnic in Athens on 14 November 1973, a series of dramatic events led to the rapid demise and fall of the junta. Three days after the student action began, an alarmed government ordered a military operation. Tearing down the neoclassical gate, tanks rumbled into the Polytechnic grounds, putting an end to the student action, 're-establishing order' as it was officially announced, and reaffirming the regime's permanence. Yet, seven months later the regime collapsed.

On 24 July 1974, Karamanlis flew from Paris back to Athens. He landed at 2 am and by 4 am was Prime Minister. The year the dictatorship fell coincided with the 'Year of European Architectural Heritage' that was declared by the Council of Europe. Architectural heritage, as well as cultural heritage generally, was a subject the junta, despite its patriotic traditionalist claims, had totally ignored, having opted for unsustainable development. The result was the demolition and abandonment of a wealth of time-honoured rural settlements. Dionysis Zivas, who had promoted the conservation of historic buildings during the junta years, welcomed the Council of Europe's declaration in a 1975 issue of *Design in Greece*, which was celebrating its first decade, with the wish that Greece would rise from years of inaction and naive nationalist rhetoric to start caring sincerely about its cultural treasures.

The declaration had an immediate impact on the Greek National Tourist Organization (EOT), overturning its policies. The change of direction received additional support from Konstantinidis, who returned to the Organization as a special advisor, having resigned from his position there and leaving Greece following the *coup d'état*. The EOT acknowledged that its previous policies favouring the construction of large tourist complexes, while financially successful, had been detrimental to the distinctive identity of Greece's architectural and landscape heritage. Examples include the massive Porto Heli hotel at Ermioni (1974–5) by C. S. Papaioannou in collaboration with C. Fines, and the Nafsika Astir Palace Hotel (1976, commissioned during the junta period) in Mikro

Nicos Valsamakis, 'Daidalos' Robinson Club Tourist Complex, Kos, 1988–91.

Prime Minister Karamanlis with ministers survey the capital from the Acropolis, September 1976.

Kavouri from Vourekas, Georgiades & Decavalla. Here the sloping form of the project, the brief claimed, 'transformed a spoiled beach into a garden resort'. Yet though the scheme fitted well into the site's contours, the naturalness of the peninsula was lost forever. The EOT consented that its conventional programmes had to be supplemented by a programme for tourism that involved conservation going beyond the preservation of isolated monuments to include whole complexes. And following precedents in Western Europe, as well as in the Balkans, it was accepted that such a programme had to take into consideration the reuse of these historic complexes.

This new direction in conservation coincided with a new trend – 'history from below',[1] which focused on the way ordinary people worked, lived and died rather than on heroic and diplomatic events. Until 1932 the law protected single buildings constructed up to 1830, while a law of 1950 was extended to include 'works of art and historical monuments' created after 1830 'needing special protection', but it still covered only isolated structures. To counter this, the 1985 General Building Regulation was aimed at promoting the preservation of the urban fabric, requiring architects to carry out special historical, sociological and ethnographic research before submitting a scheme for approval to the authorities. The new law also required that government agencies categorized building complexes according to the kind of preservation required.[2]

As independent practitioners, Alexander and Haris Calligas were pioneers when as early as 1972 they began to study the potential of the transformation of an old settlement in Monemvasia. They appropriated existing structures, including ruins, and conserved, restored and modified spaces to fit new residential uses with contemporary standards of comfort. They marketed the scheme to artists and other people in search of a small-scale place for a weekend, for a season, or even for a permanent home away from home, offering them contact with nature within a culturally enriching environment. While the idea was not especially original methodologically, for Greece it was an innovation, an alternative to the anonymous, mega-facilities of chain hotels.[3] The work met with approval by the Archaeological Services and the EOT, but it was not without problems generated by a bureaucracy insensitive to the efforts of the architects and to the complexity of the situation. Other issues concerned the conflict between the need to modernize the buildings yet preserve a traditional way of life; the desire to help an impoverished local populace; and intrusive Athenian developers and houseowners bent on introducing pseudo-traditional motifs in their efforts to blend new buildings with the surroundings.

Within the EOT, in September 1974, architects V. Bozineki and T. Zervas began transforming abandoned traditional rural settlements of cultural importance into tourist facilities, starting with Oia in Santorini and Koutsounari, a small village in Crete. The latter numbered 120 scattered houses without any central public space, inhabited by just 12 people, just 800 metres from the beach surrounded by olive groves and small patches of cultivated land. Similarly, projects of mixed success were carried out transforming nineteenth-century industrial areas in Attica, such as the Laurio Mining Company into the Laurio Technology Park (1992), the Gazi factory into a cultural centre (discussed below), and in Thessaloniki the reuse of the early twentieth-century Modiano Market and the 'Ladadika' (the former centre of the olive oil trade) into food markets with cafés, bars and taverns. The Allatini flour mill would be turned into the 'Politeia Allatini', a multi-functional complex of residences, shops and offices, by P. Makridis and A. Tombazis. Once the narrow idea of conservation of 'monuments' was broadened, new candidates emerged for preservation and restoration, structures not so much valued for their aesthetic contribution as for their place in Greek collective memory and their socio-sentimental bygone aura. This resulted in owners of many historic buildings appreciating their property as capital rather than as a dead weight, and new work for architects. The kind of buildings chosen for renewal, and the location of these buildings – urban versus countryside – varied. So did the degree of their cultural versus commercial success.

An interesting early example is the renovation by Dimitris Papacharalambous of a complex constructed between 1756 and 1860 on the island of Hydra, a fish- and sponge-processing facility, which was transformed into a hotel (the Bratsera) and mini cultural centre offering a glimpse of a workplace and the life it contained in early industrial Greece. The intervention on important buildings in the centre of Athens fuelled the discussion about renovation and conservation. One case was the 1991 transformation and fusion of the neoclassical Stathatou residence by Ziller with the older part of the Museum of Cycladic Art (1986–95). Another was the transformation of the Orfanides deli and ouzo bar in Athens, a block away from the Parliament and the Ministry of External Affairs, frequented by politicians and the intelligentsia from the first half of the twentieth century and of considerable historical significance, into a jewellery shop. Reusing the bar paraphernalia to display and store jewellery was criticized as an unsuccessful example of preservation. The general interest in conservation also drew attention to more recent buildings, such as the eight refugee apartment buildings on Alexandras Avenue, and stimulated public campaigns that did produce concrete results, clarifying the criteria for conservation, and establishing institutional structures and procedures robust enough to carry out such tasks effectively. Yet in all this there were negative implications: the gradual gentrification of historic centres (a common phenomenon around the world) consisting of renovated traditional buildings, as well as the loss of interest by the EOT in continuing to support new architectural explorations as it had during the 1950s and early '60s – a point raised by Konstantinidis.[4]

Without doubt, the attitude towards preservation in the 1970s and '80s ran in parallel to a broader tendency of the time to critically reevaluate

Nicos Valsamakis, Amalia Hotel, Olympia, Peloponnese, 1977–9.

the contribution of the modern movement and pay special attention to both context and precedent as significant factors in the development of a new approach to design. In extreme cases this tendency revealed itself to be a negative, anti-modern force (an approach taken up by some post-modernists). In other cases, however, it allowed for interesting regionalist innovations, as in Nicos Valsamakis's Amalia Hotel in Nafplion (1980–83). Here the neoclassical precedents both made the project more appropriate to the historic town and helped organize the scheme and adapt it to its specific site. The Amalia conforms to a grid structure and to a tripartite schema, but there are surprises in its spatial deviations and rhythmical inventions, born out of the need to arrange space to accommodate function. The volumes might appear opulent, but due to a tight budget the building materials were inexpensive and prudently applied. The same characteristics are present in Valsamakis's Amalia Hotel Olympia (1977–9) and the 'Daidalos' Robinson Club on the island of Kos (1988–91), an elegant tourist village built on a platform 90 metres above the Aegean panorama. The 268 rooms are grouped into 15 neighbourhoods of two- and three-storey structures, each with a view of the sea. Built to accommodate 1,000 people, Valsamakis made this large project appear familiar and playful by carefully reducing its scale, breaking down its volumes, and twisting its paths as if it were a Mediterranean village. His regionalist stance in this case could be termed traditional picturesque, but it avoids sentimentality in its appreciating the landscape in the same Mediterranean spirit as the poetry of Elytis.

Kostas Nikolaidis and Caroline Edwards, Two Bars, Imerovigli, Santorini, 1994.

Agnes Couvela-Panayotatou, 'House of the Winds', Akrotiri, Santorini, 1993–7.

Similarly, but in a more reductive manner reminiscent of Konstantinidis's Summer House in Eleusis (1938), Kostas Nikolaidis and Caroline Edwards designed a small open-air timber structure for the Two Bars in Imerovigli in Santorini (1994). The Bars are part of an apartment complex at one end of a swimming pool next to a cavernous space sculpted out of Santorini's legendary soft stone. Nikolaidis (who lived and worked on the island between 1979 and 1984), and Edwards (an Australian biologist who joined the practice in 1984) succeeded in turning a tourist facility into a refined environment. The other pools included in the scheme elegantly fit into the sloping site. Equally successful was the way the same architects inserted the new structures of the Colours ('Chromata') Apartment Complex-Hotel in Imerovigli, also on Santorini (1991), within a striking and precious group of ruined Aegean houses, arranging paths, verandas, flat roofs and 'stepped levels in response to the quirks of the terrain' into a continuous entity', a 'succession of interior and exterior spaces'.[5]

Even more grounded to the region, microclimate and the aura of the place is the 'House of the Winds' in Akrotiri, Santorini (1993–7), designed by Agnes Couvela-Panayotatou.[6] A modest holiday house appears like an abandoned ruined fragment of a medieval fortification, the thick, angular stone walls acting as shafts to channel the wind for cooling purposes; it seems to grow from the rocks, a poetic representation of the unique identity of the region: its light and its strong northerly wind. The ground floor has two residential units, with separate entrances. On the upper floor there is an empty open-air space, a kitchen and a large bedroom, a sitting-room during the winter. The materials and methods used for the construction were local: light, easily moulded bricks that offer excellent heat insulation, thick-grained, peach-coloured local sand (pozzolana) for insulation, and concrete slabs also made with local sand. Similarly, the plan of the house is adapted to the local climate and prevailing winds. What is striking at first glance is its location, above the hill of Akrotiri overlooking the village and the Aegean, with the silent volcano in the distance.

Couvela-Panayotatou also designed the In-Situ Museum on Naxos (1992–9), which was one of the first attempts in Greece to set out an archaeological site with artefacts displayed in their original location. The architect created a dialogue between artefacts, many of them 2,500 years old, which she placed at various levels and oriented towards different directions

Agnes Couvela-Panayotatou, In-Situ Museum, Naxos, 1992–9.

Alexandros Tombazis with active solar designer P. Lamaris, 'HELIOS 1', Active Solar Weekend House, Trapeza Aigialeias, Achaia, 1977–9.

in the museum, and the surrounding contemporary churches still in use and the ancient cemetery, current public spaces and past urban tissue.

The identity of a region as a set of unique constraints defining the configuration of a project became the concern also of Alexandros Tombazis. He focused less on the poetic or metaphorical representation of these constraints, preferring to concentrate on their micro-environmental implications. His involvement with environmentally sustainable structures dates back to 1977, when, with civil engineer Socrates Angelides and the solar designer Panayiotis Lamaris, he designed and built together with the structural engineer, HELIOS 1, a wood-frame, brick-clad house in Trapeza Aigialeias, the first house in Greece to be heated by solar energy. The total heated area of 80 sq m was arranged around a courtyard that in the summer was shaded by a plane tree. The different levels of the scheme were adapted to the natural slope of the site, which exploited the view of the Gulf of Corinth to the north, while inclining the roof to accommodate flat-plate solar thermal collectors on the south side, at the same time echoing the slope of the mountains in the background. According to the brief, 'the collectors with a total surface of 25 sq m, on average cover 85 per cent of the annual heating and domestic hot water demands'. An 8-cubic m water-storage tank stores the solar energy for use, mostly on weekends, providing hot water to the under-floor heating system. Back-up heating is provided by electricity on a night rate.

It's worth stressing that this pioneering project was a weekend house. The second home was a fresh trend, indicative of both the new affluence of a considerable part of the population of the country and the need to escape a capital city that was becoming an increasingly unattractive place in which to live. Paradoxically, the energy expended and the pollution created by commuting between primary and secondary homes contributed more environmental damage than the little that was retrieved by running a solar energy-saving home.

There were, however, architects who were polemically opposed to such technological explorations and experiments, and to the modern movement in general, believing as they did that it was driven by material interests and suppressed architecture's emotional and spiritual dimensions. One of the most important representatives of this position was Kyriakos Krokos. In contrast to the regionalism of Valsamakis and Couvela-Panayotatou, his search for precedents and context was driven by a question of ethnic identity; this was made explicit in both his writings and buildings, of

Kyriakos Krokos, Museum of Byzantine Culture, Salonica, 1977–93.

which the most significant and representative work of his brief career is the Byzantine Museum in Thessaloniki (1977–93). This Museum has 3,000 sq m of exhibition space, a library, and a cafeteria organized around a colonnaded courtyard. Here the spaces are lit either from above or through the courtyard itself. The design neither emulates traditional prototypes nor reinvents and recombines precedents. The light foregrounds the surface of the rustic materials, alluding to Byzantine and Roman brick walls by recalling their soft, rough and atmospheric mysteriousnous. Krokos was nostalgic not for traditional architecture's forms, but for their 'true essence'. Like Dimitris and Suzana Antonakakis's work, his scheme is organized along a path, an 'upward course', as he called it. But unlike Antonakakis's buildings, which were driven by the conceptual organization of space, Krokos's project was instead an architecture of 'mood'. The same treatment of materials and light was applied more dramatically, though less sensitively, in his conversion of an apartment building of the 1970s into a museum at the corner of Metaxa and Chiou streets, Athens (1990–95), for the Greek painter Alecos Fassianos.

Other attempts to bring identity and culture into contemporary architecture would often be rather more forced than not (the latter allowing buildings to emerge from the limits and merits of their particular region), for example later work by the Antonakakises. Their Crete Polytechnic in Chania (1982–92) and their Science Building for the University of Crete in Herakleion (1987–94), as well as the modification of Kolonaki Square in Athens – a project with serious functional and contextual problems – all fall into this category. The projects are conceived as 'collages' of themes that make allusions to a Greek 'past', especially a rural past, and a Greek 'place', but without any grounding to their site; thus they lost the crucial critical dimension that was so effective for the success of their earlier work.

Panos Koulermos, whose work in the 1960s in partnership with Kalogeras and Amourgis was discussed earlier, seems to have been driven by similar urges in the conception of the scheme for the Research and Technology Foundation, University Campus, Herakleion (1987–94). Koulermos, however, was a knowledgeable critic and historian of architecture, and this plus his international experience meant he was not going to be influenced by superficial ethnic metaphors. In addition to his remarkable early career in London (he left Greece during the dictatorship), he had been active as a teacher and architect in the USA, associated with the postmodernist movement. For the University Campus, Koulermos created a compact, high-density 'acropolis of knowledge'. In contrast to his visionary, iconoclastic design for the Army Share Fund in Athens in 1966, the white, concrete scheme housing the Institute for Molecular

Panos Koulermos, Research and Technology Foundation, University Campus, Herakleion, Crete, 1987–94.

Biology, Computer Science, and Biotechnology in Herakleion is historicist. Its monumental character, the ordered composition of the volumes and fenestration, and the use of the 75-m-long stoa were inspired by the nearby Minoan palace of Knossos, and it also borrowed from 1930s Italian Rationalism as well as from Louis Kahn's Salk Institute in California.

Less sculptural, less monumental and less preoccupied with references to heroic precedents than the projects by Krokos and Koulermos is the scheme (2001–5) of the Benaki Museum, Pireos Branch. Located in the heart of the old industrial area of Athens near Gazi, this temporary exhibition space of 8,500 sq m, is an addition and modification of an existing late 1960s building, and relates well both to the sites's industrial past and to its immediate neighbourhood. Designed by Maria Kokkinou and Andreas Kourkoulas,[7] it includes exhibition halls, an auditorium, an architectural archive, administration facilities, bookshop, restaurant,

opposite and above: Maria Kokkinou and Andreas Kourkoulas, Benaki Museum, Pireos Branch, 2001–5.

store-rooms and parking facilities. According to the official description of the project, the intention of the architects was 'to create an enclosed building' like 'a treasure chest', occupying a whole urban block. Its centre is an open atrium, intended to orientate the visitors, while the outside's red Iranian travertine-clad walls are 'closed, monolithic, vertical and smooth with few horizontal necessary openings', serving as 'a boundary'; the walls of the atrium consist of 'big wooden louvre panels, which cover three of the four facades of the atrium, act as diaphragms of light'; they 'and the glass walls', allowed visitors 'to follow the happenings in the atrium, attributing to the space a theatrical dimension'.[8]

The mood of the building is tough and cool (echoing ideas developed by Elias Zenghelis, with whom the architects' had worked in the early 1980s), but, as with many examples of this type of 'industrial chic' cultural buildings, in the end the hard reality of old industrial warehouses or mechanical workshops is refined, gentrified. While anchored to the site's local context, the atmosphere of the project is globalist. As the project description states, the 'movement' of the visitor 'is organized on a large axis, which starts from the entrance gallery, through the atrium', and 'the gaze is directed towards the big screen of metal mesh, which is the fourth facade of the atrium', leaving behind the memory of the place where the new structure was born. Part of the scheme refers dramatically to the planetary universe, the 'south orientation of the mesh reflecting the sun and making it look like falling water', but not to the past or present human condition of the neighbourhood. And, following the narcissistic norms of current global museum design, 'at night, when the lights are on, visitors moving on the ramp behind the metal mesh, which is the main path connecting the exhibition halls, become the main exhibit of the museum'; thus the status of the exhibited cultural objects is reassigned to one of benign neglect.

Sharing a similar tendency towards minimalism is the 5,500 sq m New Administrative Building ASPIS Bank, Athens, (2003–5, construction 2005–8) designed by Dimitris Papaioannou, located next to Gropius's U.S. Embassy, and the well-designed neoclassical Aegineteion and Areteeion hospitals by A. Metaxas. Constructing a bank next to the Metro line was an additional technical challenge.

Serenity and simplicity also characterize the school buildings designed by Christos Deligiannis, qualities achieved through the most elementary material means. Like Mitsakis in the 1920s and Konstantinidis in the 1950s, Deligiannis worked for the Greek government, and like them he was able to produce a series of remarkable projects, which he saw serving the public interest in offering a sense of hope and dignity. 'Today, in Greece', he wrote, 'whether we live in the centre or the periphery, we all live in an incoherent environment . . . profit-seeking, political indifference and degradation is our reality'.[9] Architecture can stand apart from this environment, he argued; the architect has to try to rediscover order and to educate. His school in Athens is an example of the same commitment. The six classrooms and auxiliary teaching areas were placed in an awkwardly shaped inclining site in Exarcheia, a densely built area in the centre of Athens, not far from Panayiotakos's Blue apartment building of

Christos Deligiannis, Fifth Gymnasium in Haidari, Attica, 1997–9.

Christos Deligiannis, Twelfth Kindergarten School, Piraeus, 2002–03.

the 1930s. Deligiannis faced the constraints posed by a highly restrictive building code and environmental requirements as a challenge that invited a creative and rigorous new scheme. His design is characterized by two entrances to allow for the difference between rear and front levels, a free zone surrounding the building and a specially designed external wall screening the children from the gaze of anonymous passers-by while allowing views out from within for the children and staff. As with the Fifth Gymnasium in Haidari, Attica, the organization of spaces is purist: white volumes are used for the massing of the building. Deligiannis continued the purist principles for the Twelfth Kindergarten, Piraeus, fitting – in a very small lot – two multi-functional classrooms. Following his larger-scale buildings, outdoor spaces were provided for learning, play and social interaction. As in his other schools, the building is enriched by works of art by the artists Nikos Alexiou, Lida Manthouli-Goritsa and Danae Stratou.

The architecture of Rena Sakellaridou and Morpho Papanikolaou also gradually shifted from monumental expression in buildings of public or institutional character to more sensitive approaches related to site and context, achieving rich effects through the calculated manipulation of apparently simple means. One could refer to the redesign of the Nafsika Astir Palace Hotel entrance mentioned earlier.

DECA Architecture, Earthworks, Four houses, Antiparos, 2005–8.

A striking example of the turn to purism and rigour was the short-lived Aphrodite outdoor cinema, Athens (1998–9), designed by Aris Zambikos and his collaborator Ismini Panayiotarou. Built on the site of a pre-existing cinema, the new, light functionalist structure was able to be transformed into an indoor winter cinema by enclosing part of the seating area of the theatre to make a restaurant, bar and exhibition space. Similar qualities characterize a three-storey office building on the Athens–Corinth National Highway designed by Kalliopi Kontozoglou. Also restrained in terms of their volumes and profile were the Earthworks, four houses on the island of Antiparos (2005–8) by DECA Architecture.[10] Design rigour characterizes the finally crafted residence (1994–9) in Psychico by Zoe Samourka, which includes many of the features found in the work of young architects in Greece today.

In pursuit of an architecture shaped by the need to minimize consumption of rare resources in harmony with the microclimatic constraints of the region, Alexandros Tombazis & Associates have created a number of inventive and technically high-quality complexes over the last twenty years. Situated in the centre of Athens, on the east side of Lycabettus, the headquarters of Avax S.A. (1992–8), a major Greek contracting company, provides a comfortable microclimate for the staff by employing a bioclimatic design: a steel frame with waffle-type reinforced concrete slabs and a raised false floor has a facade of silkscreen-printed glass panels, blinds that rotate automatically in response to sunlight, ceiling fans, lighting control systems, an ice bank in the basement for the production of off-peak electricity, and management systems controlling ventilation, shade, lighting and the back-up A/C system minimizing energy consumption.[11]

Equally successful is the Office Building Complex, at Polydrosso, Athens (1990–95), which consists of three adjoining buildings, one of which houses the offices of A. N. Tombazis & Associates.[12] The complex is organized around a central entrance courtyard that includes olive trees and a sculpture by the Greek artist G. Zongolopoulos. The Tombazis & Associates building provides 1,100 sq m of office space. The occupants designed the whole interior, including the furniture. One building is long and narrow (approximately 35 x 8 m) with a work-space adequately daylit by the side windows and by light reflected from fabric panels below the skylights of the roof. Exterior vertical electric-motor awnings provide shade. Cross-ventilation and occasionally automatically controlled ceiling fans offer ventilation and cooling, while a central BMS system records and controls energy consumption. The project also collects and channels rainwater for irrigation and toilet-flushing.

The bright blue-and-silver metal panel-clad office and retail building at Syngrou Avenue, Athens, designed (1997–9) by Tombazis, is a 63,000 m^3

Alexandros T ombazis, 'Avax' S.A. Headquarters, Athens, 1992–8.

Alexandros Tombazis, Office Building Complex, Polydrosso, Attica, 1990–95.

Alexandros Tombazis, Office and Retail Building, Syngrou Avenue, Athens, 1997–9.

facility, with natural lighting and ventilation being the primary determinates of the scheme.[13] Between the two buildings a semi-open public space is shaded by a metal superstructure providing protection from sunlight and overheating to the taller, northerly volume. Careful shading by projecting metal structures has been foreseen wherever necessary. The morphology of the building is further characterized by the exterior metal staircases.

This short overview of recent buildings shows that with very few exceptions Greek architecture has been an architecture running at two speeds, one improving the quality of selected buildings, the other leading to delays in improving the overall environment. For some this at times chaotic development is seen as a source of excitement. Other critics, however, see this inconsistency as the result of a deep structural deficiency in the Greek state. But aside from individual buildings, two major urban projects have transformed the capital, the Unification of the Archaeological Sites of Athens and the Athens Metro, the latter planned to serve 85 per cent of Attica with 200 stations.

The new Metro is a crowd-mover that occasionally also functions as a memory machine. In addition to a subway system, the project is the largest archaeological excavation ever undertaken beneath a modern city. While no one was surprised that the project unearthed so many ancient finds – settlements in the area date as far back as 3,000 BC – the confrontation between the antique and modern worlds added many unforeseen challenges to what was already the country's most ambitious public works project.

Athens was one of the earliest cities in Europe to develop an urban rail transportation system, but failed to enlarge it adequately to keep pace with a growing population. Neither the 1970s ills of traffic congestion nor the serious pollution that, as well as people and plant life, so threatened antique artefacts that they had to be removed and replaced with copies were sufficient to move the authorities to expand the Metro. Eventually, it was a bid for the 2004 Athens Olympics that obliged the government to modernize its public transportation network and in 1987 to make Metro expansion the city's priority. Construction began in 1991, the European Union subsidizing 50 per cent of the work, with the American firm Bechtel as the contractor. Alleviating congestion and pollution were primary goals of the planners and the politicians, but it was soon realized that, as in the case of the Mexico City Metro, they would have to go hand in hand with preservation of the city's heritage. Thus, along with the imported engineers, planners and consultants came foreign archaeologists and historians to advise, employing knowledge of the texts of Herodotus combined with ground-penetrating radar (GPR), scanning and satellite photography to locate hidden objects. Despite occasional disruptions, the multi-disciplinary team proved to be a great success.

The dig yielded invaluable information about everyday life in Athens and about particular events, such as the fifth-century plague. This led to a new challenge: how was this new archaeological wealth to be displayed without removing it too far from the original sites of discovery. An important decision was taken to design stations that would double as galleries for antiquities and for contemporary art. In the Syntagma and Evangelismos stations for example, ruins of the ancient aqueduct, the sewage system, a cemetery and antique workshops are displayed next to recently commissioned works by modern Greek artists.

The Metro incorporates visual elements that enhance collective memory but, by and large, the new stations are architecturally undistinguished, both above and below ground. Given city planners' ambitions to use the Metro to improve city life, it's surprising that the construction of new

Syntagma Station, Attiko Metro (design 1987, construction began 1991).

stations was not accompanied by the creation of new street-level public places, plazas or services. Apart from simple signs, nothing of structural or symbolic significance indicates the presence of the Metro's stations. The entrances and interiors of the new stations are neutral and without the poetic atmosphere of the turn-of-the-century stations at Theseion and Monastiraki. However, the Minister of Environment, Physical Planning and Public Works, Costas Laliotis, decided to specify only 'monumental and chic' materials, mostly marble and granite. The idea was that the luxuriousness of the materials would discourage vandalism; and indeed the Metro has remained remarkably clean and calm in contrast to the litter-strewn public spaces in Athens. Perhaps the absence of any commercial activity integrated within its stations serves the deeper need of providing a serene haven from the hyperactivity above. The system was planned to eventually cover 161 miles, serving 92 stations.[14]

The second most interesting contemporary Greek urban project is the Integration of the Archaeological Sites of Athens. A joint programme by the Ministry of Culture and the Ministry for Environment, Physical Planning and Public Works,[15] together with the new Metro it was the most successful and the largest urban project undertaken since the end of the Second World War. The idea of establishing a cultural-historical area in the centre of Athens dates back to the first urban planning attempts for the modern city, in the nineteenth century. Kleanthes, Schaubert and more explicitly Kaftanzoglou had envisioned a path-park meandering through the ruins of Athens to serve as an outdoor museum, school and informal meeting place. Subsequently, many Greek governments, many administrations, and many architects and scholars, including Hébrard, continued to promote the idea or initiate sympathetic projects. Finally, the idea became a concrete plan. The Grand Promenade included the restoration of heritage buildings, the elimination of billboards, enforcing the character of traditional neighbourhoods (Theseion, Psyrri, Metaxourgeion, Plaka), pavement restoration, enhancement of green spaces, street furniture, service facilities, and making the archaeological sites accessible to pedestrians. It linked the Olympeion, Acropolis, Philopappou Hill, the Ancient and the Roman Agoras, the Library of Hadrian, Theseion, Keramikos, and ended at Gazi (the gasworks in operation until 1984, thereafter the property of the city of Athens). The Gazi buildings and site were renovated under the coordination of Alkis Prepis, transforming them into an industrial museum, cultural and social centre under the name Technopolis, with the restored buildings named after major Greek poets, including Cavafy, Sikelianos, Ritsos and Palamas.

The flight to the suburbs that began during the junta, suburbs enabled by the new building codes and the economic initiatives of the regime, continued and even intensified after the return to political normalcy. Some new upper-income apartment buildings were attempts to minimize the negative impact apartment buildings had made on the city fabric. One building of 1977–80 in the northern suburb of Polydrosso, by Dimitris Biris and Tasos Biris in collaboration with Maria Kafritsa, was a serious attempt to rethink collective housing in Greece.[16] A major concern of the

Dimitris Biris and Tasos Biris in collaboration with Maria Kafritsa, Apartment Building, Polydrosso, Attica, 1977–80.

architects was no longer technical effectiveness and economic efficiency (typical priorities of the early 1930s), but the alienating effects of collective housing as applied in Greece after the Second World War. The project consisted of six one-storey apartments and nine duplexes. In order to create a neighbourhood setting, the architects organized the apartments into residential cubes that develop vertically rather than horizontally. The aim was to define a new dynamic of privacy and community. They were mostly concerned with the educational role the built environment could play in making young children understand the potentials and limits of human cohabitation and collaboration. The volumes of the housing units were organized within a strict grid, their relative position within this spatial system varying considerably by staggering the units within the building envelope, offering a variety of air circulation and lighting, and of interactions and social experiences. Interestingly, the architects remarked that in developing this open scheme of habitation within a network of homes they foresaw new and developing contacts and friendships but also conflicts, which they believed were healthy experiences in the learning process of cohabitation. The architects developed a three-dimensional grid space-structure that permitted the interpretation of the environment in many ways, introducing sunshades, flowerpots and bird-cages, even accommodating clothes-drying frames. As the architects notes, all this is a lot more than a simple play of volumes. It is a 'spatial mechanism', interplay between the individual and the collective whole.[17]

The 360-degree, four-storey apartment building by TRAC in Patras (2007) is a complex of 30 units located at the border of the city by the sea. TRAC is a diverse group, founded in 2005 in Patras by Dimitris, Nicholas and Takis Travasaros but with affiliated offices in Athens under the name Divercity. In their Patras project they sought to acknowledge the relation of the project to the sea and the urban background. The quality of the surfaces and the spatial orderliness makes the building stand apart from the characteristically grimy look of the Greek townscape.

As for the compact *polykatoikia* in the centre of Athens, it appears that there were not many new ideas about by the end of the 1970s. In a short article in *I Kathimerini*,[18] Panos Dragonas, like many Greek architects fascinated with the 'unexpected success' of the Athenian apartment 'meeting the needs of post-war Greek society' – its 'small scale, focus on function, and direct relation to street life' – made the point that 'today's needs are very different', and that the average apartment was unable to 'be adapted to bioclimatic design and [was] dependent on air conditioners'. He concluded that 'a radical reappraisal is needed', and that examples of a new direction had already appeared in 'some privileged suburbs'. His apartment building on Vassilios Georgiou and Spyrou Mercouri streets, designed in

Dimitris, Nicholas and Takis Travassaros (TRAC), 360 Apartment Building, Patras, 2007.

collaboration with Varvara Christopoulou, is an unusual, congenial volume of seven residential units rising amidst of the chaotic archipelago of apartments in Athens. The lowest part, which extends the full length of the plot, is occupied by a women's gym that offers a view of the street for its users. The middle part has an idiosyncratic meandering appearance generated by arbitrary joins in the frame of the apartment balconies to form a pattern. The summit of the building is designed to offer 'spectacular views of the city'. Dragonas believes that 'the spirit of place has more to do with the urban landscape, which we need to understand and interpret' without

Panos Dragonas and Varvara Christopoulou, Apartment Building, Pangrati, Athens, 1999–2002.

Dimitris Tsakalakis, Double Residential units in the old part of Sitia, Crete, 1987–94.

excluding the international 'spirit of the times' and globalism. However, the interesting configuration of his '*polykatoikia*' above all is an elegant play of solids and voids that takes no notice of the spirit of place, a very vague term but minimally defined as having to do with attributes such as height, silhouette, relation between open and built spaces as well as life style, attributes ignored by Dragonas's building, whatever its other merits. Quite the opposite can be seen in the approach of Dimitris Tsakalakis. In the prismatic volume of his double-unit residential project in the old part of Sitia, Crete (1987–94), in a tight 4 x 16 m site with narrow dead-end side street, he took advantage of the open and closed surrounding spaces, skilfully allocating the open courtyard, vertical circulation and the building's balconies. Neither project, however, offers what Dragonas demanded: 'a radical reappraisal' of urban collective living combining the spirit of place with the spirit of the times.

Without doubt the *polykatoikia*, as an architectural-economic solution enabled by means of legislation by the Greek state, satisfied the need for housing a large part of the population within the economic and technological constraints that followed each world war and the Civil War. Mushrooming in Athens, Thessaloniki and other towns it offered flexibility within the framework of highly informal, small-scale private development rather than large-scale governmental planning. The outcome attracted the admiration and praise of local as well as foreign architectural critics, who compared the emerging disorganized and vibrant urban environment of the Greek capital to the well-ordered but gloomy welfare state-planned estates and settlements in other countries. In an interview in 1985, Guy Burgel, a French academic, enthused: 'When I gaze at Athens from the top

Residential and commercial building block, Kolonaki, Athens, 2008, drawing from survey by Alcestis Rodi.

of Lycabettus . . . I see a sea of *polykatoikies* and I know that behind each one stands a single transaction. I find this amazing'. He contrasted it with La Défense in Paris.[19] However, a quarter of a century later the situation was perceived differently both by Greeks and foreigners. The whole legal / economic framework that had produced the *polykatoikia* became suspect, and the *polykatoikia* itself began to be doubted as a good building type, disparaged as an incomplete and non-sustainable solution.[20] Most occupants of urban apartments tolerate them because they own a second home in the countryside. No wonder that Athens empties out during weekends and holidays, with all the negative economic and ecological consequences that this entails.

A new generation of middle- and even high-income Greeks has become nostalgic of urban life in the centre of the city with its social and service amenities, minimizing daily commuting or weekend trips to the country. The problem then is how can the decline of the city centre be turned around so as to offer an environment that in terms of amenities is as good as the suburbs? Is a truly new type of urban collective residential structure required? Though large-scale interventions that renew and modify existing apartment units and increase access to open spaces might be imagined, the reality remains to be seen. The economic crisis of 2008 onwards has

opposite and above: Georgia Daskalaki and Yiannis Papadopoulos, consultant Tasos Biris. Residential and Commercial Complex, Metaxourgeion, Athens, 2007–9.

brought much construction to a halt. There have been, however, modest attempts to design new kinds of urban collective, helping to generate a counter-movement back to the city. One example in Athens is a residential and commercial complex at Metaxourgeion (2007–9), commissioned following a competition required by the developers and the architectural review *Domés* by Georgia Daskalaki and Yiannis Papadopoulos, with Tasos Biris as key consultant. The scheme consists of a 'cellular formation' of residential duplexes arranged in a 'lego' manner, providing a more airy environment than the traditional residential building blocks of the downtown city. It also provides a sense of community in its public, plaza-like atrium. The fabric of the building recalls the industrial buildings of the area, using industrial materials and rugged exposed surfaces. What is especially interesting about the project is that it develops further the ideas to be found in their embryonic stage in the apartment buildings designed by D. and S. Antonakakis on Benaki Street and by the Biris brothers in Polydrosso.

chapter eight

Whither Young Architect?

Over the last decade in Greece there has been an unparalleled improvement in construction techniques, including the lavishness of spatial arrangements and the quality of interior details. But these accomplishments are characterized by an overridingly unadventurous, if not conservative, spirit favouring 'minimalist' prismatic volumes, 'clean' rectilinear plans, a simple palette of colours, matters that are also applied in works in France, Switzerland and the Netherlands. The search for identity seems to be lacking, as is identifying the uniqueness of each problem and the correct resources with which to solve it (features of the contemporary regionalist spirit found in earlier decades in the work of Pikionis and Konstantinidis, to give two examples). There also seems to be a lack regarding the spirit of invention that was so typical of Zenetos and his contemporaries of the 1950s and 1960s. Moreover, we find few projects that engage with new situations, such as the homeless, the poor, immigrants and refugees, today making up at least 10 per cent of Greece's population. A rare exception was Twenty Four Houses by Olivia Karagianni, Olympia Hatzopoulou and Myrto Chronaki (1998–2000). These 'shells' were conceived to accommodate Roma while respecting their way of life, requiring minimum maintenance and servicing costs, using sustainable, easily demountable, materials, and with the flexibility to accommodate multiple arrangements.

The works discussed in chapter Seven use modernist forms, their designers diligently in agreement with the works by so-called 'starchitects'. But their contribution to the development of a more specifically *Greek* modern architecture and to the modernization of Greece seems to have been limited. Without doubt, the conventionality of current Greek architects is the result of the conformism of their clients, whether in the public or private domain. Like the generation of clients that commissioned the cornucopia of projects from Ziller at the end of the nineteenth century, the clients of the early twenty-first century – despite bursts of conspicuous consumption expressed without any embarrassment – appear pragmatic, with a bias towards the familiar rather than the extraordinary, the sensible

Olivia Karagianni, Olympia Hatzopoulou and Myrto Chronaki. Bio-climatic Unit from Twenty-four Houses to accommodate Roma, Menemeni, Salonica, 1998–2000.

rather than the extravagant, as demonstrated in numerous private homes, apartments and school buildings.

Even the numerous well-designed projects spread over the country tend to be drowned out by the mass of buildings produced by such companies as BVIC. Founded in 1974 during the construction boom of the junta period, BVIC, headed by Babis Vovos, grew to become the leading development enterprise in Greece. Its clients have been major multinational corporations (Coca-Cola, Sun Microsystems, Microsoft, Siemens, as well as the Greek state), and its offices (more than 30 major buildings), commercial centres and tourist facilities among the most important in Greece. Yiannis Vikelas has been the designer of many of the buildings (for example, the Atrina Centre, 1980; the Galleria Shopping Centre, 1980–83; the Agora, 1987; POLIS, 1995; and the Monumental Plaza, 1999). The scale of these operations was without precedent in Greece, and the sheer physical presence of his buildings is overpowering, given their mass, central location and to some degree their aggressive unsuitability for the region – often with highly reflective exteriors and an overwhelming disregard for site conditions. Beyond size what made the firm unique was its total package of services ranging from real estate development, financing, architecture, construction, supervision, as well as interior design, running the services of the facility, and acting as a landlord, owning and renting out parts of the complexes. Occasionally, this centralization of controls and power has led to architectural innovations, as was the case of John Portman with his mega-atrium hotels; but this is not the case with Vovos and his collaborators.

Neither the culturally interesting buildings nor the commercially successful ones discussed earlier add up to what we might call environmental happiness. Instead, they have consumed a disproportional amount of the available spatial, economic and ecological resources that could have been allocated to public and environmental domains, as has happened with most Western European countries. The figures describing the levels of social and environmental quality in Greece, especially Athens, are grim indeed. A study carried out by the Economist Intelligence Unit in cooperation with Siemens, and presented during the UN Climate Change Conference in Copenhagen in 2009, compared the environmental quality of 30 major cities in 30 European countries, using data drawn from official sources – categories including consumption of water and energy per capita, air quality, efficiency standards for buildings, waste and land use, use of public transportation, and environmental governance. Athens ranked 22nd in the European Green City Index, with Copenhagen 1st and Kiev 30th.[1]

Additional contributions to this poor performance were the chaotic scattering of buildings, a substantial number of which were illegal. After the fall of the junta, following its spectacular failure to develop the urban and rural environment of the country, relying instead on the initiatives of the market, the new Constitution of 1975 established that the protection of the environment was an obligation of the state, the only agent controlling urban growth, requiring the creation of a rational spatial plan on the regional and urban level. The plan, however, was not respected: land speculation and illegal construction continued to be major determinants of the built environment. In 1977 new legislation deprived illegal structures of the right to be connected to the national electricity grid, and introduced other severe penalties, such as the confiscation of equipment that was used in illegal construction. The measures had no effect.[2]

In a speech of 11 January 2008, Stefanos Manos, under-secretary of Public Works (1977–80) and subsequently minister of Planning, Housing, and the Environment (1992–3), credited with founding the first pedestrian streets in Athens, pointed out that illegal construction, initially carried out by the underprivileged as a means of obtaining basic shelter, by the 1980s was simply facilitating the wealthy to obtain a second home (2,000 illegal high-quality buildings were constructed in the Hymettus area alone). In the same speech Manos discussed his failed efforts to reduce the permissible density footprint[3] and to control the growth of Athens through rigorous legislation, obliging landowners and speculators to participate in the cost of development by contributing to the infrastructure and the provision of public and green spaces. His efforts were interpreted as collectivization by the members of his own conservative party, and he was soon replaced by Georgios Plytas, who froze the application of the law in 1980. Several of the policies set forth by S. Manos were resurrected by Antonis Tritsis, Plytas's successor. Tritsis (an ex-student of Ludwig Hilberseimer at IIT and a supporter of sustainable planning) had a new law on city and regional planning passed,[4] which introduced new tools and procedures and optimistically provided for the integrated design of the entire territory and suppression of illegal building activity. In less than four years in the post he was, like Manos, replaced.

The socialist opposition headed by George Papandreou, grandson of the minister of education under whom the pioneering schools of the early 1930s were built, questioned the little time the law permitted for consultation, evaluation and discussion between its presentation and adoption as well as the competence of the government to implement such a programme in the context of overwhelming corruption, which according to a timely special report published in July 2009 by the Greek General Inspector of Public Administration, was rooted to a great extent within the urban planning offices of the country. Soon after, on 4 October 2009, elections took place in Greece, with the conservative party suffering its worst electoral defeat ever, the outcome to a great extent the result of public disgust with corruption.

Following the landslide victory of the socialists, on 6 October 2009 George Papandreou was sworn in as Prime Minister of Greece. One of his first initiatives was to invite the Barcelona architect Josep Acebillo, one of the top planners of the city, to visit sites where environmental failure was coupled with the potential for an urban and ecological renaissance. In his statement to the press Papandreou argued that there was huge potential that remained untapped and which could be used to give local residents and the Greek people 'self-evident rights' towards a good environment.

The need for a good environment is more urgent than ever before but it will not come about by just adding piecemeal individual buildings, even if these are good buildings. However, the kind of holistic construction that involves the much-needed major interventions is more difficult than at any time in the past, not only because the complexity of the problem increases the accumulation of errors and omissions, but because of the current world crisis that makes resources more expensive, and also because of the diminishing potential of Greece to bring it about – financial, moral and intellectual. This becomes clear when reading the 10 December 2009 issue of the newspaper *Estia*, noting that Greece broke three records almost at the same time: it was recognized as the most corrupt European nation (a view the majority of Greeks shared); it had the lowest debt ratio within the 16-member Eurozone, which according to Fitch Rating was the worst in the Eurozone (a statistic further borne out in 2010 and 2011 with the ongoing economic crisis), as well as the worse environmental qualities among Western European countries. The 2007 Mercer Survey of Worldwide Quality of Living placed Athens 25th in the European Union and 138th worldwide. On 20 December 2009, the *Times* reported that 'after the bonanza of European Union development aid and the euphoria of hosting the Olympics' responsible for the 'sumptuous villas (that) have sprouted around Athens on altogether more lavish government spoils . . . Greeks are shocked to realize that their gravy train has rolled off the tracks'.[5] Perhaps even more serious was the announcement that according to EurLIFE the participation of Greece in life-long learning activities – a prerequisite to change and modernization – was the lowest in the EU.

'Whither young architect?' was Saporta's rhetorical question at the Athens opening of the IV Congress of CIAM in 1933. It is doubtful that accepting with 'unconditional realism the architecture of Athens', its illegal housing, unfinished construction works, abandoned sites, TV aerials, as an expression of 'third world dynamism', 'a laboratory of our time' (an idea actually celebrated by the Greek participation in the 2002

Venice Biennale of Architecture in Venice, with the support of the Ministry of Culture and Union of Architects), can offer a viable direction for the future of urban and rural Greece.[6] Nor can 'starchitects' or celebrity projects bring about a solution, as the Greek press has occasionally suggested. The point was clearly put by Josep Acebillo during his October 2009 visit to Greece: after stressing the global nature of the environmental crisis and the global potentials of technology and architectural expertise to overcome it, he remarked that each region requires its own special solutions and that the solutions for Greece depended on the Greeks themselves, who have a deeper knowledge of their country.[7]

The well known economic – and moral – crisis that erupted 'unexpectedly' at the beginning of 2010, the most serious crisis since 1857 and 1893 in the history of modern Greece, risks forcing the problem of development into secondary importance. Yet, while history has shown that the current economic crisis in Greece has its precedents that were to a great extent reversible, the history of Greek modern architecture shows that the current environmental, cultural, social and physical predicaments are unprecedented and may be irreversible.

References

Introduction

1 Leo von Klenze, 'Memorabilien', II (1838), pp. 64–5, quoted in Αλέξανδρος Παπαγεωργίου-Βενετάς, *Ο Leo von Klenze στην Ελλάδα* (Athens, 2000), pp. 107–8. Klenze's 'Memorabilien', kept in the Bavarian Library of Munich, is rich in architectural, cultural and political observation. Venetas has made an excellent selection and translation in Greek of parts that refer to Greece.

2 'Ελλη Σκοπετέα, *Το 'Πρότυπο Βασίλειο' και η Μεγάλη Ιδέα: όψεις του εθνικού προβλήματος στην Ελλάδα 1830–1880* (Athens, 1988), pp. 21–49.

3 Sia Anagnostopoulou, '"Tyranny" and "Despotism" as National and Historical Terms in Greek Historiography', in *Clio in the Balkans: The Politics of History Education*, ed. Christina Koulouri (Thessaloniki, 2002), pp. 81–90.

4 Κατερίνα Μυστακίδου, *Η Μεγάλη Ιδέα στον Τύπο του Γένους: Ο Τύπος στην Ελλάδα και στην οθωμανική αυτοκρατορία 1800–1923* (Athens, 2004), p. 35.

5 A term borrowed from Benedict Anderson, *Imagined Communities* (London, 1983). See Paschalis Kitromilidis, '"Imagined Communities" and the Origins of the National Question in the Balkans', *European History Quarterly*, XIX/2 (1989), pp. 149–92, and *Modern Greece: Nationalism and Nationality*, ed. Martin Blinkhorn and Thanos Veremis (Athens, 1990).

6 Anagnostopoulou, '"Tyranny" and "Despotism" as National and Historical Terms', pp. 81–90.

7 Richard Clogg, ed., *Minorities in Greece* (London, 2002).

8 As noted by Anastasios Orlandos in Αναστάσιος Ορλάνδος, 'Αι ημέραι του συνεδρίου εν Ελλάδι', *Τεχνικά Χρονικά*, 44–46 (1933), p. 1002.

9 'Ελλη Σκοπετέα, *Το «Πρότυπο Βασίλειο» και η Μεγάλη Ιδέα.'Οψεις του εθνικού προβλήματος στην Ελλάδα 1830–1880* (Athens, 1988), p. 199.

chapter one: Architecture of Revolution

1 Kapodistrias is also known as Conte Capo d'Istria (1776–1831). See also Christopher Montague Woodhouse, *Capodistria: The Founder of Greek Independence, 1821–1829* (London, 1973).

2 Ιωάννης Καποδίστριας, *Κείμενα*, ed. Κώστας Δαφνής (Athens, 1976).

3 Μάρω Καρδαμίτση -Αδάμη, 'Οι πρώτοι Έλληνες Μηχανικοί', *Τεχνικά Χρονικά*, 4 (October–December 1988), pp. 63–8.

4 Όλγα Μπαδήμα-Φουντουλάκη, *Κλεάνθης 1802–1863* (Athens, 2001); Αλέξανδρος Παπαγεωργίου-Βενετάς, *Εδουάρδος Σάουμπερτ 1804–1860* (Athens, 1999).

5 Μάρω Καρδαμίτση-Αδάμη, 'Οι πρώτοι Έλληνες Μηχανικοί', *Τεχνικά Χρονικά*, 4 (October– December 1988), pp. 63–8; Anne Marie Claire Godlewska, *Geography Unbound: French Geographic Science from Cassini to Humboldt* (Chicago, 1999). See also *Το Έργο της Γαλλικής Επιστημονικής Αποστολής του Μοριά, 1829–1838, Α' Μέρος, Τμήμα Φυσικών Επιστημών, επιμέλεια Γιάννης Σαΐτας* (Αθήνα 2011); simultaneously published in

French and English editions: *L'Œuvre de l' Expédition Scientifique de Morée, 1829–1838, Première Partie, Section des Sciences Physiques*, ed. Yanis Saitas, trans. Jeanne Roques-Tesson and Marcel Durand; *The Work of the French Scientific Expedition to the Morea, 1829–1838, Part I, Natural Sciences Section*, ed. Yanis Saitas, trans. John C. Davis.

6 Nauplion, 3 October 1829. Ιωάννης Καποδίστριας, *Κείμενα*, ed. Κώστας Δαφνής (Athens, 1976).

7 Κική Καυκούλα, Νίκος Παπαμίχος and Βίλμα Χαστάογλου, *Σχέδια πόλεων στην Ελλάδα του 19ου αιώνα* (Thessaloniki, 1990).

8 Θωμάς Δρίκος, *Οι πωλήσεις των Οθωμανικών Ιδιοκτησιών της Αττικής 1830–1831* (Athens, 1994), pp. 41 and 142.

9 Georgios Katakouzinos quoted in Θωμάς Δρίκος, *Οι πωλήσεις των Οθωμανικών Ιδιοκτησιών της Αττικής 1830–1831* (Athens, 1994), p. 113.

10 Γιώργος Δερτιλής, *Ελληνική Οικονομία και Βιομηχανική Επανάσταση 1830–1910*, (Athens, 1984), p. 125.

11 Hans Hermann Russach, *Deutsche Bauen in Athen* (Berlin, 1942).

12 Γεώργιος Πανέτσος, 'Η συγκρότηση του αθηναϊκού νεοκλασικισμού' in *Αθήναι. Από την Κλασική Εποχή έως Σήμερα*, eds, Χ. Μπούρας, Μ.Β. Σακελλαρίου, Κ. Στάικος, Ε. Τουλούπα (Athens, 2000).

13 Αλέξανδρος Παπαγεωργίου-Βενετάς, *Εδουάρδος Σάουμπερτ 1804–1860* (Athens, 1999); Κωνσταντίνος Η. Μπίρης, 'Η μετάθεσις της Καθέδρας εις τας Αθήνας', *Αθηναϊκαί μελέται*, vol. II (Athens, 1939), pp. 18–21; General State Archives , Αρχείο Περιόδου Όθωνος, Υπουργείο Εσωτερικών, file 219, 16 (Nauplion 1830, September 1834).

14 Klenze comments on the confusion and conflicts of Otto's court, 15 July 1835, in Leo von Klenze, 'Memorabilien oder Farben zu einem Gemälde, welches sich die Nachwelt vom Könige Ludwig von Bayern machen wird', undated manuscripts in the Bayerischen Staatsbibliothek, Munich, Klenzeana I, I–VII, pp. 419–46.

15 Αλέξανδρος Παπαγεωργίου-Βενετάς, *Ο Leo von Klenze στην Ελλάδα: Τεκμήρια για τη νεοελληνική ιστοριογραφία* (Athens, 2000).

16 Leo von Klenze, 'Memorabilien', I–VII, p. 419 (15 July 1835).

17 Letter to the Greek vice-regency, in Leo von Klenze, 'Memorabilien', I–VII, pp. 419–46 (23 August to 3 September 1834).

18 Leo von Klenze, *Aphoristische Bemerkungen gesammelt auf seiner Reise nach Griechenland* (Berlin, 1838), pp. 484–7.

19 General State Archives, Αρχείο περιόδου Όθωνος, Υπουργείο Εσωτερικών, file 220, Athens.

20 Κωνσταντίνος Η. Μπίρης, 'Η μετάθεσις της Καθέδρας εις τας Αθήνας', Αθηναϊκαί - Μελέται, ιι (Athens 1939), pp.18–21. See also General State Archives, Αρχείο περιόδου Όθωνος, Υπουργείο Εσωτερικών, file 219, 16 (Nauplion 1830, September 1834) (on the transfer of the capital to Athens).

21 Oswald Hederer, *Friedrich Von Gärtner 1792–1847. Leben–Werk–Schuler* (Munich, 1976).

22 Hederer, *Friedrich Von Gärtner*, p. 199.

23 Henry-Russell Hitchcock, *Architecture: Nineteenth and Twentieth Centuries* (Baltimore, MD, 1958).

24 Hederer, *Friedrich Von Gärtner*, p. 190.

25 Leo von Klenze, *Aphoristische Bemerkungen gesammelt auf seiner Reise nach Griechenland*, pp. 355–6.

26 Hans Hermann Russach, *Deutsche Bauen in Athen* (Berlin, 1942).

27 Κανονιστικόν 'Περί του Κτιρίου της Εθνικής Βιβλιοθήκης', *Εφημερίς της Κυβερνήσεως*, άρθρον 1, 225 (Athens, 20 August 1886).

28 Όλγα Φουντουλάκη, 'André Couchaud, 'Ο αρχιτέκτων του Καστέλου της Ροδοδάφνης στην Πεντέλη', *Archeologia* 112 (September 2009).

29 Παντολέων Καμπούρογλου, *Ιστορία του Πειραιώς από του 1833–1882 έτους* (Athens, 1883); Νικόλας Σ. Ντόριζας, *Τα κτίρια του Πειραιά κατά τον 19ο αιώνα: δημόσια*

κτίρια και κατοικία (Athens, 1997); Λίζα Μιχελή, *Πειραιάς: Από το Πόρτο Λεόνε στη Μαγχεστρία της Ανατολής* (Athens, 1989), pp. 64–82 and 137–42.

30 Αχιλλέας Χατζόπουλος, *Τα Καφενεία του Ελληνισμού* (Athens, 2001); Άρτεμις Σκουμπουρδή, *Καφενεία της παλαιάς Αθήνας* (Athens, 2001).

31 Ιωάννης Τραυλός and Αγγελική Κόκκου, *Ερμούπολη: Η δημιουργία μιας νέας πόλης στη Σύρο στις αρχές του 19ου αιώνα* (Athens, 1980); Μάνος Ελευθερίου, ed., *Νεοκλασσική Ερμούπολη* (Athens, 1998); Χριστίνα Αγριαντώνη , Αγγελική Φενερλή and Ιωακείμ Καρακουλίδης , *Ερμούπολη-Σύρος: Ιστορικό-Οδοιπορικό* (Athens, 1999); Τιμολέων Αμπελάς , *Ιστορία της νήσου Σύρου από των αρχαιοτάτων χρόνων μέχρι των καθ' ημάς* (Hermoupolis, 1874) (facsimile edition, Hermoupolis, 1998).

32 Ελένη Καλαφάτη, *Τα σχολικά κτήρια της πρωτοβάθμιας εκπαίδευσης 1821–1929* (Athens,1988).

33 General State Archives, 'Κατάλογος των Μαχαλάδων, οσπιτίων, εργαστηρίων, κατοίκων και παροίκων της πόλεως των Αθηνών', Υπουργείο Αστυνομίας, file 16 (Athens, 26 October 1824); Άρης Κωνσταντινίδης, *Τα παλαιά αθηναϊκά σπίτια* (Athens, 1950); Μάρω Καρδαμίτση-Αδάμη, 'Το αθηναϊκό σπίτι στα πρώτα μετά την απελευθέρωση χρόνια', *Αρχιτεκτονική και πολεοδομία από την αρχαιότητα έως σήμερα. Η περίπτωση των Αθηνών,* conference proceedings 15–18 February 1995 (Athens,1997), pp.142–9; Αγγελική Κόκκου, 'Τα πρώτα αθηναϊκά σπίτια: 1832–1860', *Αρχαιολογία και Τέχνες,* 2 (February 1982), pp. 50–64; *Exteriors of Athenian Houses,* intro. Manos G. Biris (Athens, 1992); Παύλος Κυριαζής and
Μιχάλης Νικολινάκος, eds, *Οι πρώτοι Έλληνες τεχνικοί επιστήμονες της περιόδου της Απελευθέρωσης* (Athens, 1976).

34 Μπίρης Κ.Η., *Αι αθήναι από τόν 19ου εις τόν 20ο αιώνα* (Athens, 1966/1995). See also Κώστας Η. Μπίρης, 'Τα αναφιώτικα', *Ό Πάν* (June–July 1947).

chapter two: 'Forward': Infrastructure, City Plans and Buildings

1 It was carried out by Hungarian civil engineers István Türr and Béla Gerster who had also been involved with the Panama Canal. Though the engineers were foreign, the workers and many of the supervisors were Greek. The project was seen in Greece as a national technological achievement of the new state.

2 From Κωνσταντίνος Ασώπιος, *Αττικόν Ημερολόγιον,*' cited in Έλλη Σκοπετέα, *Το 'Πρότυπο Βασίλειο' και η Μεγάλη Ιδέα. Όψεις του εθνικού προβλήματος στην Ελλάδα 1830–1880* (Athens,1988), p. 360.

3 Μάρω Καρδαμίτση-Αδάμη, *Ο Δ. Καλλίας και το σχολικό κτίριο* (Athens, 1986), p. 19.

4 Γιώργος Β. Δερτιλής, *Ιστορία του Ελληνικού Κράτους 1830–1920* (Athens, 2005), p. 350. See also George B. Leon, *The Greek Socialist Movement and the First World War: The Road to Unity* (New York, 1976).

5 Ανδρέας Συγγρός, *Απομνημονεύματα* (Athens, 1908).

6 A speech on Greece and the Don Pacifico case was given by Lord Palmerston at London's House of Commons on 25 June 1850.

7 *Ακρόπολις,* 4072 (5 June 1893).

8 Χριστίνα Αγριαντώνη and Μαρία Χριστίνα Χατζηιωάνου, eds, *Το Μεταξουργείο της Αθήνας* (Athens, 1995).

9 Γιώργος Β. Δερτιλής, *Ιστορία του Ελληνικού Κράτους 1830–1920* (Athens, 2005), p. 489–90.

10 Μάρω Καρδαμίτση-Αδάμη, *Ernst Ziller. Αναμνήσεις,* (Athens, 1997); Δημήτριος Παπαστάμος, *Ερνέστος Τσίλλερ. Προσπάθεια Μονογραφίας* (Athens, 1973).

11 Αχιλλέας Χατζόπουλος, *Τα Καφενεία του Ελληνισμού* (Athens, 2001); Άρτεμις Σκουμπουρδή, *Καφενεία της παλαιάς Αθήνας* (Athens, 2001).

12 Έλλη Σκοπετέα, *Το «Πρότυπο Βασίλειο» και η Μεγάλη Ιδέα. Όψεις του εθνικού προβλήματος στην Ελλάδα (1830–1880)* (Athens, 1988), p. 166.

13 A structure of 329 BCE, improved by Herodus Attikos (139–194 CE).

14 Theophil Hansen, 'Austellungsgebäude in Athen (Olympion) auf Kosten des Herrn Zapas nach Plänen des Architekten Boulanger modifizirt von Hansen', *Allgemeine Bauizetung*, 7, (Vienna, 1884), p. 64.

15 Ρ. Ρίτσαρδσον, 'Το ανοικοδομηθέν Παναθηναϊκόν Στάδιον' in *Η Ελλάς κατά τους Ολυμπιακούς Αγώνες του 1896. Πανελλήνιον Εικονογραφημένο Λεύκωμα* (Athens, 1896), pp. 127–9.

16 Γιώργος Β. Δερτιλής, *Ιστορία του Ελληνικού Κράτους 1830–1920* (Athens, 2005), pp. 640–42.

17 Γιώργος Β. Δερτιλής, *Ιστορία του Ελληνικού Κράτους 1830–1920*, pp. 366–7.

18 In 1961, it was republished in the form of a book in full and uncensored as Περικλής Γιαννόπουλος, *Η Ελληνική Γραμμή* (Athens, 1961).

19 Frustratingly, we know that kept in a box with other unpublished material was an unpublished text on architecture, from which he had read passages to the historian Kambouroglou. He burned it the day before his suicide.

20 'Πρός τους καλλιτέχνας μας: Ζωγράφους, γλύπτας, αρχιτέκτονας και μουσικούς', *Ανατολή*, 12 (February 1903), pp. 392–6.

21 Βασίλης Κολώνας, *Έλληνες Αρχιτέκτονες στην Οθωμανική Αυτοκρατορία 19ος–20ος αιώνας* (Athens, 2005).

22 Anonymous, 'Παραγραφάκια', *Ο Νουμάς*, VIII, 373 (3 January 1910), p. 4; Στρατοκόπος, 'Ο Ένας', *Ο Νουμάς*, VIII, 376 (24 January 1910), p. 1; Δ. Π. Ταγκόπουλος, 'Αντίς Επινίκια', *Ο Νουμάς*, VIII, 402 (22 September 1910), p. 49.

23 Ρένα Σταυρίδη-Πατρικίου, *Γλώσσα Εκπαίδευση και Πολιτική* (Athens, 1999).

24 Margaret Olwen MacMillan, *Paris 1919: Six Months that Changed the World* (Toronto, 2002). Originally published as *Peacemakers* (London, 2001).

25 'Σχέδιο για ένα σύντομο υπόμνημα' in Δημήτρης Γληνός, *Άπαντα*, ed. Φίλιππος Ηλιού, vol. II: *1910–1914* (Athens, 1983), p. 549.

26 Ηλίας Αγγελόπουλος, 'Επί του σχεδίου της πόλεως Αθηνών', *Αρχιμήδης*, 11 (November, 1920), pp. 83–8.

27 For example, around the time of the Cretan crisis, Pavlos Vakas, aspiring to transform Athens into a 'European metropolis', proposed a plan conforming to his discovery that the arrangement of Athens followed an arcane spatial pattern, a perfect octagon, as recommended by Vitruvius. See Παύλος Βακάς, *Μελέται και σχέδια δια την συγκοινωνίαν, τον εξωραϊσμόν, την εξυγίανσιν των Αθηνών* (Athens, 1898).

28 Hartig Schmidt, 'Ludwig Hoffmann's Athens Master Plan', *Design in Greece*, 11 (Athens, 1980), pp. 50–59.

29 Αριστείδης Μπαλάνος, *Μελέτη σχεδίου Πόλεως Αθηνών. Τμήμα συνοικιών Κολωνού-Σεπολίων-Κολοκυνθούς-Ιεράς Οδού* (Athens, 1917).

30 T. H. Mawson, *The Art and Craft of Garden Making* (London, 1900). It seems that Mawson had already received several commissions in Greece, as a *New York Times* article reveals. See 'Tells of his Work Replanning Cities', *New York Times*, 16 December 1913. See also Mawson's own *The Life and Work of a English Landscape Architect* (London, 1927) and Janet Waymark, *Thomas Mawson: Life, Gardens and Landscapes* (London, 2009).

31 T. H. Mawson, *Αι Αθήναι του μέλλοντος και η Θεσσαλονίκη της αύριον* (Athens, 1918); T. H. Mawson, 'The Replanning of Athens', *Architectural Review*, 47 (March 1919), pp. 48–52.

32 Mark Mazower, *Salonica, City of Ghosts: Christians, Muslims and Jews, 1430–1950* (New York, 2004).

33 Αλέκα Καραδήμου-Γερόλυμπου, 'Φτώχεια και περιθωριοποίηση σε έναν μεταβαλλόμενο αστικό χώρο. Οι εβραϊκές συνοικίες στη Θεσσαλονίκη 1870–1920', in *Ο Ελληνικός Εβραϊσμός*, Conference Proceedings, 3–4 April 1998 (Athens, 1999), pp. 172–203; Αλμπέρτος Νάρ, 'Μία ανέκδοτη έκθεση του 1942 για τη δομή της Ισραηλιτικής Κοινότητος Θεσσαλονίκης στην περίοδο 1912–1940', in *Η Θεσσαλονίκη μετά το 1912*, Conference Proceedings, 1–3 November 1985 (Thessaloniki, 1986), pp. 303–23.

34 Αλέκα Καραδήμου-Γερόλυμπου, 'Φτώχεια και περιθωριοποίηση σε έναν μεταβαλλόμενο

αστικό χώρο. Οι εβραϊκές συνοικίες στη Θεσσαλονίκη 1870–1920', pp. 179–83; Ρένα Μόλχο, *Οι Εβραίοι της Θεσσαλονίκης 1856–1919* (Athens, 2001), pp. 110–20.

35 Αλέκα Καραδήμου-Γερόλυμπου, *Η ανοικοδόμηση της Θεσσαλονίκης μετά την πυρκαγιά του 1917: Ένα ορόσημο στην ιστορία της πόλης και στην ανάπτυξη της ελληνικής πολεοδομίας* (Thessaloniki, 1985–6).

36 Bernard C. Pierron, *Juifs et chrétiens de la Grèce moderne: Histoire des relations Intercommunautaires de 1821 à 1945* (Paris, 1996).

37 Βασίλης Κολώνας and Λένα Παπαματθαίου, *Ο αρχιτέκτονας Vitaliano Poselli: Το έργο του στη Θεσσαλονίκη του 19ου αιώνα* (Thessaloniki, 1980).

38 Associated with the emergence of the union movement in Thessaloniki was the city's long history in printing. The first printing house was established in 1510 by Sephardic refugees and by the twentieth century there were dozens of Ladino newspapers covering the whole political spectrum. One of the founders of *Federation* was Avraam Benaroya, a printer by profession. See also Ραφαήλ Φρεζής, *Ο Εβραϊκός Τύπος στην Ελλάδα* (Volos, 1999).

39 Marjorie Housepian, *Smyrna 1922: The Destruction of a City* (London, 1972).

40 Henry Morgenthau, *I was Sent to Athens* (Garden City, NY, 1929). The Relief Fund for Refugees ('Ταμείο Περιθάλψεως Προσφύγων') was founded in 1923.

41 Υπουργείο Κοινωνικής Πρόνοιας, *Η αποκατάσταση των προσφύγων του 1922*, ed. Ι. Αγγελή (Athens, 1960).

42 Υπουργείο Κοινωνικής Πρόνοιας, *Η αποκατάσταση των προσφύγων του 1922*; Ιωάννης Πολύζος, *Η εγκατάσταση των προσφύγων του 1922: Μία οριακή περίπτωση αστικοποίησης* (Athens, 1984); Maria Mantouvalou, *Production des logements et rapports de pouvoir en Grèce*, thesis dissertation, EHESS, Paris (1980).

43 The 'erker' law was introduced by law in 1923 imported from Berlin building regulations for economic and functional reasons, and as improvement to the traditional Mediterranean balcony. Royal Decree 24 August 1922: 'Περί τροποποιήσεως του από 27.11.1919 δια τας εντός του σχεδίου της πόλεως των Αθηνών οικοδομάς εκτελεστικάς του νόμου 858 Β. Διατάγματος'; law 1923: 'Περί οικοδομικών προεξοχών (erker)'.

44 Legislative Decree 17 July 1923: 'Περί σχεδίων πόλεων, κωμών και συνοικισμών του Κράτους και οικοδομής αυτών', *Εφημερίς της Κυβερνήσεως*, ΦΕΚ 228 (16 August 1923).

chapter three: Open Wide the Windows – Let the Sun Come In!

1 Ιωάννης Καποδίστριας, *Κείμενα*, ed. Κώστας Δαφνής (Athens, 1976).

2 Quoted in the introduction in Πάτροκλος Καραντινός, *Τα νέα Σχολικά Κτίρια*, (Athens, 1938).

3 Margaret Olwen MacMillan, *Paris 1919: Six Months that Changed the World* (Toronto, 2002), p. 349.

4 *Στατιστική Επετηρίς της Ελλάδος* (Athens,1933), p. 418; Χαράλαμπος Νούτσος, *Ιστορία της εκπαίδευσις και Ιδεολογία: Όψεις του Μεσοπολέμου* (Athens, 1990); Κωνσταντίνος Σβολόπουλος, ed., *Κωνσταντίνος Β. Γόντικας 1870–1937: Θεσμικές αλλαγές κατά τον μεσοπόλεμο* (Athens, 2003).

5 Ελένη Καλαφάτη, *Τα σχολικά κτήρια της πρωτοβάθμιας εκπαίδευσης 1821–1929* (Athens, 1988); Κυριακή Τσουκαλά, *Τάσεις στη Σχολική Αρχιτεκτονική* (Athens,1998).

6 M. Mantoudis, 'Les Bâtiments scolaires en Grèce', *L' Hellenisme contemporaine*, 5 (March 1936), pp. 450–56.

7 Δημήτριος. Ι. Σαράτσης, 'Περί υπαιθρίων σχολείων και υπαιθρίου διδασκαλίας', copy from the proceedings of *Β' Ελληνικό συνέδριο κατά της φυματιώσεως* (Volos, 1913), p. 35.

8 Book-review, vol. II (1913), p. 373 in *Δημήτρης Γληνός Άπαντα*, vol II: *1910–1914*, ed. Φίλιππος Ηλιού (Athens, 1983). The limitations of universal types in architecture were expressed more polemically by a young architect, Emmanuel Kriezis, in his article 'Popular Architecture' in a professional monthly review *Archimedes:* Εμμανουήλ

A. Κριεζής, 'Δημώδης αρχιτεκτονική', *Αρχιμήδης* (May 1912), pp. 1–8. The monthly review was published from 1 January 1899 by the Club of Engineers of the Greek Polytechnic, edited by the State Engineer, Ilias Angelopoulos.

9 Τζόκας Σπύρος, *Ο Ελευθέριος Βενιζέλος και το Εγχείρημα του Αστικού Εκσυγχρονισμού, 1928–1932* (Athens, 2002), pp. 165–75.

10 In a letter (1 February 1923) to the author Penelope Delta, Glinos declared that Venizelos would soon fail, as he did in 1917, when he withdrew many of the reforms he had initiated in 1910 and 1913. Even more extreme was the criticism by a young historian and sociologist Yannis Kordatos, who maintained that those who are in search of a national identity through language were misguided: 'There is no such a thing as a national education; only a nationalist one.' See Ιωάννης Κ. Κορδάτος, *Δημοτικισμός και Λογιωτατισμός* (Athens, 1927).

11 Mantoudis, 'Les Bâtiments scolaires en Grèce', pp. 450–56.

12 Στέφανος Ι. Στεφάνου, ed., *Τα κέιμενα του Ελευθερίου Βενιζέλου*, vol. III (Athens, 1981–83), p. 468.

13 Γεώργιος Θεοτοκάς, 'Ο Γιώργος Σεφέρης οπως τον γνώρισα', *Εποχέες*, 10 (February, 1964), pp. 11–17.

14 Γεώργιος Θεοτοκάς, *Ελεύθερο πνεύμα* (Athens, 1929).

15 It was legally established during the brief premiership of Papanastassiou in 1925. The first appointment was the radical critical philosopher Theodoridis, a promoter of the demotic language.

16 Among the architects were: Ioannis Despotopoulos, Vassilios Douras, Patroklos Karantinos, Rennos Koutsouris, Kimon Laskaris, Pavlos Michaleas, Kyriakos Panayiotakos, Angelos Siagas, Thucydides Valentis, Pericles Georgakopoulos and Dimitris Pikionis.

17 In his autobiographical notes he says that he quit Munich for Paris within a year. He notes this shift occurred after seeing three paintings by Cezanne, especially impressed with their representation of three-dimensional space through colour.

18 Δημήτρης Πικιώνης, 'Αυτοβιογραφικά σημειώματα', in *Δημήτρη Πικιώνη Κείμενα*, eds. Αγνή Πικιώνη and Μιχάλης Παρούσης (Athens, 1986), pp. 30–31. First published in *Ζυγός*, 27–28 (January–February 1958), pp. 4–7.

19 Δημήτρης Πικιώνης, 'Αυτοβιογραφικά σημειώματα', pp. 31–5.

20 Κούλα Πράτσικα, *Έργα και Ημέρες* (Athens, 1991).

21 Loos' own motifs on the Villa Müller were arguably drawn from precedents from Skyros with which Kontoleon was certainly familiar.

22 Γιώργος Θεοτοκάς, 'Η διαύγεια', *Ο Κύκλος*, (1 November 1931), p. 65 in Γιώργος Θεοτοκάς, *Αναζητώντας τη διαύγεια: Δοκίμια για τη νεότερη ελληνική και ευρωπαϊκή λογοτεχνία*, ed. Δημήτρης Τζιόβας (Athens, 2005).

23 Κυπριανός Μπίρης , 'Η αστική πολυκατοικία', *Τεχνικά χρονικά* 11 (1 June 1932), pp. 563–71.

24 Legislative Decree 19 March 1927: 'Περί της κατ' ορόφους ή διαμερίσματα ιδιοκτησίας' and generalized for any kind of appartment in 9 January 1929, Law 3741, 'Περί της ιδιοκτησίας κατ΄ορόφους'.

25 The 'erker' had been introduced by law in 1923.

26 Σέμνη Παπασπυρίδη-Καρούζου, 'Ακνίσωτοι Οίκοι' *Νέα Εστία*, 202 (15 May 1935), p. 464 .

27 Decades later, Saporta commented that the list was improvised rather than the product of some reflection. Michaelidis and Mitsakis should have been included in the group and certainly Pikionis, maintained Saporta who dared to ask Pikionis why he was not in the list and even why he did not lead the delegation. See Ισαάκ Σαπόρτα, *Επάγγελμα Αρχιτέκτων*, ed. Γιώργος Σημαιοφορίδης, Γιώργος Σαρηγιάννης (Athens, 1996), pp. 34–5.

28 One can argue also that it was influential for designing the path to the Weitzman house in Rohovot, in Israel. Pikionis translated and published the article in his revue *To Trito Mati*, p. 65 and continued to correspond with Mendelsohn. Erich Mendelsohn's articles were 'Mysterien-Strasse' and 'Akropolis und Parthenon', *Berliner Tageblat* (May 1931).

Translated in *Erich Mendelsohn: Letters of an Architect*, ed. Oskar Beyer, trans. Geoffrey Strachan, intro. Nikolaus Pevsner (London, 1979), pp. 110–20.

29 Ιωάννης Γ. Δεσποτόπουλος, 'Πολεοδομική', *Τεχνικά Χρονικά*, 39 (1 August 1933), pp. 756–73.

30 Στάμος Παπαδάκης, 'Τα διεθνή αρχιτεκτονικά Συνέδρια', *Τεχνικά Χρονικά*, 27 (1 February 1933), pp. 136–7.

31 Νίκος Κιτσίκης, 'Αι ημέραι του συνεδρίου εν Ελλάδι, Πρόποσις', *Τεχνικά Χρονικά*, 44–45–46 (15 October–15 November 1933), pp. 998–9.

32 Κιτσίκης, 'Αι ημέραι του συνεδρίου εν Ελλάδι, Πρόποσις', pp. 998–9.

33 Ισαάκ Σαπόρτα, 'Αι ημέραι του συνεδρίου εν Ελλάδι, Ομιλία', *Τεχνικά Χρονικά* 44–45–46 (15 October–15 November 1933), pp. 1003–5.

34 Παύλος Σαντορίνη, 'Συμβολή εις το Διεθνές Συνέδριον Γεφυρών και Κατασκευών, Παρισίοι 19–25 Μαΐου', *Τεχνικά Χρονικά*, 18 (15 September 1932), pp. 921–30.

35 G. Vlachos, G. Yannitsaris and E. Hadjicostas, 'Housing the Asia Minor Refugees in Athens and Piraeus between 1920 and 1940', *Architecture in Greece*, 12 (Athens, 1978), pp. 117–24.

36 In fact his study was prepared before the CIAM Congress and was mailed to Karl Moser, honorary president of CIAM. It ultimately resulted in the invitation to form a Greek CIAM group. See Στάμος Παπαδάκης, 'Ο συνεταιρισμός "Νέας Αλεξάνδρειας" και η εδαφική οικονομία των Αθηνών', *Τεχνικά Χρονικά*, 31 (1 April 1933), pp. 361–4.

37 Ιωάννης Γ. Δεσποτόπουλος, 'Πολεοδομική', *Τεχνικά Χρονικά*, 39 (1 August 1933), pp. 756–73.

38 Mark Mazower, *Η Ελλάδα και η οικονομική κρίση του μεσοπολέμου* (Athens, 2002).

39 Τζόκας, Σπύρος, *Ο Ελευθέριος Βενιζέλος και το Εγχείρημα του Αστικού Εκσυγχρονισμού: 1928–1932* (Athens, 2002).

40 Mazower, *Η Ελλάδα και η οικονομική κρίση του μεσοπολέμου*, p. 310.

41 Γεώργιος Θεοτοκάς, *Αργώ*, vol. ι (Athens, 1933), p. 182.

42 Klaus Vrieslander and Τζούλιο Καΐμη, *Το σπίτι του Ροδάκη στην Αίγινα*, ed. Μισέλ Φάις (Athens, 1997), p. 38 (first edition 1934).

43 Άγγελος Σικελιανός, 'Αφορμαί και αίτια (των αντισημιτικών επεισοδίων της Θεσσαλονίκης)', *Ελεύθερον Βήμα* (6 July 1931).

44 Δημοσθένης Δώδος, *Οι Εβραίοι της Θεσσαλονίκης στις εκλογές του Ελληνικού Κράτους 1915–1936* (Athens, 2005), pp.180–84.

45 Τζόκας, Σπύρος, *Ο Ελευθέριος Βενιζέλος και το Εγχείρημα του Αστικού Εκσυγχρονισμού: 1928–1932* (Athens, 2002), pp. 175–85.

46 Mazower, *Η Ελλάδα και η οικονομική κρίση του μεσοπολέμου*, p. 311.

47 Mazower, *Η Ελλάδα και η οικονομική κρίση του μεσοπολέμου*, p. 360.

48 Mazower, *Η Ελλάδα και η οικονομική κρίση του μεσοπολέμου*, p. 362.

49 Γεώργιος Θεοτοκάς, *Αργώ* (Athens, 1933), p. 81.

50 Κώστας Καραβίδας, *Το Συντεχνιακόν Κράτος* (Athens, 1936).

51 Vlachos, Yannitsaris and Hadjicostas, 'Housing the Asia Minor Refugees in Athens and Piraeus between 1920 and 1940', pp. 117–24; Ι. Αγγελής, ed., *Η αποκατάσταση των προσφύγων του 1922* (Athens, 1960); Ιωάννης Πολύζος, *Η εγκατάσταση των προ*

chapter four: Hard Times: The Third Hellenic Civilization, War and Reconstruction

1 Bert Birtles, *Exiles in the Aegean: A Personal Narrative of Greek Politics and Travel* (London, 1938), chap. 1.

2 Aegina, August 1936: Γιώργος Σεφέρης, *Μέρες Β′: 24 Αυγούστου 1931 – 12 Φεβρουαρίου 1934* (Athens, 1975).

3 Mark Mazower, *Η Ελλάδα και η οικονομική κρίση του μεσοπολέμου* (Athens, 2002), p. 264.

4 His right-hand man for these tasks was Kostis Bastias, an experienced journalist and playwright of leftist beginnings, who was appointed by Metaxas as Director of the new-founded division of Letters and Fine Arts at the Ministry of Education (August 1937).

5 Seferis in his Diary, Saturday 14 May 1942; Γιώργος Σεφέρης, *Μέρες Δ΄: 1 Γενάρη 1941 – 31 Δεκέμβρη 1944* (Athens, 1977).

6 Γιάννης Κ. Μπαστιάς, *Ο Κωστής Μπαστιάς στα χρόνια του Μεσοπολέμου*, vol. II (Athens, 1997). See also 'Τα μυστικά του άρματος: πως στήνεται και πως λύνεται', *Τα Παρασκήνια* (16 September 1939), p. 1. Published interview with Constantinos A. Doxiadis about the technology used for the demountable outdoor theatre.

7 His dissertation, was immediately published in Germany as *Raumordnung im griechischen Staedtebau* (1937), and published in English edited and translated by Jacqueline Tyrwitt as *Architectural Space in Ancient Greece,* without the introduction of the German edition by the notorious Minister of Culture of the Third Reich, Alfred Rosenberg, who grabbed the opportunity for 'Aryan' propaganda (Cambridge, MA, 1972). Doxiadis' thesis, however, was not only alien to Rosenberg's ideas and intentions, but stood on its own and, for a short period, Doxiadis became a household name in Berlin discussed even among Nobel-winning scholars in the internationally prestigious Kaiser Wilhelm Gesselschaft. (Personal testimony of K. Tzonis.)

8 Γιώργος Θεοτοκάς, *Αναζητώντας τη Διαύγεια: Δοκίμια για τη νεότερη ελληνική και ευρωπαϊκή λογοτεχνία,* ed. Δημήτρης Τζιόβας (Athens, 2005).

9 According to Georgios A. Panetsos, Malaparte saw the gypsum model of the Kyriakides house in Kontoleon's studio during one of his visits to Athens during the 1930s. Malaparte was a frequent traveller to Athens as the *Corriere* correspondent, but also as the friend of Galeazzo Ciano (Mussolini's son-in-law, minister of press and propaganda and, subsequently, of foreign affairs) and, later, personal envoy to Emanuele Grazzi, the Italian ambassador to Greece. Panetsos also mentions that the Villa Loverdo in Psychico by Kontoleon, the property of his wife Ioanna, had been rented as the Italian ambassador's residence at the time. See Γεώργιος Α. Πανέτσος, 'Από την Ελλάδα στην Ευρώπη: οι περιπτώσεις A. Loos και C. Malaparte', paper presented at *Ανατολή και Δύση στη Μοντέρνα Αρχιτεκτονική*, 3rd Do.Co.Mo.Mo. (Greek Section) Conference (Patras, 6–8 May 2004).

10 City planning council meeting reported in 'Ο λόγος του κ. Πρωθυπουργού', *Η Καθημερινή*, 7878 (19 June 1938); August 1937 recommendations recorded in Ιωάννης Π. Μεταξάς, *Λόγοι και σκέψεις: 1936–41* (Athens,1969), p. 239.

11 Konstantinidis records the background to the commission in his journal: Άρης Κωνσταντινίδης, *Αρχιτεκτονική της Αρχιτεκτονικής: Ημερολογιακά σημειώματα* (Athens, 1992).

12 Konstantinidis journal entry of 21 April 1937.

13 Ηλίας Φ. Ηλιού, 'Κουτιών Εγκώμιον', *Νεοελληνικά Γράμματα*, 33–36 (1937).

14 The fact is that the Greek Company for Sewage Construction was offered the job earlier, on 22/23 January 1936, before Metaxas took over, but his regime continued with the construction. See *Τεχνικά Χρονικά*, (December 1938). See also Γεώργιος Σαρηγιάννης, *Αθήνα 1830–2000: Εξέλιξη, πολεοδομία, μεταφορές* (Athens, 2000).

15 G. Vlachos, G. Yannitsaris and E. Hadjicostas, 'Housing the Asia Minor Refugees in Athens and Piraeus between 1920 and 1940', *Architecture in Greece,* 12 (Athens, 1978), pp. 117–24.

16 Βασίλειος Τσαγρής, 'Αι Αθήναι ως πόλις', *Αρχιμήδης*, 7 (July 1918), pp. 73–81.

17 Stavros B. Thomadakis, 'Black Markets, Inflation, and Force in the Economy of Occupied Greece', in *Greece in the 1940s: A Nation in Crisis*, ed. John O. Iatrides (Hanover, NH, 1981), pp. 61–80.

18 Οδυσσέας Ελύτης, 'Το χρονικό μιάς δεκαετίας' *Ανοιχτά Χαρτιά* (Athens, 1974), pp. 255–361.

19 Key members were Alexander Svolos, a professor of constitutional law with a history in the protection of minorities in Greece, the economist Angelos Angelopoulos and the physician

Petros Kokkalis, both professors of the University of Athens, Nikos Karvounis, a writer, and the Chief Rabbi of Athens. Much inspired by Marxist central planning ideas and industrialization they also promoted equally strong administrative regional autonomy.

20 Ελύτης, 'Το χρονικό μιάς δεκαετίας', pp. 255–361.

21 In haste, before the departure of the Germans, on 18 April 1944, Rallis, the Prime Minister rushed through an ambitious law assigning new responsibilities to the Ministry of Transportation. It included 'research on cities, towns, and settlements and in general districts and supervision of their physical development'. He also requested new research to be carried out on the problem of shelter, a new industrial map of the country to be drawn, and asked for a study on the control and approval of new plans for existing cities, towns and settlements. See 'Αρμοδιότης της Υπηρεσίας Δημοσίων Έργων', *Εφημερίς της Κυβερνήσεως* 86 (18 April 1944). On 12 October 1944 Athens was liberated and Rallis resigned.

22 Ελύτης, 'Το χρονικό μιάς δεκαετίας', pp. 255–361.

23 Rena Molho, *Jewish Sites in Thessaloniki: Brief History and Guide* (Athens, 2009); Yomtov Yacoel, *The Holocaust in Salonika: Eyewitnesses Accounts,* ed. Steven Bowman, trans. Isaac Benmeyer, n.d.; Asra Kadisha, 'A Report on Preventing any Further Desecration of the Jewish Cemetery of Thessaloniki, Greece: Findings, Concerns and Recommendations', *Conference of Academicians for the Protection of Jewish Cemeteries and the Central Rabbinical Congress* (July 2008); Michael Molho, 'El cementeriojudío of Salónica', *Sefarad*, 9/1 (1949) pp. 124–8.

24 Reported in 'Greece offers lists of German crimes: pictures and data are submitted in Paris as preliminary to exhibition', *New York Herald Tribune* (30 March 1945).

25 Signed Archbishop Damaskinos, Prime Minister Sofoulis, Compulsory Law 768: 'Περί συστάσεως Υπουργείου υπό τον τίτλο «Υπουργείο Ανοικοδομήσεως»' and Decree 'Περί διορισμού του κ. Κωνσταντίνου Δοξιάδη ως Υφυπουργού επί της Ανοικοδομήσεως' in *Εφημερίς της Κυβερνήσεως*, 317 (27 December 1945).

26 Renée Hirschon, *Heirs of the Greek Catastrophe: The Social Life of Asia Minor Refugees in Piraeus* (Oxford, 1989).

27 Δημήτρης Πικιώνης, 'Η ανοικοδόμηση και το πνεύμα της παράδοσης', *Εκλογή*, II/9 (September 1946), pp. 64–71.

28 In his articles 'Αρχιτεκτονημένη Οικοδόμησις', *Η Καθημερινή*, 10715–7 (24–26 July 1947).

29 Report to the Foreign Ministry by Athanassios I. Sbarounis, who represented Greece during this meeting (Athens, 31 January 1946).

30 'Report of the Chief, Special Mission to Greece, Economic Cooperation Administration, September 1949 to November 1950'; 'The Story of the American Marshall Plan in Greece: July 1, 1948 to January 1, 1952', papers in the Paul R. Porter Collection, Harry S. Truman Library, Independence, Missouri.

31 Porter understood the larger framework that linked the post-war reconstruction to the local Civil War, the global Cold War, and the long-term process of modernization and development of the country. He did not hesitate to spell out his opinions even if they were controversial and contradicted powerful local politicians. As Adviser on Labor Affairs to the Allied Control Commission in Germany after World War Two he was involved with matters of occupation policy and the establishment of free trade unions at variance with the American military, who at that time, according to Porter, were impressed by the communists and influenced by the Soviets.

32 Juergens, George, *The Journal of American History*, LXV/3 (December 1978), pp. 832–3, review of *Concerned about the Planet: The Reporter Magazine and American Liberalism, 1949–1968* by Martin K. Doudna (Westport, CT, 1977).

33 As reported in *To Vima,* 14 December 1950.

34 *Ministry of Reconstruction, Weekly Report,* 7 June 1950.

35 Ελύτης, 'Το χρονικό μιάς δεκαετίας', pp. 255–361.

36 Άρης Κωνσταντινίδης, *Τα παλαιά αθηναϊκά σπίτια* (Athens, 1950).

1 See Alexander Tzonis, 'Critical Regionalism' in *The Oxford Companion to Architecture*, ed. Patrick Goode, vol. I (New York, 2009), and Liane Lefaivre and Alexander Tzonis, *Critical Regionalism, Architecture and Identity in a Globalised World* (Munich, 2003); also by the same authors with Anthony Alofsin, 'Die Frage des Regionalismus' in *Für eine andere Architektur*, ed. M. Adritzky, L. Burckhardt and Hoffmann, vol. I (Frankfurt, 1981), pp. 121–34.

2 Foreign capital increased from 3.4 per cent in 1955 to 8 in 1958 and to 31.8 in 1965. Between 1952 and 1963 agricultural production doubled. In 1954, 9,810 new cars were imported into Greece, in 1961 there were 42,139, and in 1967 there were 135,142. In 1962, for the first time the industrial sector exceeded the agricultural in GNP. In 1954, 9,810 new cars were added, since 1961 there were 42,139, and the legendary, increasingly crowded Syngrou Avenue served 135,142 cars in 1967 and was declared at last congested – a strange but objectively accepted 'measure' of success and progress.

3 Mark Mazower, *After the War was Over: Reconstructing the Family, Nation and State in Greece 1943–1960* (Princeton, NJ, 2000).

4 For more on the *polykatoikia* see: Απόστολος Μπουρνιάς, *Περί της οριζοντίου ιδιοκτησίας* (Athens, 1982); Δημήτρης Γ. Χριστοφιλόπουλος , *Κάθετος Συνιδιοκτησία* (Athens, 1976); Dimitris Philippides, 'Apartment Houses and Life in Modern Greece', *Architecture in Greece*, 12 (1978), pp. 102–8; Anastasia Tzakou, 'The Apartment House. Its Postwar Development in Athens', *Architecture in Greece*, 12 (1978), pp. 131–43; Giorgos Sariyannis, 'The Commercialization of Housing. Its effects on housing and city form', *Architecture in Greece* 12 (1978), pp.108–16 and 'Contemporary building legislation. The standing of housing in the production process', *Architecture in Greece* 12 (1978), pp. 144–50; Dimitris Antonakakis and Suzanna Antonakaki, 'Apartment houses in Athens, The architect's role', *Architecture in Greece* 12 (1978), } pp. 151–3; Δημήτρης Αντωνακάκης , 'Πολυκατοικία, όνειρο ή εφιάλτης;', *Δελτίο Συλλόγου Αρχιτεκτόνων* 6 (Athens, 1981), pp. 68–78.

5 See Constantinos A. Doxiadis, *Ekistics: An Introduction to the Science of Human Settlements* (New York, 1968); Constantinos A. Doxiadis, *Anthropopolis: City for Human Development* (New York, 1974); Constantinos A. Doxiadis, Action for Human Settlements (New York: W.W. Norton, 1976); and the academic journal *Ekistics* started by Doxiadis and published since the mid-1960s by the Athens Center of Ekistics.

6 Its directors were P. Vassiliadis and A. Spanos, with architects C. N. Decavalla, S. Condaratos, B. Bogakos, N. Sapountzis and B. Grigoriadis.

7 These included Dourgouti, Drapetsona, Koundouriotika, Kaisariani, Aegaleo, Asyrmatos, Korydallos, Tavros and Peristeri.

8 According to UN sources, around 1961 Greece had only 647 rooms available per 1,000 inhabitants while countries that were also severely damaged in World War Two had the following: UK 1,423, Netherlands 1,260, Belgium, 1,060, France 955, Italy 858, East Germany 832, Czechoslovakia 762 and USSR 685. In terms of density Greece was overcrowded: 1.45 persons per room in relation to UK 0.65, Netherlands 0.76, France 1.01, East Germany 1.19, Czechoslovakia 1.30 and USSR 1.5. Greek houses also remained under-equipped. The percentage of Greek dwellings with piped water within the dwelling was 29 percent in comparison to UK 96 per cent, Netherlands 90 per cent, France 78 per cent, Italy 35 per cent, Czechoslovakia 49 per cent, and Yugoslavia 42 per cent. See UN Major Problems cited by D. V. Donnison, *The Government of Housing* (1967).

9 Aris Konstantinidis, 'Architecture of Xenia Hotels', *World Architecture 3: Art and Technology: Towards a Third Culture in Architecture*, ed. John Donat (London, 1966), pp. 144–7.

10 Άρης Κωνσταντινίδης, *Η Αρχιτεκτονική της Αρχιτεκτονικής: Ημερολογιακά σημειώματα* (Athens, 1992), pp. 304–9. Record of 10 June 1988.

11 Royal Decree of 30 August / 9 September 1955: 'Περί όρων δομήσεως εν Αθήναις', Article 5.

12 Vincent Scully, 'The Athens Hilton: A Study in Vandalism', *Architectural Forum* (July, 1963), pp.101–2.
13 Δημήτρης Πικιώνης, 'Συναισθηματική Τοπογραφία', *Το 3ο μάτι*, 2–3 (November–December 1935), pp. 13–17.
14 Characteristically, he published his article next to extracts from Pericles Giannopoulos's *Greek Line* (1903) and John Ruskin's *Modern Painters* (1843), both texts stressing the close link between sensuality and morality. See Περικλής Γιαννόπουλος, 'Ελληνική γραμμή', *Ανατολή*, 1 (23 May 1903), pp. 416–22, and Ruskin's *Modern Painters*.
15 Dimitris Pikionis, Letter to Constantine Karamanlis, 12 May 1955, in Δημήτρης Πικιώνης, *Κείμενα* , ed. Αγνή Πικιώνη and Μιχάλης Παρούσης (Athens, 2000). See also *Dimitris Pikionis: The Landscaping of the Archaeological Site around Acropolis 1954–57* (Athens, 1994), pp. 31–3.
16 Ζήσιμος Λορεντζάτος, 'Πρόλογος', in *Δημήτρη Πικιώνη: Κείμενα* eds. Αγνή Πικιώνη and Μιχάλης Παρούσης (Athens, 1986), pp. 7–13.
17 Lewis Mumford, *The City in History* (Harmondsworth, 1961). Graphic Section One, Plates 10–12.
18 Lewis Mumford, unpublished letter to Artur Glikson, 6 May 1965. With permission from Sophia Mumford and Andrew Glikson.
19 Δημήτρης Πικιώνης, "Διά την προστασίαν του τοπίου: Ομιλία', *Τεχνικά Χρονικά*, 58 (15 May 1954), pp. 3–7.
20 Letter of 12 May 1955 to the Minister of Public Works, 'Επιστολή προς τον Υπουργόν Δημοσίων Έργων- Εν Αθήναις τη 12 Μαΐου 1955', in *Δημήτρη Πικιώνη, Κείμενα*, eds. Αγνή Πικιώνη and Μιχάλης Παρούσης (Athens, 1986), pp. 266–9.
21 Directed by Frantzis Frantziskakis, its board of advisors included the architects Nikos Moutsopoulos, Dimitris Fatouros and Dionysios Zivas, associated with a modern art gallery with the same name.
22 Decavalla, Konstantinidis, Papailiopoulos, Valsamakis and Zenetos.
23 John Liapis and Elias Skroubelos, 'Passenger Terminal at the Port of Piraeus', *Architecture in Greece*, 5 (1971), pp. 170–77.
24 Wilbur Smith & Associates, *Έρευνα και μελέτη κυκλοφορίας Λεκανοπέδιου Αθηνών* (Athens, 1964).
25 Lila Leontidou, *The Mediterranean City in Transition: Social Change and Urban Development* (Cambridge, 1990), p. 149.
26 Αιμιλία Καραλή, *Μια ημιτελής άνοιξη…:Ιδεολογία, πολιτική και λογοτεχνία στο περιοδικό Επιθεώρηση Τέχνης 1954–1967* (Athens, 2005).

chapter six: Architecture of the Junta

1 Αλέξανδρος Λ. Ζαούσης, *Ο Εμπαιγμός* (Athens, 1997).
2 Christopher Montague Woodhouse, *Karamanlis: The Restorer of Greek Democracy* (Oxford, 1982).
3 Law 395/68, 'Περί του ύψους των οικοδομών και του συστήματος της ελεύθερης δομήσεως'.
4 Νικόλαος Μακαρέζος, *Η οικονομία της Ελλάδος:21η Απριλίου 1967 – 8η Οκτωβρίου 1973* (Athens, 2006).
5 Personal communication to the authors. Among the members of the journal board were A. Aravantinos, T. Argyropoulos, I. Dergalin, D. Fatouros, I. Liapis and K. Michailidis.
6 Takis Ch. Zenetos, 'City Planning and Electronics', *Architecture in Greece*, 3 (1969), pp. 114–25.
7 Alexander Tzonis and Liane Lefaivre, 'The Grid and the Pathway. An Introduction to the Work of Dimitris and Suzana Antonakakis. With Prolegomena to a History of the Culture of Modern Greek Architecture', *Architecture in Greece*, 15 (1981), pp. 164–78.
8 Tzonis and Lefaivre, 'The Grid and the Pathway', pp. 164–78.

9 Liane Lefaivre and Alexander Tzonis, 'The Grid and the Pathway: An Introduction to the Work of Dimitris and Suzana Antonakakis in the Context of Greek Architectural Culture', *Atelier 66* [Athens] (1985).

10 Law 395/ 1968: 'Περί του ύψους των οικοδομών και του συστήματος της ελεύθερης δομήσεως', *Εφημερίς της Κυβερνήσεως*, 95, A (4 May 1968).

11 Μαριέλλα Ο. Δουμάνη, 'Γυμνάσιο-λύκειο Αγ. Δημητρίου, Μπραχάμι', *Αρχιτεκτονικά Θέματα*, 13 (1979), pp. 195–7.

12 Compulsory Law 625/1968: 'Περί συμπληρώσεως και τροποποιήσεως των γενικών περί σχεδίων πόλεων διατάξεων', *Εφημερίς της Κυβερνήσεως*, 266, A (14 November 1968).

13 Μαρία Μαντουβάλου and Λουΐζα Μάρθα, 'Το "οικοδομικό θαύμα" και οι παγίδες του', *Αντί* 199 (19 February 1982), p. 39.

14 Κέντρο Προγραμματισμού και Οικονομικών Ερευνών (ΚΕΠΕ), *Σχέδιον Προτύπου μακροχρονίου Αναπτύξεως της Ελλάδας 1973–1987*, vol. II (Athens, 1972).

15 Renée Hirschon, *Heirs of the Greek Catastrophe: The Social Life of Asia Minor Refugees in Piraeus* (Oxford, 1989).

16 *European Yearbook*, 17 (The Hague, 1969), p. 315.

17 Παπαδόπουλος Γεώργιος, *Το Πιστεύω μας. Λόγοι-συνεντεύξεις-δηλώσεις-μηνύματα και εγκύκλιοι από 29 Ιουλίου 1968 έως 31 Ιανουαρίου 1969*, vol. III (Athens, 1969), p. 147.

18 Compulsory Law 410: 'Περί αυθαιρέτων οικοδομικών κατασκευών', *Εφημερίς της Κυβερνήσεως*, B, 110 (16 May 1968).

19 Legislative Decree 8/9/1973: 'Περί Γενικού Οικοδομικού Κανονισμού', more specifically articles 118–124, explicitly addressing the problem of illegal construction.

chapter seven: Modern Architecture Comes of Age

1 A history promoted by Lucien Febvre in the 1930s that remerged in the 1960s through E. P. Thompson's writings. See Thompson's 'History from Below', *Times Literary Supplement* (7 April 1966), pp. 279–80.

2 See Regulatory Law 5351/1932: 'Περί αρχαιοτήτων', Law 1469/1950: 'Περί προστασίας ειδικής κατηγορίας οικοδομημάτων και έργων τέχνης μεταγενέστερων του 1830', and Law 1577/1985 legislation respectively. In Ιωάννα Στεριώτου, 'Η ισχύουσα νομοθεσία για την προστασία ιστορικών μνημείων και συνόλων στην Ελλάδα. Προθέσεις, πρακτικές και αποτελέσματα της κρατικής πολιτικής' in Χάρις Καλλιγά and Αλέξης Μάλλιαρης, eds., *Θεωρία και Πρακτική για την αποκατάσταση ιστορικών οικισμών με σκοπό τις νέες χρήσεις*, proceedings of the 9th Symposium of History and Art, Monemvasiotikos Homilos, July 20–22 (Athens, 2004), pp. 147–60.

3 Αλέξανδρος Γ. Καλλιγάς and Χάρις Καλλιγά, 'Απόψεις και εκτιμήσεις', *Architecture in Greece* 23 (1989), p. 108, and Alexandros G. Kalligas and Haris A. Kalligas, 'Hotel in Monemvasia', *Architecture in Greece* , 26 (1989), pp. 156–61.

4 'Αρης Κωνσταντινίδης, 'Αρχιτεκτονική και παράδοση. Αναφορά στο πρόγραμμα του ΕΟΤ για τους παραδοσιακούς οικισμούς', *Δελτίο Συλλόγου Αρχιτεκτόνων*, 4 (July–August 1977), pp. 11–6.

5 Sinan Özgen, 'Designing for sustainable Tourist Development, Case Studies of Greek Islands', paper presented at the 5th European Academy of Design conference, Design Wisdom, 28–30 April (Barcelona, 2003).

6 Similar to Valsamakis, Agnes Couvela graduated from the Athens Polytechnic (Couvela in 1966) in time to experience the impact of the dictatorship.

7 Collaborators: A. Halari, D. Korres, G. Peponis, S. Vasiliou, G. Nikolopoulos, K. Keoglou and N. Paplomatas.

8 From the architects' brief.

9 Χρήστος Δεληγιάννης, 'Παρουσίαση Προσωπικού έργου – η Σχέση του με το Φως', lecture in the seminar *Αρχιτεκτονική και Φως*, Center of Mediterranean Architecture, 19–21 May, (Chania, 2006).

10 The principals of the DECA Architecture team were Alexandros Vaitsos, Carlos Loperena and Elena Zabeli. The working team consisted of Maria Doxa, Kyle Gudsell, Katerina Chrysanthakopoulou and Thomas Ragousis.
11 Meletitiki – A. N. Tombazis & Associates Architects Ltd. According to the brief the project was part of the THERMIE – EC 2000 (Energy Comfort 2000) programme and was partly funded by the European Commission – Directorate General XVII for Energy. Its total energy consumption is being monitored and it is anticipated that it will be significantly less than 50 percent of the energy consumption of equivalent conventional buildings.
12 Assisted by A. Demetriou, S. Paraskevopoulou and J. Romanos.
13 Meletitiki – Alexandros N. Tombazis & Associates Architects Ltd.
14 Alexander Tzonis and Alcestis Rodi, 'Rubble-Rousing', *Architecture* (1 October 2000), pp. 71–3.
15 Under the general direction of Y. Kalantides with Ioannis Patronis as director of Architecture, both of whom were succeeded by Dora Galani.
16 Interestingly the Biris brothers were sons of Kyprianos Biris whose pioneering lecture on the modern apartment building (15 April 1932), design of Logothetopoulos Apartment Building (1930) and article in *Τεχνικά Χρονικά*, 11 (1 June 1932) were discussed in chapter 3.
17 'Apartment building at Polydrosso, Athens', *Design and Art in Greece*, 15 (1984), pp. 132–6.
18 Πάνος Δραγώνας, 'Μετά την πολυκατοικία;', *Η Καθημερινή* (11 January 2009).
19 Guy Burgel, *Η Νεοελληνική Πόλη* (Athens, 1989). See also Guy Burgel, *Αθήνα: η ανάπτυξη μιάς μεσογειακής πρωτεύουσας* (Athens, 1976), and Ιωάννης Αίσωπος and Γιώργος Σημαιοφορίδης, eds., *Μετάπολις 2001: Η σύγχρονη (ελληνική) πόλη* (Athens, 2001).
20 Γεώργιος Πανέτσος, 'Επτά θέσεις και μια πρόταση για την ανασυγκρότηση της Αθήνας', *Αρχιτέκτονες* 9/10, (Athens May/June/July 1997), pp. 64–9, and Γεώργιος Πανέτσος, 'Η εκδίκηση της υψηλής αρχιτεκτονικής', *Αρχιτέκτονες* 37, (Athens January/February 2003), pp. 55–8

chapter eight: Whither Young Architect?

1 *European Green City Index*, a research project conducted by the Economist Intelligence Unit (Munich, 8 December 2009).
2 Αριστείδης Γ. Ρωμανός, *Αθήνα: Το πολεοδομικό ζήτημα από τη μεριά του πολίτη* (Athens, 2004).
3 See Law 947: 'Περί Οικιστικών Περιοχών', *ΦΕΚ* 169/Α' (26 July 1979).
4 See Law 1337: 'Επέκταση των πολεοδομικών σχεδίων, οικιστική ανάπτυξη κα σχετικές ρυθμίσεις', *ΦΕΚ* 33/A (14 March 1983).
5 See Matthew Campbell, 'Party's over for Greek graspers. A black mood has settled upon Athens', *The Sunday Times* (Sunday 20 December 2009).
6 Orestis Doumanis, 'The "Architectural Idiom" in Danger', *Architecture in Greece*, 37 (2003), p. 27.
7 'Papandreou visit to coastal Olympic facilities', *Athens News Agency: Daily News Bulletin in English*, 3321 (13 October 2009).

Select Bibliography

Abbott, John Nelson, *Sketches of Modern Athens, Describing its Manners, Customs and Laws* (London, 1849)

Alderfer, Harold F., *I Like Greece* (New York, 1956)

Angelomatis-Tsougarakis, Helen, *The Eve of the Greek Revival: British Travellers' Perceptions of Early Nineteenth-century Greece* (London, 1990)

Bastea, Eleni, *The Creation of Modern Athens: Planning the Myth* (Cambridge, 1999)

Birtles, Bert, *Exiles in the Aegean* (London, 1938)

Clogg, Richard A., *A Concise History of Greece* (Cambridge, 1992)

—, ed., *Minorities in Greece: Aspects of a Plural Society* (London, 2002)

Cofano, Paola and Dimitri Konstantinidis, *Aris Konstantinidis: 1913–1993* (Rome, 2010)

Cranaki, Mimica, 'Journal d'exil', *Les Temps Modernes*, 58 (August 1950), reprinted as *'Ματαρόα' σε δύο φωνές – Σελίδες ξενητιάς* (Athens, 2007)

Djélépy, Panos N., *Villages d' enfants* (Paris, 1947)

—, *L'Architecture populaire en Grèce* (Paris, 1952), reprinted as *Λαϊκή Ελληνική Αρχιτεκτονική* (Athens, 1971)

Dodwell, Edward, *A Classical and Topographical Tour through Greece during the Years 1801, 1805 and 1806* (London, 1819)

Doumanis, Orestis B., ed., *Architecture in Greece*, annual review (Athens, 1967–2012) [Greek-language journal with summaries in English]

—, ed., *Design in Greece*, annual review (Athens, 1970-2012), now published as *Design + Art in Greece* [Greek-language journal with summaries in English]

—, ed., *Takis Ch. Zenetos: 1926–1977* (Athens, 1978)

—, ed., *Post-War Architecture in Greece* (Athens, 1984)

Dumont, Paul, 'La Correspondance de Joseph Nehama avec l' "Alliance Israélite Universelle", in *Οι Εβραίοι στον ελληνικό χώρο. Ζητήματα ιστορίας στη μακρά διάρκεια: Πρακτικά του Α' Συμπόσιου Ιστορίας της Εταιρείας Μελέτης Εβραϊκού Ελληνισμού: Θεσσαλονίκη, 23–24 Νοεμβρίου 1991*, ed. Έφη Αβδελά and Οντέτ Βαρών – Βασάρ (Athens, 1995), pp. 131–50

Fessas-Emmanouil, Helen, *Essays on Neohellenic Architecture* (Athens, 2001)

—, and Emmanouel V. Marmaras, *12 Greek Architects of the Interwar Period* (Heraklion, 2005)

Gallant, Thomas W., *Modern Greece* (London, 2001)

Giacumakatos, Andreas and Ezio Godoli, *L'Architettura delle scuole e il razionalismo in Grecia* (Florence, 1985)

Hederer, Oswald, *Friedrich von Gärtner, 1792–1847. Leben, Werk, Schüler* (Munich, 1976)

Henderson, George Patrick, *The Revival of Greek Thought, 1620–1830* (Edinburgh, 1971)

Horton, George, *Modern Athens* (New York, 1901)

Housepian, Marjorie, *Smyrna 1922: The Destruction of a City* (London, 1972)

Juergens, George, in *The Journal of American History*, LXV / 3 (December 1978), pp. 832–3, a review of *Concerned About the Planet: The Reporter Magazine and American Liberalism, 1949–1968* by Martin K. Doudna (Westport, CT, 1977)

Koliopoulos, John S., *Brigands with a Cause: Brigandage and Irredentism in Modern Greece, 1821–1912* (Oxford, 1987)

Kouvertaris, George A. and Betty A. Dobratz, *A Profile of Modern Greece in Search of Identity* (Oxford, 1987)

Lavedan, Pierre, 'L'œuvre d'Ernest Hébrard en Grèce', *Urbanisme*, 14 (May 1933), p. 159
—, 'Un problème d' urbanisme: la reconstruction de Salonique', *La Gazette des Beaux-Arts* (September–October 1922), pp. 230–48
Lefaivre, Liane and Alexander Tzonis, *Critical Regionalism, Architecture and Identity in a Globalized World* (Munich, 2003)
Leon, George B., *The Greek Socialist Movement and the First World War: The Road to Unity* (New York, 1976)
Leontidou, Lila, *The Mediterranean City in Transition: Social Change and Urban Development* (Cambridge, 1990)
Lidderdale, Harold A., ed. and trans., *Makriyannis: The Memoirs of General Makriyannis, 1797–1864* (London, 1966)
Lincoln, Francis F., *United States Aid to Greece, 1947–1962* (1975)
Loyer, François, *Architecture de la Grèce Contemporaine*, Thèse de Doctorat, Faculté de Lettres et Sciences Humaines, Université de Paris (Paris, 1966)
MacMillan, Margaret, *Peacemakers: The Paris Peace Conference of 1919 and its Attempt to End War* (London, 2001), also published as *Paris 1919: Six Months That Changed the World* and as *Peacemakers: Six Months That Changed the World*
Mantouvalou, Maria, *Production de logements et rapports de pouvoir en Grèce,* These 3eme cycle Sociol., EHESS (Paris, 1980)
Mawson, Thomas H., 'The Replanning of Athens', *Architectural Review*, 47 (March 1919), pp. 48–52
Mazower, Mark, *Greece and the Inter-War Economic Crisis* (Oxford, 1991), also published in Greek by MIET (Athens, 2002)
—, *After the War was Over: Reconstructing the Family, Nation and State in Greece, 1943–1960* (Princeton, NJ, 2000)
Mouzelis, Nicos P., *Modern Greece, Facets of Under-development* (New York, 1978)
Otto, Christian F., 'Modern Environment and Historical Continuity: The Heimatschutz Discourse in Germany', *Art Journal* XLIII / 2 (Summer 1983), pp. 148–57
Panetsos, Georgios A., 'Architecture' in *About Greece*, co-ord. A-J. D. Metaxas, ed. Anthony J. Bacaloumis (Athens, 2007)
Papanikolaou-Christensen, Aristea, *The Panathenaic Stadium: Its History over the Centuries*, trans. Alexandra Doumas, ed. Aliki Solomou-Prokopiou (Athens, 2003)
Phiippidis, Dimitris, *Urban Housing of the '30s: Modern Architecture in Pre-war Athens* (Athens, 1998)
Pierron, Bernard, *Juifs et Chrétiens de la Grèce moderne. Histoire des relations intercommunautaires de 1821 à 1945* (Paris, 1996)
Popescu, Carmen, *Le Style National Roumain. Construire une Nation à travers l'architecture 1881–1945* (Rennes, 2004)
Porter, Paul R., *The Story of the American Marshall Plan in Greece: July 1, 1948 to January 1, 1952* [foreword by Roger D. Lapham, Chief of Mission]
—, *Report of the Chief, Special Mission to Greece, Economic Cooperation Administration, September 1949 to November 1950* [Paul R. Porter's report to his successor, Roger D. Lapham]
Rodi, Alcestis, *Creating the Creative Block: Towards a Design Tool for Urban Regeneration*, PhD dissertation, School of Architecture, Delft University of Technology (Delft, 2008)
Russach, Hans Hermann, *Deutsche Bauen in Athen* (Berlin, 1942)
Sartoris, Alberto, *Gli elementi dell' architettura funzionale* (Milan, 1932)
Sfaellos, Charalambos, *Le Fonctionnalisme dans l'architecture contemporaine* (Paris, 1952)
Sisa, Jozsef, 'Joseph Hoffer and the Study of Ancient Architecture', *The Journal of the Society of Architectural Historians*, XLIX / 4 (December 1990), pp. 430–39
Schmidt, Hartwig, 'Ludwig Hoffmann's Athens Master Plan', *Design in Greece*, 11 (Athens, 1980), pp. 50–59
Svoronos, Nicos, '1940–1950: The Main Problems', in *Greece in the 1940s: A Nation in Crisis*, ed. John O. Iatrides (Hanover, NH, 1981), p. 11
Travlos, John, 'Athens after the Liberation: Planning the New City and Exploring the

Old', *Hesperia, Greek Towns and Cities: A Symposium,* L / 4 (October–December 1981), pp. 391–407
Tzonis, Alexander and Liane Lefaivre, 'Introduction', in *Post-War Architecture in Greece*, ed. Orestis Doumanis (Athens, 1984)
—, 'Dimitris Pikionis. Régionaliste des années 50', *Le Moniteur Architecture AMC*, ed. Dominique Boudet, 99 (Paris, June–July 1999), pp. 60–69
Woodhouse, Christopher Montague, *Capodistria: The Founder of Greek Independence, 1821–1829* (London, 1973)
Zachos, Aristoteles, 'Aeltere Wohnbauten auf griechischem Boden', *Wasmuths Monatshefte für Baukunst*, 7/1922–23, H. 7/8 (Berlin, 1922), pp. 247–50
Zivas, Dionysis A., 'The Future of the Old Sector of the City of Athens: Plaka', in *The Conservation of European Cities*, ed. Donald Appleyard (Cambridge, MA, 1979), pp. 154–63

Publications in Greek

Anon., *Οι ιστορικοί λόγοι του Ε.Κ. Βενιζέλου:1909–1936. Κοινοβουλευτικές αγορεύσεις – λόγοι προς το λαό – ιστορικές δηλώσεις – άρθρα – συνεντεύξεις*, vol. I: p. 144, vol. II: pp. 145–288 (Athens, 1936)
Αίσωπος, Γιάννης and Γιώργος Σημαιοφορίδης, eds, *Τοπία Εκμοντερνισμού: Ελληνική Αρχιτεκτονική '60 και '90* (Athens, 2002)
—, eds, *Η Σύγχρονη (Ελληνική) Πόλη* (Athens, 2001)
Αντωνιάδης, Αντώνης, *Σύγχρονη Ελληνική Αρχιτεκτονική* (Athens, 1979)
—, *Ο φωταγωγός: Η αρχιτεκτονική του άγχους* (Athens, 1982)
Αραβαντινός, Αθανάσιος, 'Προβλήματα Χωροταξίας, Πολεοδομίας και Κατοικίας εις την Ελλάδα', *Τεχνικά Χρονικά*, 5–6 (May–June 1967), pp. 76–87
Βασιλείου, Ιωάννης, *Η λαϊκή κατοικία, Κοινωνικές, τεχνικές και οικονομικές απόψεις. Η λαϊκή κατοικία σε διάφορες ξένες χώρες και στην Ελλάδα* (Athens, 1944)
Βεντούρα, Λίνα, *Έλληνες Μετανάστες στο Βέλγιο* (Athens, 1999)
Βεργόπουλος, Κωνσταντίνος, *Κράτος και Οικονομική Πολιτική στον 19ο αιώνα* (Athens, 1978)
Bourgel, Guy, *Αθήνα, η ανάπτυξη μιας μεσογειακής πρωτεύουσας* (Athens, 1978)
—, *Η Νεοελληνική Πόλη* (Athens, 1989)
Γέροντας, Δημήτριος and Νικόλαος Νικολούδης, *Αθήνα 1456 μ. Χ. – 1686 μ. Χ.: Η προσωπογραφία μιας πόλης* (Thessaloniki, 2007)
Γιακουμακάτος, Ανδρέας, *Η Αρχιτεκτονική και η Κριτική* (Athens, 2001)
Γιακουμής, Χάρης, Αλεξάνδρα Γεροδήμου-Γερόλυμπου and Christian Pedelahore de Loddis, *Ερνέστ Εμπράρ – Ernest Hébrard, 1875–1933* (Athens, 2001)
Γιαννόπουλος, Περικλής, *Άπαντα*, ed. Δημήτρης Λαζογιώργος-Ελληνικός (Athens, 1963)
Γιοχάννες, Χάιντς (Johannes Heinz) and Κώστας Η. Μπίρης, *Αι Αθήναι του Κλασσικισμού* (Athens, 1939)
Γκιζελή, Βίκα Δ., *Κοινωνικοί μετασχηματισμοί και προέλευση της κοινωνικής κατοικίας στην Ελλάδα, 1920–1930* (Athens, 1984)
Γληνός, Δημήτρης, *Άπαντα*, vol. I: 1898–1910, vol. II: 1910–1914, ed. Φίλιππος Ηλιού (Athens, 1983)
Δεμενεγή-Βιριράκη, Αικατερίνη, *Παλαιά Ανάκτορα Αθηνών, 1836–1986* (Athens, 1994)
Δερτιλής, Γιώργος, *Ελληνική Οικονομία και Βιομηχανική Επανάσταση, 1830–1910* (Athens, 1984)
—, *Ιστορία του Ελληνικού Κράτους, 1830–1920* (Athens, 2005), 2 vols
—, Δημαρας, Αλεξης, ed., *Παιδεια και Κοινωνια – Αρχειο Δ. Ι. Σαρατση – Αλληλογραφια, Μαρτυριες, Δημοσιευματα* (Athens, 1995), 2 vols
Δοξιάδης, Κωνσταντίνος, *Οικιστική πολιτική για την ανοικοδόμηση της χώρας με ένα εικοσάχρονο σχέδιο* (Athens, 1947)
—, *Η πρωτεύουσα μας και το μέλλον της* (Athens, 1960)
Ελευθερίου, Μάνος, *Νεοκλασική Ερμούπολη* (Athens, 1998)
Ελύτης, Οδυσσέας, *Ανοιχτά Χαρτιά* (Athens, 1974)
Ζήβας, Διονύσης Α., *Η Επέμβαση στην Πλάκα: Διαπιστώσεις και Συμπεράσματα* (Athens, 1983)

Θεοτοκάς, Γιώργος, *Αναζητώντας τη Διαύγεια: Δοκίμια για τη νεότερη ελληνική και ευρωπαϊκή λογοτεχνία*, ed. Δημήτρης Τζιόβας (Athens, 2005)

Καλαφάτη, Ελένη, *Τα σχολικά κτήρια της πρωτοβάθμιας εκπαίδευσης, 1821–1929* (Athens, 1988)

Καλλιγά, Χάρις and Αλέξης Μάλλιαρης, eds, *Θεωρία και Πρακτική για την αποκατάσταση ιστορικών οικισμών με σκοπό τις νέες χρήσεις* [Theory and Practice for the Restoration of Historic Settlements for New Use], proceedings of the 9th Symposium of History and Art, Monemvasiotikos Homilos, 20–22 July (Athens, 2004)

Καλογήρου, Νίκος Σ., *Αρχιτεκτονική και πολεοδομία στη μεταπολεμική Θεσσαλονίκη* (Thessaloniki, 1992)

Καραβία, Μαρία, *Κηφισιά: ομορφιά και μνήμη* (Athens,1988)

Καραδέδος, Γιάννης, ed., *Νεοκλασσική Πόλη και Αρχιτεκτονική*, National Conference Proceedings, Aristotle University of Thessaloniki, 2–4 December (Thessaloniki, 1983)

Καραδήμου-Γερόλυμπου, Αλέκα, *Επανασχεδιασμός και ανοικοδόμηση της Θεσσαλονίκης μετά την πυρκαγιά του 1917: Ένα ορόσημο στην ιστορία της πόλης και την ανάπτυξη της ελληνικής πολεοδομίας*, Doctoral thesis, School of Architecture, Aristotle University (Thessaloniki, 1985)

—, *Μεταξύ Ανατολής και Δύσης: Βορειοελλαδικές πόλεις στην περίοδο των Οθωμανικών Μεταρρυθμίσεων* (Athens, 1997)

—, *Το χρονικό της μεγάλης πυρκαγιάς Θεσσαλονίκη, Αύγουστος 1917* (Thessaloniki, 2002)

Καραδήμου-Γερόλυμπου, Αλεξάνδρα and Βασίλης Κολώνας, 'Η ανοικοδόμηση της Θεσσαλονίκης μετά το 1917', in *Οι Εβραίοι στον ελληνικό χώρο. Ζητήματα ιστορίας στη μακρά διάρκεια: Πρακτικά του Α' Συμπόσιου Ιστορίας της Εταιρείας Μελέτης Εβραϊκού Ελληνισμού: Θεσσαλονίκη, 23–24 Νοεμβρίου 1991*, ed. Έφη Αβδελά and Οντέτ Βαρών-Βασάρ (Athens, 1995), pp. 231–54

Καραντινός, Πάτροκλος, *Τα νέα Σχολικά Κτίρια* (Athens, 1938)

Καρδαμίτση-Αδάμη, Μάρω, *Ernst Ziller. Αναμνήσεις* (Athens, 1997)

—, *Έρνστ Τσίλλερ, 1837-1923. Η τέχνη του κλασσικού* (Athens, 2006)

—, *Η μπλε πολυκατοικία* (Athens, 2006)

Καυκαλάς, Γρηγόρης, Λόης Λαμπριανίδης and Νίκος Παπαμίχος, eds, *Η Θεσσαλονίκη στο μεταίχμιο: Η Πόλη από τη Σκοπιά των Αλλαγών* (Athens, 2008)

Καυκούλα, Κική, Νίκος Παπαμίχος and Βίλμα Χαστάογλου, *Σχέδια πόλεων στην Ελλάδα του 19ου αιώνα* (Thessaloniki, 1990)

Κόκκου, Αγγελική, *Αθήνα: Η ιστορία της πόλης* (Athens,1984)

Κολώνας, Βασίλης Σ., ed., *Θεσσαλονίκη, 1912–1992: 8 δεκαετίες νεοελληνικής αρχιτεκτονικής* (Thessaloniki, 1993)

—, *Έλληνες αρχιτέκτονες στην οθωμανική αυτοκρατορία 19ος–20ός αιώνας* (Athens, 2005)

Κονταράτος, Σάββας, *Αρχιτεκτονική και παράδοση* (Athens, 1986)

Κύρτσης, Αλέξανδρος-Ανδρέας, ed., *Κωνσταντίνος Α. Δοξιάδης. Κείμενα, Σχέδια, Οικισμοί* (Athens, 2006)

Κωνσταντινίδης, Άρης, *Τα παλαιά αθηναϊκά σπίτια* (Athens, 1950)

—, *Αμαρτωλοί και Κλέφτες ή η απογείωση της Αρχιτεκτονικής* (Athens, 1987)

—, *Για την Αρχιτεκτονική: Δημοσιεύματα σε εφημερίδες, σε περιοδικά και σε βιβλία, 1940–1982* (Athens, 1987)

—, *Σύγχρονη Αληθινή Αρχιτεκτονική, Ομιλία στην Πολυτεχνική Σχολή Αριστοτελείου Πανεπιστημίου Θεσσαλονίκης* (Thessaloniki, 1978)

—, *Τα Θεόκτιστα* (Heraklion, 1995)

Κωτσάκη, Αμαλία, *Αλέξανδρος Νικολούδης, 1874–1944: αρχιτεκτονικά οράματα, πολιτικές χειρονομίες* (Athens, 2007)

Λεονταρίτη, Γιώργος Β.,'Εθνικισμός και Διεθνισμός: Πολιτική Ιδεολογία', in *Ελληνισμός και Ελληνικότητα*, ed. Δημήτρης Γ. Τσαούση (Athens, 1983)

Λεοντίδου, Λίλα, *Πόλεις της Σιωπής: Εργατικός εποικισμός της Αθήνας και του Πειραιά, 1904–1940* (Athens, 1989)

Μαρμαράς, Μανώλης, *Η αστική πολυκατοικία της Μεσοπολεμικής Αθήνας* (Athens, 1991)

Μαυρογορδάτος, Γιώργος and Χρήστος Χατζηιωσήφ, eds, *Βενιζελισμός και αστικός εκσυγχρονισμός* (Heraklion, 1988)
Mawson, Thomas H., *Αι Αθήναι του μέλλοντος και η Θεσσαλονίκη της Αύριον* (Athens, 1918)
Μόλχο, Ρένα, *Οι Εβραίοι τις Θεσσαλονίκης, 1856–1919* (Athens, 2000)
Μπαδήμα-Φουντουλάκη, Όλγα, *Κλεάνθης, 1802–1863* (Athens, 2001)
Μπαστιάς, Γιάννης Κ., *Ο Κωστής Μπαστιάς στα χρόνια του Μεσοπολέμου*, vol. I: Χρονογραφία – Εργογραφία, vol. II: Βιβλιογραφία (Athens, 1997)
Μπάτσης, Δημήτρης, *Η Βαρειά Βιομηχανία στην Ελλάδα* (Athens, 1947)
Μπίρης, Κώστας Η., 'Κλασσικισμός και Ρωμαντισμός στην Αρχιτεκτονική των Αθηνών', *Αθηναϊκαί Μελέται*, vol. III (Athens, 1940), pp. 17–23
—, *Τα πρώτα σχέδια Αθηνών: Ιστορία και ανάλυσις των* (Athens, 1933)
—, *Αι Αθήναι από τον 19ου εις τον 20ο αιώνα* (Athens,1966 / 1995)
Μπίρης, Μάνος, *Μισός Αιώνας Αθηναϊκής Αρχιτεκτονικής, 1875–1925* (Athens, 1987)
Μπίρης Μάνος and Μάρω Καρδαμίτση-Αδάμη, *Νεοκλασσική Αρχιτεκτονική στην Ελλάδα* (Athens, 2001)
Μπουρνιάς, Απόστολος, *Περί της οριζοντίου ιδιοκτησίας* (Athens, 1982)
Νούτσος, Χαράλαμπος, *Ιστορία της εκπαίδευσης και Ιδεολογία: Όψεις του Μεσοπολέμου* (Athens, 1990)
Πανουσάκης, Χρήστος, *Νικόλαος Μητσάκης, 1899–1941* (Athens, 1999)
Παπαγεωργίου-Βενετάς, Αλέξανδρος, *Εδουάρδος Σάουμπερτ, 1804–1860* (Athens, 1999)
—, *Ο Leo von Klenze στην Ελλάδα: Τεκμήρια για τη νεοελληνική ιστοριογραφία* (Athens, 2000)
Παπαδάτου-Γιαννοπούλου, Χαρά, *Εξέλιξη του σχεδίου πόλεως των Πατρών: 1829–1989* (Patras, 1991)
Παπαδημητρίου-Ζιρώ, Χριστίνα, *Ο αρχιτέκτων Αριστοτέλης Ζάχος, 1872–1939* (Athens, 1988)
Πικιώνη, Αγνή and Μιχάλης Παρούσης, eds., *Δ. Πικιώνη Κείμενα* (Athens, 1986)
Πολύζος, Ιωάννης, *Η εγκατάσταση των προσφύγων του 1922: Μία οριακή περίπτωση αστικοποίησης* (Athens, 1984)
Ρωμανός, Αριστείδης Γ., *Αθήνα: Το πολεοδομικό ζήτημα από τη σκοπιά του πολίτη* (Athens, 2004)
Σακελλαρόπουλος, Χριστόφορος Π., *Μοντέρνα αρχιτεκτονική και πολιτική της αστικής ανοικοδόμησης, Αθήνα, 1945–1960*, Doctoral thesis, School of Architecture, National Technical University of Athens (Athens, 2003)
Σαπόρτα, Ισαάκ Η., *Επάγγελμα Αρχιτέκτων*, ed. Γιώργος Σημαιοφορίδης and Γεώργιος Σαρηγιάννης (Athens, 1996)
Σαρηγιάννης Γεώργιος, *Αθήνα 1830–2000: Εξέλιξη, πολεοδομία, μεταφορές* (Athens, 2000)
Σκοπετέα, Έλλη, *Το πρότυπο Βασίλειο και η Μεγάλη Ιδέα. Όψεις του Εθνικού προβλήματος στην Ελλάδα* (Athens, 1988)
Τζίκα-Χατζοπούλου, Αλίκη, *Πολεοδομικό δίκαιο* (Athens, 1998)
Τζιόβας, Δημήτρης, *Οι μεταμορφώσεις του εθνισμού και το ιδεολόγημα της ελληνικότητας στο Μεσοπόλεμο* (Athens, 1989)
Τζόκας, Σπύρος, *Ο Ελευθέριος Βενιζέλος και το Εγχείρημα του Αστικού Εκσυγχρονισμού: 1928–1932* (Athens, 2002)
Τραυλός, Ιωάννης, *Πολεοδομική εξέλιξις των Αθηνών. Από των προϊστορικών χρόνων μέχρι των αρχών του 19ου αιώνος* (Athens, 1960)
—, *Νεοκλασσική Αρχιτεκτονική στην Ελλάδα* (Athens, 1969)
Τσουκαλά, Κυριακή, *Τάσεις στη Σχολική Αρχιτεκτονική* (Athens, 1998)
Τσουκαλάς, Κωνσταντίνος, *Κοινωνική ανάπτυξη και κράτος. Η συγκρότηση του δημόσιου χώρου στην Ελλάδα* (Athens, 1983)
Φεσσά-Εμμανουήλ, Ελένη, ed., *Αρχιτέκτονες του 20ού αιώνα Μέλη της εταιρείας: Αρχιτέκτονες – μηχανικοί διπλωματούχοι των ετών, 1905–1933: Περίοδος πρώτη* (Athens, 2009)
Φιλιππίδης, Δημήτρης, *Νεοελληνική Αρχιτεκτονική* (Athens, 1984)
—, *Μοντέρνα Αρχιτεκτονική στην Ελλάδα* (Athens, 2001)
Χέλμης, Γεώργιος, *Ταραγμένη Διετία: 1973–1974* (Athens, 2006)
Χολέβας, Νίκος Θ., *Αρχιτεκτονική του μεσοπολέμου στα Βαλκάνια* (Athens, 1994)

Acknowledgements

Greece is a small country but its history is unusually complex and few books have been written about it. We acknowledge the work of François Loyer, Dimitri Philippides, Yorgos Simeoforidis, Anthony Antoniades, Helen Fessas-Emmanouil, Nikos Cholevas, Andreas Giakoumakatos and Vassilis Kolonas, and the contributions by Alexander Papageorgiou-Venetas, Maro Kardamitsi-Adami, Aleka Karadimou-Gerolympou, Manos Biris, Dimitri Fatouros, Georgios Panetsos, Manolis Marmaras, Rena Molho and Mark Mazower as most helpful for writing this book. We also acknowledge the help of the Neohellenic Architecture Archives of the Benaki Museum and the Hellenic Institute of Architecture, as well as to the architects of works published, for supplying visual documents.

We are also indebted for advice to Michael Lykoudis, Agnes Pikioni and Giorgos Sariyannis; and to Stathis Eustathiadis, many thanks for the endless supply of documentation. Special acknowledgements also to Orestis Doumanis for his generous assistance.

Many generic ideas contained in this book have their origin in conversations held by Alexander Tzonis with Kyprianos Biris, Spyros Papaloukas, Yannis Tsarouchis, Dimitri Pikionis and Aris Konstantinidis, all teachers or friends, none knowing at that time that they would appear as part of the history covered in this book.

Our deepest appreciation to our editor Vivian Constantinopoulos for her enthusiastic support, which made this book possible.

Photo Acknowledgements

The authors and publishers wish to express their thanks to the below sources of illustrative material and/or permission to reproduce it:

Courtesy of Dimitris and Suzana Antonakakis: pp. 208, 209, 210, 211, 214; from *Architektonika Themata*, 1 (1967): p. 206; from *Architektonika Themata*, 29 (1995): p. 213; from *Architektoniki* (1957): p. 185; photo Erieta Attali: pp. 234, 235, 238, 246; courtesy of Attiko Metro S.A.: p. 243 (left and right); Benaki Museum, Athens: pp. 9; Benaki Museum (Photographic Archive): p. 40; Benaki Museum, Neohellenic Architecture Archives: pp. 59, 80, 89, 91, 92 (above), 92 (below), 94, 95 (above), 95 (below), 96 (above), 96 (below), 97 (below), 102, 103, 104, 110, 130, 131, 132, 173 (above), 186; from K. Biris, 'I Astiki Polykatoikia', in *Technika Chronika*, 11 (1 June 1932): p. 100; courtesy of Tassos Biris: p. 244; from Pierre de Coubertin, Timoleon J. Philemon, N. G. Politis and Charalambos Anninos, *The Olympic Games, BC 776–AD 1896* (Athens and London, 1897): p. 52; courtesy of Agnes Couvela-Panayotatou: pp. 228, 229; courtesy of Constantin Decavalla Archive: pp. 170, 174; courtesy of Christos Deligiannis: pp. 236, 237 (above and below); courtesy of Domes: pp. 109, 204 (from I. Vikelas archive), 250, 251; courtesy of Orestis Doumanis: pp. 157, 158-9, 176, 177, 179, 183 (above and below), 195 (above), 196, 197 (above), 198, 218, 227; courtesy of Constantinos A. Doxiadis Archives: pp. 150, 171, 175, 215; courtesy of Panos Dragonas and Varvara Christopoulou: p. 247; Emporiki Bank of Greece, Athens: pp. 24, 26 (above), 27, 34, 35, 36; ERT Museum Archive: pp. 44 (P. Poulidis Photo Archive), 78 (Megalokonomou Brothers' Photo Archive); Helen Fessas-Emmanouil, Photographic Archive: pp. 75, 105 (above left), 134, 136 (photo D. Harissiadis); Filekpaideftiki Etaireia Archive: p. 26 (below); courtesy of The Hellenic Institute of Architecture, Athens: pp. 68, 98 (below), 105 (above right) 105 (below), 106 (above), 106 (below), 107, 111 (below), 126, 133, 135, 136, 166, 188, 216, 248, 252; The Hellenic Literary and Historical Archive: p. 49; courtesy of Lazaros Kalyvitis and Yorgos Leonardos Archive: p. 217; from P. Karantinos, *Ta Nea Scholika Ktiria*, Athens, 1938: pp. 97 (above), 98 (above), 99 (below); from *I Kathimerini*, 'Istoriko Leukoma 1961': p. 155; from *I Kathimerini*, 'Istoriko Leukoma 1976': p. 224; from E. Kazantzaki, *O Asymbibastos* (3rd edn, Athens, 1998): p. 108; from Kostas Kitsikis, *I Ktiriologiki Apopsis tou Neou Schediou this Thessalonikis* (Athens, 1919): p. 73 (below); photo Boris Kirpotin: p. 237 (above and below); courtesy of Dimitris Konstantinidis: pp. 138, 139, 181 (above and below), p. 182; courtesy of Dimitris Konstantinidis and Agra Publications: p. 180; courtesy of Koulermos Amourgis Kalogeras: pp. 172, 200, 233; Kyriakos Krokos Archive: p. 231; photo Charalambos Louizides: p. 247; I. Loverdou-Vassiliadis: pp. 105 (above left), 134; Manolis Marmaras: p. 60 (below); from Thomas H. Mawson, *The Athens of the Future and the Thessaloniki of Tomorrow* (Athens, 1918): p. 63; from S. Meletzis, *Antistasi: Apo to epos tis Ethnikis Antistasis. Fotografies tou Spyrou Meletzi* (Athens, 1982): p. 147; Municipal Gallery of Athens: pp. 20–21; Thessaloniki History Centre: p. 64; National Gallery–Alexandros Soutzos Museum, Athens: pp. 31, 50, 51; from *Neos Aristofanes* (10 March 1891): p. 55; courtesy of Georgios A. Panetsos: p. 32; photo Dimitris Papademos: pp. 26 (above), 34, 36; courtesy of Agnes Pikioni: p. 99 (above), 190 (above and below), 192, 193; Private collection: p. 163; photo Alcestis Rodi: pp. 110 (below), 165, 249; Secretariat General of Communication and Information, Athens, Photo Archive: pp. 67, 73 (above); photo Paul Sotiriadis: p. 140; photo Richard Sowersby / Rex Features: p. 6; from P. Santorini, 'Symboli eis to diethnes synedrion gefyron kai kataskevon', in *Technika Chronika* (15 September 1932): p. 111 (above); from *Technika Chronika* (1 July 1936): p. 124; Thessaloniki Planning Office Archives: p. 71; courtesy of Alexandros Tombazis: pp. 212, 230, 240 (above and below), 241; photo Alexander

Tzonis: p. 191; courtesy of Nicos Valsamakis: pp. 160, 167, 168, 169, 222, 226; photo Manolis Vernardos: p. 24; from Marino P. Vréto, *Athènes Moderne*, vol. II (Paris, 1861): p. 28 (above); from Klaus Vrielander and Julio Kaimi, *To Spiti tou Rodaki stin Aigina* (Athens, 1934): pp. 120 (above), 120 (below); photo Yorgis Yerolymbos: p. 117; courtesy of Takis C. Zenetos Archive: pp. 197 (below), 199.

Index

Numerals in *italics* indicate figures